D0991814

THE AUTHORITY OF SCRIPTURE

THE
AUTHORITY OF SCRIPTURE

A Study of
the Reformation and Post-Reformation
Understanding of the Bible

BY

J. K. S. REID

LONDON
METHUEN & CO., LTD.
36 ESSEX STREET · STRAND

First published in 1957
Reprinted 1962
Printed in Great Britain by litho-offset by
William Clowes and Sons Ltd.,
London and Beccles

I·2

CATALOGUE NUMBER 2/5968/10

Contents

Preface

———

C H. Dodd's *The Authority of the Bible* appeared in 1928
—a long time ago. Besides being a notable contribution to the understanding of the Bible, this book may
be said to mark the beginning in this country of a renewed
and deepened interest in Holy Scripture. Since its appearance, a succession of books, increasing in volume and showing
as yet no sign of cessation, has both expressed and stimulated
the fresh attention which theology has recently paid to this
pre-eminently great and important subject. The so-called
'Theology of the Word' has contributed largely to this development. Yet when Dr Dodd led the way, Barth and Brunner
were hardly known in this country; their names do not appear
in his book, and the influence they were to exert upon current
theological thought was still in the future.

The Authority of Scripture is an ambitious title—perhaps too
ambitious, since it may seem to invite comparison with the
important work just mentioned. From such a comparison,
the present work could only emerge the loser. But a glance at the
table of contents will remove any suspicion that comparison
is courted; for the plan is quite different. The present writer
is, however, acutely aware that he enters a field in which
eminent theologians have already taken position, with whose
biblical scholarship he would never dream of competing. He
is their debtor rather than their rival; and he cherishes the
hope that, if he has little that is new to say, he may have
learned something of what they have taught, and perhaps
succeeded in imparting to others some of what he has thus
learned.

Whatever may be thought of the book, the subject is of
lasting importance for Christians of all types and all denomina-
tions. The revived interest in the Bible already mentioned has
faced theologian and evangelist alike with all the profound

questions concerning its nature which must one way or another find answer if it is to be both norm and nourishment for men's faith. It is of the utmost importance that these questions should be answered rightly. This is the situation in which there is perhaps justification for surveying historically some of the classic views on the subject. We are ourselves heirs of the past, and we can well borrow from earlier views what is true and living, and also learn from their errors what is to be avoided. Hence, after a brief account of the position as it appears today, a start is made with Cálvin, in whose work the concern for the Bible rediscovered at the Reformation comes to clearest expression. Luther's treatment is also highly instructive and differs less than is usually supposed from that of the Reformed Church. An even closer resemblance between Lutheran and Reformed Churches, alas! appears, as in Protestant Orthodoxy the living and (if the word be permitted) dynamic quality of the understanding, with which both Luther and Calvin construed the Bible, becomes mislaid or overlaid, and a rigid torpor takes its place. Here is a lesson which must be taken to heart if the renewed interest in the Bible is not to run out into the sands of oracularism or bibliolatry, in which a living voice is replaced by a textbook of doctrine and morals.

Alongside the reformed witness concerning the Bible there is the impressive testimony of the Roman Church. Despite its massiveness, it suffers from certain defects which render inarticulate what the Bible has to say to us, and fuses it too simply with what the Church says. It is not the Roman view that can be recommended to men whose interest in the Bible has been newly stirred.

One would not be wrong in seeing in the Theology of the Word the most powerful single theological influence inviting Christians of all kinds to reckon seriously with the Bible. A study of the Bible today must try to state and assess what the contribution is which Barth and Brunner make, and this is attempted in the penultimate chapter. But before the importance of this contribution can be appreciated it is necessary to deal with two views concerning the Bible which interpret its importance respectively in terms of Inspiration and of Progressive Revelation. That these concepts do help in rightly assessing the Bible cannot be denied, but their contribution is by no means so great or permanent as is often thought. Both involve inadequacies which disable them from giving satisfaction today. One may venture to say that they were useful 'caretaker' interpretations, tiding over a period in which traditional views were so shattered that little or no authority seemed to be left to the Bible.

In a final chapter there is offered a statement of how, in the light of the finer insights of Calvin, Luther and the Theology of the Word, we may validly construe the authority of the Bible for Christians today. This attempt may be successful or unsuccessful; *verbum autem Domini manet in aeternum*, and it is at any rate worth making.

For Chapter III, three works were found particularly useful: R. Seeberg's *Lehrbuch der Dogmengeschichte*, vierter Band, erster Teil; W. Köhler's *Dogmengeschichte*, das Zeitalter der Reformation; and R. Preus' *The Inspiration of Scripture*, A Study of the Theology of the Seventeenth-century Lutheran Dogmaticians. For Chapter VII, Otto Weber's *Karl Barth's Church Dogmatics*—an introductory Report on Vols. I/1-III/4 was found helpful. Some of the material in Chapter IV appeared in a review by the present writer of *A Catholic Commentary on Holy Scripture* in *The Scottish Journal of Theology*, Vol. 7, 83ff., and he encountered no editorial opposition to its inclusion here.

The author is most grateful to the Committee of Selection of the Kerr Lectureship, under whose auspices the material was originally given as lectures in the University of Glasgow in the Christmas Term, 1954, and especially to the late Dr Millar Patrick of Edinburgh and Professor G. H. C. Macgregor of Trinity College, Glasgow, successive conveners of the Committee, for help and encouragement. His thanks are also due to the publishers for both courtesy and competence in seeing this volume through the various stages of publication.

Preface to the 1962 Reprint

The issue of a second edition has given opportunity to correct some purely typographical errors which the first regrettably contained, and to clear up a confusion concerning the identity and date of Sebastian Franck (pp. 97–100) to which the kindness of one reader drew attention.

If the book were being rewritten, greater prominence would have to be given to what is too casually stated in a footnote (p. 241 [1]). To admit an 'inspired' character to the response made to the impact of Christ seems to open to the ideas of inspiration, dictation, inerrancy and infallibility the door which the doctrine of Scripture as primarily witness shut against them. I have no doubt that something to which these ideas testify has a rightful place in a doctrine of Scripture. But it looks as if the place they are to have can only be properly discussed within certain limits. Discussion about inspiration and the range of theologically cognate ideas has historically been exposed to the temptation of excess and exaggeration and has far too frequently yielded to it. If it be recognized that scriptural authority resides substantially in Jesus Christ and formally in the human witness to Jesus Christ, at least the right perspective is provided for proper discussion of the way in which the scriptural documents themselves may properly be said to be inspired and authoritative.

I

The Modern Attitude to the Bible

———

That the Bible has lost face in modern days is a common-place. Even the recent revival of biblical interest bears indirect testimony to its truth: it is a position endangered and to some extent lost that is being recovered. Much has still to be done before the recovery is anything like complete. Few people today would care to say that authority is ascribed to the Bible so readily or certainly or widely as once it was. It is of course true that in practice the Bible is read and loved by countless Christians, and also at least highly regarded by many who do not profess the Christian faith. It is true that officially the Bible holds its place undisturbed in the Churches as the standard of Christian faith and life, acknowledged by both subordinate ecclesiastical standards and by a ministry of word and sacraments. It is probably still true that 'the Bible takes a place and exercises a power far greater than we commonly realise'.[1] But it is incontestable that interest in the Bible has generally receded, the practice of Bible reading steadily declined, and knowledge of the Bible rapidly diminished. This is one of the features of modern religious life which, like decreased Church attendance, all Churches, Roman and reformed[2] alike, have to report and to deplore. It is a Roman Catholic who writes:[3] 'The Bible

[1] W. T. Cairns: *The Bible in Scottish Life and History.* The writer has just quoted from Henry Rogers' *The Eclipse of Faith* the story of 'The Blank Bible', in which 'under the similitude of a dream' the entire obliteration of every scriptural passage and word, wherever occurring, forces on people a realization of the astonishingly wide and deep influence of the Bible in literature and in life.

[2] The term 'reformed' is used throughout to denote Churches often, with unhappy negativeness, contrasted with the Roman Church as Protestant or non-Roman; the term 'Reformed' denotes those among the reformed Churches which historically followed the pattern of Geneva rather than that of Wittenberg.

[3] R. A. Knox: *The Belief of Catholics,* 14.

was never so little believed as it is today; I doubt if it was
ever so little read.'

The question may therefore be appropriately raised: Why
do we of today find it difficult, apparently more difficult than
an earlier age, to concede to the Bible the authority which it
claims? The difficulty we experience is not necessarily dis-
creditable to us. It is suggested that people today want to
know the meaning of the Bible. But in fact they find great
difficulty in making the Bible intelligible to themselves. Writing in 1928, C. J. Cadoux declares:[1] 'For the most part the
doubt [of today] is not that of moral slackness or religious
indifference; it is the doubt of honest and truth-loving intellect, concerned to be scrupulous in creed as in scientific judgment.' Applying this to the Bible, we may be tempted to find
here the reason why the Bible suffers from neglect today.
This looks like a rationalization of the situation—a rationalization that turns the neglect to the credit of the man of today.
It is creditable that he should wish to find intelligible meaning
in the Bible. That he finds the Bible remarkably unintelligible
and for this reason neglects and even rejects it, is not only
natural but right.

There is, of course, some truth in what is here said. The
Bible is not easy to understand. The most obvious difficulty
which is met with is the archaic language in which it is written.
This fact has been much in the minds of those who are concerned about the present neglect, and many have recently
taken in hand the work of translating the Bible, so that it may
be given to people in a language that is their own. There has
been a notable output of modern versions of Holy Scripture.
Publishers tell us that these versions are good sellers, and it is
evident that they are meeting a felt need.[2]

---

[1] *Catholicism and Christianity*, 201f.

[2] It is a long time, for example, since the ordinary church-goer slipped a Bible
into his pocket on his way to weekday work; yet I have seen, and I do not doubt
that others have seen, Dr Rieu's Penguin edition of the four Gospels read by
passengers in bus and tube. It ought here also to be mentioned that the major
Churches of this country, with the exception of the Roman Church, are engaged
in an enterprise which resembles what took place at the beginning of the seventeenth century and culminated in the Authorized Version of King James' Bible.
Building now, as the scholars of the earlier period did, on the unauthorized work
of individuals, the attempt is being made to prepare a translation in as nearly
'timeless English' as may be, which will be capable of being 'understanded of
the people'. This production may be expected to appear, the New Testament
first, within the next few years.

Yet, while not minimizing the importance of what is being done along these lines, few will think that this is a complete answer to the situation of today. The admitted language difficulty is not the only source of that distaste and neglect of the Bible which are evident. After all, if fifty or a hundred years ago Bible reading was much more an accepted discipline of professing Christians, it has to be remembered that the language difficulty cannot then have been so much less as to account for the difference now. The fact seems to be that, despite the language difficulty, which must then too have been considerable, the Bible was used more faithfully and regularly. It would be a hazardous judgment to suppose that we of today bring with us minds so much more eager for intelligibility, that a difficulty which then was overcome or overlooked has now almost suddenly become insuperable. We cannot really suppose that people of an earlier time continued to read the Bible simply because they knew it was the right thing to do, even if, finding it unintelligible, they derived no discernible profit for themselves. It seems necessary to conclude that our forefathers, despite the language difficulty and the unintelligibility which they too found, read the Bible because they profited from it. They realized when doing so that they stood, not only where they ought to stand, but where the word of life was available.

Thus the question, Why is the Bible not credited with an equal authority today? is still unanswered. Putting it in a slightly different form, we may ask: What has made the difference between that earlier day and this? The ground of the difference cannot be located in the Bible itself. When a man reads the Bible, it is always a 'strange new world', to use a phrase of Karl Barth in an early essay,[1] into which he is ushered. It is a world of which we should hardly know apart from the Bible, and one in which we cannot feel quite at home, for all that it may be the place where we would rather be than any other.

If the ground for the difference cannot be located in the Bible itself, is it located in us who come to the Bible? Do we of today come to the Bible with an outlook different from our forefathers, which causes the difficulty which we seem to find and they did not? No doubt the most notable feature of our

[1] *The Word of God and the Word of Man*, Essay 2.

age is the rise of modern science, with the astonishing achievements that are due to it and the immense prestige it has acquired. Have we to look here for the source of this perplexing difference?

We do not find in the fact that our minds are 'scientifically conditioned' the immediate reason and source. There is in all ages some kind of conditioning of the mind of the age which makes the message of the Bible hard to decipher. After all, the mind of the eighteenth century is conditioned by rationalism, and the mind of the nineteenth century by materialism. And it would be difficult to make out that the mind conditioned by science is in a situation of unique difficulty when confronted by the Bible. It is always despite some kind of adverse conditioning that the mind grapples with the Bible and its message; for the conditioning, since it is provided by the world around us, is never particularly favourable to what the Bible has to say. Its message is always 'strange' enough to make it hard going at the best of times.

But if it is not directly to the scientifically conditioned mind of our age that the peculiar difficulty has to be attributed, we do stand, when we say this, very near to what is the source of the difficulty. The source is not so much that we read the Bible with a mind conditioned by the scientific age in which we live, but that certain scientific methods have been applied to the study of the Bible, and the effect has been to put even the believer in a position in which he does not quite know how much of the Bible is left to him. Two scientific methods, or applications of scientific method, have to be taken into account: Criticism and Evolution.

a) *Criticism.* 'We must recognize the fact', says W. Sanday,[1] 'that a change has come over the current way of thinking on this subject of the authority of the Bible. The maxim that the Bible must be studied "like any other book" has been applied. For good or ill, the investigations to which it has given rise are in full swing, and it would be hopeless to stop them, even if it were right to do so. Truth has this advantage, that any method that is really sound in itself can only help to confirm it.' This was written in 1893. Criticism, however, did not begin as a method of studying the Bible. It was first applied

[1] *Inspiration*, 1.

to secular literature. The classics, for example, were examined in order to discover how far a pure text could be reconstructed from which would be excluded all the errors that had in various ways crept in during the course of transmission through the years. These errors being removed, the original text, as it may be supposed to have left the hand of the author, was obtained. Criticism was also applied in another way—not only to discover a pure original text, but, as an extension of this enterprise, also to discover the sources from which this text took its rise and to distinguish between different sections of the text which had to be ascribed to different authors. If Homer is the author of the *Odyssey*, it still remained possible to ask the question: What were his sources and from where did he come by the material which he then 'wrote up'?[1] 'The task of the higher (or literary) and historical critic is to consider questions concerned with the date, authorship, composition, purpose, meaning, and religious and historical value of the various books.'[2]

Textual criticism of the Bible was practised widely in the Church of the Middle Ages. A full account of the many ventures on which medieval biblical scholars embarked is given by Miss B. Smalley in her *The Study of the Bible in the Middle Ages*. The interest was real but restricted: real, as is testified by the *Correctoria Biblica* or lists of emendations compiled by the scholastics; restricted, in that they concerned themselves with the genuineness of the Latin version.[3] Especially 'it seems clear that anti-Jewish controversy was a considerable stimulus to the study of the Old Testament. Unfortunately, the particular direction imparted by that stimulus cannot be regarded as having been healthy either for the life or theology of the Church. Nor is its legacy yet departed from us.'[4] It did, however, have at least one good result: it obtained a more accurate knowledge of the text. The Renaissance stimulated further study, and here Reformers joined hands with the doctors of the unreformed Church. Luther and Calvin, and especially

[1] Wolf's *Introduction to Homer* at the end of the eighteenth century was a pioneer work.

[2] R. H. Lightfoot in *The Interpretation of the Bible*, 78.

[3] See *Providentissimus Deus*, xiii (English translation in 1914 edition of the Douai Bible).

[4] M. F. Wiles: 'The Old Testament in Controversy with the Jews', in *The Scottish Journal of Theology*, Vol. 8, 126.

Melanchthon, owe much to the inspiration and influence of Erasmus the humanist.[1] Yet despite this study, the Bible contrived to retain its authority unimpaired. Thus, interested as he was in the text, 'for Luther there was no sacred text; God's Word depended not on the letter, but lay in the meaning'.[2] The real impact of criticism upon the authority of the Bible still remained to be made.

It came about in this way. Though textual criticism had been widely applied to the Bible, in the case of higher criticism the distinction between sacred and secular literature was scrupulously observed up till perhaps the middle of the eighteenth century. Then almost suddenly the barrier this distinction interposed between Holy Scripture and the critic gave way, and, slowly at first, but with increasing momentum, his attention was turned to the Bible. In Professor Jowett's phrase in *Essays and Reviews* of 1860, one could now 'interpret the Scriptures like any other book'. The claim is made[3] that Richard Simon (1638-1712), a French priest of the Roman Catholic Oratory, may be justly called the 'father of biblical criticism'.[4] It is much more certain that J. G. Eichhorn was at the end of the eighteenth century the first to use the phrase 'higher criticism' with reference to the Scriptures, and that the most notable name in the early course of the events that followed is that of J. Wellhausen.

The immediate results were full of interest. Two illustrations must suffice.

Perhaps the most notable example in the Old Testament is the case of the Pentateuch. The observant reader of the Authorized Version cannot fail to notice discrepancies and even inconsistencies in the narrative contained in the very first book of the Bible, and this is already to be doing the work of a critic. Higher criticism carried the examination of this and other phenomena further, when it claimed (as in the Graf-Wellhausen hypothesis) that four different documents can be distinguished, denied the traditional Mosaic authorship of the first five books of the Bible, regarded the Davidic authorship of the Psalms and the Solomonic authorship of the Wisdom literature as rather literary devices than historical

---

[1] W. Köhler: *Dogmengeschichte*, II, 112f.   [2] Op. cit., 113.
[3] *A Catholic Commentary on Holy Scripture*, §43f.
[4] 'Le père de la critique biblique'—J. Coppens: *L'histoire critique des livres de l'Ancient Testament*, 28.

judgments, and traced the dominant part played by prophetic influence in at least the compilation of the books of the Old Testament as we have them. As for the New Testament, in 1835 Carl Lachmann, comparing the four Gospel narratives together and discovering how much they had in common, suggested that in fact Mark must have been the first to appear and that at least two other evangelists made use of Mark. This conclusion has stood the test of time and is largely accepted today, except by those who have a special interest in maintaining something different. Similarly, it is as certain as anything based on criticism can be that the writer of the Epistle to the Hebrews is not St Paul. The situation is not that there are no scholars who decline to accept these findings: the most recent Roman Catholic commentary in English, already referred to,[1] refuses to commit itself about the earliest Gospel, and holds that St Paul probably did write Hebrews.

If the immediate findings of criticism were interesting, the more indirect consequences of the application of the method were not less than shattering. They can be classed as in the main two, a major effect and a lesser but none the less important corollary. It was felt that since the Bible had concealed these and many other facts now by the method of criticism being brought to light, the *authenticity* of the Bible was impugned and impaired. It is true that the substance of the Bible remains the same whoever wrote it, and that what is true is true whether it is the hand of Moses or of an eighth-century prophet that wrote it. Macpherson's 'Fingal' is good or bad poetry quite independently of the question whether Ossian wrote it or not; and the facts stated in the Decretals of the ninth century are true or false whether it was Isidore of Seville or Marius Mercator who wrote them. Yet the matter is not so easily disposed of as this. It is not merely for the recital of true things that men went to the Bible. They were accustomed to turn to the Bible as the record of things and judgments committed to writing by those who were conceived to have the right to speak, and to speak authoritatively, in cases where it is not a matter of demonstrable truth or falsity. In such circumstances, there are laid in the mind the seeds of suspicion that a book that can assume so unauthentic a form may also be involved in error in its contents. But this is to anticipate. Suffice it to

[1] *A Catholic Commentary on Holy Scripture.*

say here that where the case of the authenticity of the Bible could not be made good, there its authority received a damaging blow.

The corollary that follows from the work of the critics is only a little less important than what has just been said. It is that the *unity* of the Bible is undermined. An 'atomistic criticism' succeeds in concealing all evidence of a 'unity of design'.[1] Where once one document stood under each of the titles of the first five books of the Bible, four or more documents interwoven with each other have now to be acknowledged. The unity formerly assumed has been shown to be composite; from it layers of different kinds, extent and age, can be successively peeled off. The Bible not only can be studied in short passages, but must be studied in this way if its composite character is to be understood. In place of the single voice with which Scripture was supposed to speak, we have now to listen to a chorus of voices, reaching us from different backgrounds and ages, and by no means concordant in what they say. When this is accepted, it may not be absolutely necessary to go further, but certainly the next step lies very near at hand and in fact frequently proves irresistible. When the unity is broken up and different not wholly congruent voices make themselves heard, it is easy to think that we must make our choice between these voices, accepting some and rejecting others. To do this, we bring some kind of extraneous standard and apply it to the voices we hear, and by this standard some of the voices are judged worth listening to, and others are condemned. In practical terms, what this means is that we feel it right and indeed necessary to turn to certain parts of the Bible and read there, and at the same time to ignore and decline to read certain other parts. This constitutes a further blow to the authority of the Bible. Upheld as a unity, the Bible wields an impressive authority. Broken down into small fragments different from one another rather than harmonious, as criticism has taught it must be, this impressive authority is sensibly shaken if not irrecoverably lost. The student of the Bible is then 'like a man turning over an immense heap of variously shaped fragments. What the original design may have been does not concern him. He merely fits them together as

[1] Dom Ralph Russell: ' "Humani Generis" and the "Spiritual" Sense of Scripture', in *The Downside Review*, 1951, 10f.

his fancy prompts him into wholly unexpected patterns.'[1] As Brunner says,[2] 'what we have begun to question is less the biblical record as such than the unity of the biblical record; and this of course affects our belief in the trustworthiness of that harmony of history which represents the traditional view of "biblical history" '.[3]

Thus the indirect effects of criticism are even more profound and extensive than its more direct results. The authority of the Bible for men of today has been severely impaired, not because it is likely that the prophets have more to do with the formation of Deuteronomy than Moses, but because the Bible seems now on the evidence of criticism to have been masquerading under false colours and wielding an authority to which its claims are now refuted. The readiness with which modern man may be expected to reckon with a book of this kind is much diminished.

b) *Evolution* is the second major influence contributing to the present situation and the difficulties felt by modern man in reading Holy Scripture. Little need be said here to recall the violent conflict that broke out between science and religion over the issues raised by Darwin and the theory of evolution. Under the impact of the Copernican revolution which displaced the earth from the centre of the universe, Christian

---

[1] The words are quoted by Hugh Pope in *St Thomas Aquinas* (being papers read at the celebrations of the sixth centenary of the canonization of St Thomas Aquinas, held at Manchester, 1924), in the contribution 'St Thomas as an Interpreter of Holy Scripture', 111, from *The Journal of Theological Studies*, July 1915, in an article on St Ambrose. They apply here also, the difference being that in the case of St Ambrose the unity of an imposed spiritual meaning made him indifferent to the unity actually represented in Scripture, whereas the modern is apt to lose interest in any unity real or factitious, discovered or imposed.

[2] *Revelation and Reason*, 287. The translation has been slightly altered to make the meaning plainer.

[3] Brunner even hazards the opinion that 'the most important result of the whole work of biblical criticism' is the discovery that 'between the synoptic Gospels and the Fourth Gospel, as well as between the teaching of Jesus and that of the apostles, there is a great, and indeed, a radical difference' (op. cit. 288). The result of the whole tendency Brunner expresses strongly: in the case of the Old Testament, 'there is no "theology of the Old Testament" ' (290); in the case of the New Testament, 'at some points the variety of the apostolic doctrine, regarded purely from the theological and intellectual point of view, is an irreconcilable contradiction' (loc. cit.). The situation is redeemed for Brunner by recognition that, while there is no self-contained unity, there is harmony; and that what unity the Bible does possess reposes in 'the one God who encounters us in the Book of Judges and in the Gospel of John' (op. cit., 293).

belief seemed to reel; but a recovery was made, and it was still possible to have faith and to read the Bible. Then, just as balance was being regained, there was administered this further blow. It appeared that man is not the immediate creation of a Creator who calls him into being at a certain point in time and in some such way as Genesis relates; rather he ascends from a humble origin among the brute beasts to his present unique status. Here contradiction seemed to be involved: it could not be true both that man was made on the sixth of seven first days and also that he evolved from a simian ancestry. It was a clear choice between man fallen and man risen. The hypothesis of evolution was soon supported by such a formidable array of facts which it satisfactorily explained, that it seemed to be virtually unassailable. The Bible in this case had simply to be discarded or it had to be shut up in a compartment by itself where the contagion of Darwinism would not reach it.

But once again it is the indirect consequences of this major event in Christian history that are really more important than the immediate effects; and again there is a major consequence to take into account, and a lesser corollary. The major consequence is that it now appeared that the *veracity* of the Bible was threatened. This final indignity had been spared the Bible by the critics; the evolutionists now inflicted it. Between what Genesis seemed to say and what evolution in the full flush of initial success was declaring, there seemed little chance of agreement. It seemed necessary to suppose that one was true and the other false. And if these were the alternatives offered, how could the remarkable edifice erected upon the hypothesis of evolution be easily overthrown? Must it not be the lore of an ancient people and literature that had to give way? And once the veracity of the Bible is thus seriously challenged at any point, it is impossible to hold the Bible as a whole in the same reverence, or to ascribe to it the same authority, as it had formerly enjoyed.

A corollary follows. Disunity had already affected the formerly unified witness of Holy Scripture. This disunity was now to be exploited. The characteristic feature of evolution is the discarding of anything that does not stand on the way of advance. It is not so much the brave that evolutionary fortune favours as those that are astute enough to trim their sails to the prevailing wind. The unsuccessful is rooted up and thrown away. Only that which is successful persists and needs to be reckoned with. This rubric worked with ruinous effect on the respect accorded to the Bible. The Scriptures, already fallen into fragments under the assault of criticism, are now easily divided up into the valuable and the valueless. What stands at the summit of the path of progress need alone concern us; all the rest has been superseded and need detain us no longer. Since the Gospels are the last word in revelation, Genesis can well remain a closed book. Thus another nail is driven into the coffin of biblical authority. So far from residing in the whole of Holy Scripture, such authority as is left is exercised only by a small selection of late writings, while the rest are relegated to the lumber room or to the study of the historian of religion. Even this position is difficult to maintain. The charge of mendacity is so serious, that it must seem to involve the whole of the work against any portion of which it could be substantiated.

The two factors just mentioned seem sufficient to account for the perplexity that exists today even among believers concerning the place that the Bible occupies or should occupy. They do not even have the meagre satisfaction of knowing for certain that the Bible has been denuded of all authority; for this has not been clearly established. They are left in the unsatisfactory position of knowing that the Bible and its authority have suffered severe shocks, and they are not quite sure what is left of the imposing authority it once claimed. In fact, a remarkable recovery has on the whole been made, the disturbed equilibrium has been restored, and much of the territory lost to science regained. The claim is being made good that criticism can do nothing finally harmful to the truth, but only help to elucidate it more firmly and purely. Further, a growing wisdom has entered into the exchanges between science and religion. On the one hand, science has checked its own presumptions; on the other, religion has realized that it is no integral part of faith to hold that the world was made in six days of twenty-four hours each. Brunner puts the point with much assurance. There is, he says, no real conflict at all. So far as higher criticism is concerned, 'all conflicts between historical criticism and faith, when more closely examined, turn out to be nonexistent; such "difficulties" are caused

either by an unjustifiable dogmatic statement of traditional
historical views on the part of the Church, or by a sceptical
distortion on the part of critical science'.[1] So far as the impact
of science is concerned, the solution, Brunner says, is to be
found by the Church simply taking its 'own truth seriously';
it is possible to have an understanding of Holy Scripture like
that of the Reformers, which 'wholly excluded a conflict with
natural science'.[2] Perhaps the matter is not quite so easily
resolved as this suggests. In the case of criticism, is not Bultmann to be regarded as standing beyond the point at which
the concessions to criticism have to be halted if the Gospel is
to remain recognizable, and is there no difficulty in defining
where the stand has to be made? Again, science and theology
seem to conflict in more than appearance: man must come to
be in one specific way and not in another; Christ must have
been incarnate in one particular way and not in another;
and the world must end in one certain way and not in another. At these crucial points it is difficult to think that the
accounts of science and of faith will not substantially differ,
since here the two planes of the natural and the supernatural
actually intersect. However this may be, the admitted *détente*
that has more recently been taking place between science and
religion has not impressed the ordinary man, believer or unbeliever, with anything like the same force as the initial clash
between them did. Both at this point and also in the case of
criticism, the impression that some damage has been done to
the Bible and its authority has not been erased. The arguments by which the faith has not without success tried to
restore the position which science and criticism seemed to
imperil have been too subtle to carry full conviction. The
attacks upon the authenticity and upon the veracity of the
Bible have left scars and exposed weaknesses. Men do not
hear in the Bible, as apparently former generations did, the
voice of God speaking to them. T. W. Manson says that
the result of extruding miracle from the order of nature and the
closing of the iron ring of cause and effect

'is to establish a thick plate-glass window between God and
the world. The eye of faith can see through the window
and observe that there is a God and that He appears to

---

[1] *Revelation and Reason*, 282.   [2] Op. cit., 280.

be benevolently disposed towards men; but nothing more substantial than signals of paternal affection and filial trust and obedience can get through.'[1]

If the Bible is further written off as no longer a means of and for God's Word, then, as the same writer goes on to say, 'the plate-glass window set up between heaven and earth is sound-proof' as well.

A comment may be made about each of these major influences which have contributed so substantially to the modern situation. Even if they have in fact weakened biblical interest and regard, they do not necessarily work in this way. The first comment refers to the influence of evolution. It may be that among the writers of Scripture nothing at all resembling the idea of progress embodied in the theory of evolution appears. But Christ does give a centre to the whole of history, and history thereby acquires a whence and a whither, or in other words a direction. This direction it derives from the saving plan of God. When this latter fact is forgotten, the idea of progress may still remain. The more recent idea of progress can be interpreted as a secularized reconstruction of this biblical process, in which history itself is credited with an inherent power of advance, while God is extruded. It may then seem a remarkable thing if this secularized view of progress, originating as it does from a misconstruction of a view which takes its rise from within Christianity, should be in principle hostile to Christianity and to the Bible in which Christianity has its foundations. It would be more in accord with probability that there should be no essential and irresolvable opposition between the two, and that the actual collision between them should be the result of misunderstanding.

The second comment must be made at greater length. It refers to the other major factor, the rise of criticism. It is not true that, up to the time when criticism was first methodically applied to the sacred writings about the end of the eighteenth century, all the facts that were then so compellingly revealed were unknown to students of the Bible. As has been mentioned, at least some of them had already been ascertained and acknowledged. For example, the Reformers exercised a critical insight when they studied the Scriptures. It is well known that Luther

[1] In *The Interpretation of the Bible*, 93f.

holds the later prophets to build, not only gold and silver on the foundation afforded by Moses and the earlier prophets, but also wood and hay and stubble, that he says the Fourth Gospel account of the denial of St Peter contains many inaccuracies, and that he judges the Epistle of James to be an epistle of straw. Calvin similarly is well aware of errors in Scripture, as when Jeremiah is credited in Matt. xxvii. 9 with words he never spoke. Before the Reformers, many errors had already been detected. Thus Irenaeus[1] argues against the literal meaning of the story of the Fall. Gregory of Nyssa[2] denies that the opening chapters of Genesis are historical. St Chrysostom[3] is aware of incongruities in the story as told by the evangelists and maintains that only the cardinal facts of the narrative remain intact. With Clement of Alexandria and Origen, the allegorical method of interpretation is employed without restraint, and its employment seems not merely to obscure the literal meaning of Scripture, but to conceal their doubts concerning its truth. (And who will deny that many allegorical sermons today have just the same effect, and that many hearers are thereby confirmed in their doubts concerning the truth of the Bible?) After the Reformers again, many of the results of later criticism are anticipated. Thus, to quote R. H. Lightfoot,[4]

> 'Dean Colet's letters, written before the discoveries of Copernicus, show that he regarded the first chapters of Genesis as containing poetical rather than scientific truth. ... Thomas Hobbes in his *Leviathan*, published in 1651, maintained that the first five books of the Bible must have been written after the time of Moses, and that the Old Testament, as we have it now, was first put forth after the return of the Jews from their captivity in Babylon.'

It is of course true that such anticipations of later critical conclusions were by no means fully and methodically worked out. Yet there is a discrepancy here to be accounted for. At the earlier time, it was apparently possible to maintain such conclusions without abandoning the authority of the Bible, whereas at the later date this seems to be no longer possible. Why should such a difference exist? It looks as if some other

[1] *Fragm.* 14.
[2] *Oratio Catechetica*, ch. 5.
[3] *Homilies on St Matt.*, 1. 2.
[4] In *The Interpretation of the Bible*, 79.

hitherto unmentioned factor were simultaneously at work. What can this factor be?

The suggestion may here be made that this other factor, present today and absent at the earlier period, consists in a certain literal rigidity with which the Bible has come to be regarded. It is repeatedly alleged that the view of biblical authority held in the Christian Church from the second century to the eighteenth rested on the assumption that Holy Scripture was verbally dictated and accordingly inerrant. Thus Augustine[1] says that the writers of Holy Scripture were preserved from every error in writing them. And 'such indeed', says C. J. Cadoux,[2] 'was the general assumption of Catholic and Protestants alike down to the dawn of modern criticism'. Similarly, Charles Gore affirms[3] that this is the 'constant assumption of the early centuries'; and so many others have said the same thing, that it has come to be widely accepted as incontestable. The allegation is much too general and is in its simple form unacceptable. What is true is that there appears over the years a recurrent movement from living authority to literal authority. Walter Lippmann says in a notable phrase, that insecurity 'welcomes manacles to prevent its hands shaking'.[4] The remark is applicable here. It is as though ordinary men found the faith that consists in lying 'constantly out upon the deep and with 70,000 fathoms of water under him', as Kierkegaard puts it,[5] too much of a venture and longs to put his trust in something more tangible and accessible. The movement towards literal inerrancy can repeatedly be diagnosed as the sickness or torpor that succeeds a 'first fine careless rapture'. It is the mark of the ebbtide setting in, when the flood having reached its peak subsides. It is observable when the age of rabbinical exegesis follows the age of the prophets and the commission to writing of their message. It is seen at an early stage in the history of the Christian Church. There are traces of it in the New Testament itself, where the Gospel is regarded as a *depositum fidei*; while later,

'almost from the very first the inspiration of the witness of the Old Testament and of the New is commonly regarded as "verbal" and commonly identified with infallibility. This

[1] *Ep.*, lxxxii. 3, Migne, *P.L.*, xxxiii, 277.   [2] *Catholicism and Christianity*, 273.
[3] *The Doctrine of the Infallible Book*, 35.
[4] Qtd. in G. T. Bellhouse: *Immortal Longings*, 69.   [5] *Stages on Life's Way*, 402.

was to be expected, for the Jews had commonly identified inspiration with verbal infallibility, and the Christians learned it from them.'[1]

Further, it can be detected as Protestant Orthodoxy succeeds the work of the Reformers.[2] The danger is inherent in the commission of the Gospel to writing at all, as Calvin often says, and as Karl Barth has recently reasserted.[3] But it is the sign of decadence and of a recession from true understanding of what Scripture offers us. From this decadence, however, there is from time to time a recovery, as when a Luther or a Calvin interprets the authority of the Bible in a living way, not as the deposit of faith to be assented to, but as the means through which God makes His Word heard in the present day.

If this decadent tendency is observable 'from the second century to the eighteenth', it is not unmitigated and unalleviated. The fact is that it was throughout this long period usually supplemented by methods of interpretation.

'In the Middle Ages, as represented by the twelfth and thirteenth centuries, for instance, the emphasis of, say, a preaching friar was on the spiritual and moral meaning of Scripture for the hearers, rather than on any question of the verbal inspiration and inerrancy of the text. Indeed, the literal meaning was often almost completely obscured by the current method of interpretation, based as it was on the idea of a multiple sense of Scripture.'[4]

In earlier ages, then, where the idea of literal inerrancy was maintained, it was helped out by a multiple interpretation which dissolved, for practical purposes at least, the verbal rigidity. This, as will later be said at greater length, is the official view of the Roman Church, though it 'observes the rule so wisely laid down by St Augustine, not to depart from the literal and obvious sense, except only when reason makes it untenable or necessity requires'.[5] Flexibility returned to Scripture, though it was a flexibility different from that imparted by a God whose living voice is heard in it. This latter

---

[1] Gore: *The Doctrine of the Infallible Book*, 46 and note 1.
[2] See what is later said in Chapter III.   [3] *Kirchliche Dogmatik*, I/1, 117f.
[4] Raymond Abba: 'Recent Trends in Biblical Studies', *The Scottish Journal of Theology*, Vol. 4, 227.
[5] *Providentissimus Deus*, xviii, qtg. *De Gen ad litt*, viii. 7. 13.

view, the Reformers recovered, as will be seen in the next
two chapters. Then the need for multiple interpretation disappeared, and the simple meaning re-established itself as
dominant and normative. Allegorical interpretation, with the
massive construction of fanciful and arbitrary exegesis which
from the time of Origen so preoccupied the Church, was jettisoned. Yet flexibility remained, since in Scripture the Reformers
saw the vehicle of God's speech with men.

The position of those who today subscribe to biblical infallibility in 'fundamentalist' terms is quite different. They have
been encouraged by a scientific age to adopt a literalism, and
at the same time to abandon the allegorism with which it
could be and traditionally was defended. In this sense, as
A. G. Hebert rightly observes,[1] 'the inerrancy of the Bible,
as it is understood today, is a new doctrine, and the modern
fundamentalist is asserting something that no previous age has
understood in anything like the modern sense'. Gore affirms
the same thing when he says[2] that 'those who would force us
to retain the ancient literalism without the ancient allegorism
seem to be behaving unreasonably'.

It is this fundamental change in the meaning of biblical
inerrancy which at least partly accounts for the profound
effect which the rise of science and of criticism has had upon
the modern man's understanding of and confidence in the
Bible. In earlier ages, a view of the Bible was held that possessed enough suppleness to accommodate such critical discrepancies as were discovered, and still to retain the authority
of the Bible. In the later period, the Bible was regarded in
terms of a type of literal inerrancy which, when the discoveries
were remade and extended, made it impossible for biblical
authority to survive. A view of the Bible was held which no
longer had the resilience necessary to meet the fresh challenge,
and authority seemed to suffer a mortal blow. If the authority
of the Bible be construed in the sense that every isolated
word of Holy Scripture is inerrant, to call in question of even
one of these words is enough to shatter that authority.

This is a point which Brunner realises clearly.[3]

'So long as the ecclesiastical principle which governed
the view of the Scriptures was understood in terms of the

---

[1] *The Authority of the Old Testament*, 98.
[2] *The Doctrine of the Infallible Book*, 51.   [3] *Revelation and Reason*, 274.

orthodox doctrine of verbal inspiration, even the smallest concession to "biblical criticism"—whether from the side of natural science or from that of historical science—was a catastrophe for the whole fabric of the doctrine of the Church. If the Bible is an infallible book, written down under the dictation of the Holy Spirit, then no biblical criticism could exist—no admission of any inconsistencies, errors, or mistakes in the Bible. Here the slogan was: "Everything must be believed, or nothing will be believed." '

With equal clarity he realizes that the position of the Reformers was not thus exposed to attack:[1] 'the Reformers had gained— or regained—a knowledge of the Holy Scriptures, which, taken seriously, wholly excluded a conflict with natural science'. As said above, this slightly exaggerates the security of the Reformers' position.

The grievous loss in authority which the Bible has sustained in modern days is then the result of a combination of factors —of the incidence of the conclusions of criticism and science upon a view which attaches authority to the word and the letter of Holy Scripture. If this is true, then the remedy is also clear. If the authority of the Bible be located, not in the words of Holy Scripture, but rather in the Word itself, if it be located not in the printed page, but in Him to whom the printed page bears witness, Jesus Christ Himself the Word incarnate, cruci- fied, risen, and regnant, in the transmitted message rather than in the transmitted letter, it will be possible to accommodate the results of criticism of the words, and yet to credit the Bible with all the authority of Him to whom it testifies.

[1] *Revelation and Reason*, 280.

II

Calvin on the Authority of Holy Scripture

To begin with a study of Calvin is chronologically wrong but tactically right. Two reasons may be mentioned here. The first is that, just as Luther and the theology to which he gives rise are popularly and justifiably held to be summarized by the phrase *sola fide*, so Calvin and his theology are associated with the phrase *sola scriptura*. For both Luther and Calvin and their respective theologies, Scripture and the authority of Scripture are of the greatest importance. It may be that the importance in each is about equal. But Calvin gives Scripture a clearer and more explicit status than Luther. This is illustrated by what Calvin says of the *Institutes*,[1] that it is 'the sum of what we find God wished to teach us in His Word'. Luther's view would not substantially differ, but he would not have found it natural to make so explicit and formal a profession.

The other reason is this. In Calvin, the theology of the Reformation achieved systematization at a remarkably early date. This is due to the astonishing powers of Calvin, who had so incisive an insight that he saw little need to revise an opinion he had once formed and expressed. If then the theologies of Luther and Calvin be compared, it may be said that the very fixity of the systematization achieved by Calvin discouraged development, whereas the multitudinous and uncoordinated works of Luther prompted it. It follows that the line of development for doctrines in which Lutherans and Calvinists were not involved in contentious debates, and the doctrine of Holy Scripture is of this class, has Luther as point of departure in a more marked degree than Calvin. Hence a start is made here with Calvin, and this is followed by consideration of

[1] Preface to the French edition.

Luther, before going on to Protestant orthodoxy and scholasticism.

The chief objective must here be to examine the widespread opinion that the biblicism of Calvin is based on literal or verbal inerrancy. If this is found to be a false understanding of Calvin, the secondary aim will be to discover what other view can be constructed out of the material which Calvin supplies.

It may be helpful at the outset to present in examples the different views held of the matter.

'If God's revelation was confined to this volume [the Bible], if its contents were to be the infallible touchstone of truth, if the perfect harmony of its parts was to be depended upon, it must be that Providence, which preserved the constituent books and secured their compilation into a canon, took care that no error should creep into its pages. For the assurance of faith, it was necessary to be able to trust the accuracy of every word of the record.'

This amounts to the 'assertion of the inerrancy of Scripture'.[1] Further:

'Anticipating the Quakers, Münzer held that "God still speaks to His own today, as once He spoke to Abraham, Isaac, and Jacob". To that Calvin, of course, could not agree; to do so would have deprived him of his infallible criterion and touchstone of truth, and he could then no longer clinch an argument or silence an opponent by the final words, Thus saith the Lord, with his finger on a text.'[2]

'The Scripture being regarded as not merely containing but being the very Word of God, it was a matter of the utmost moment that its interpretation by expositors should be such as to provoke confidence in their readers that they are actually learning what the Lord would say to them.'[3]

More hesitant is the view expressed by A. Dakin,[4] who maintains that Calvin's view is of 'Scripture as the infallible Word of God. It is the very Word which God has spoken for

[1] A. Mitchell Hunter: *The Teaching of Calvin*, 72.
[2] Op. cit., 71.
[3] Op. cit., 85. This is open to a diametrically opposite use: if Scripture is so directly the Word of God, the function of the expositor is reduced to vanishing importance—but this is as may be.
[4] *Calvinism*, 189.

the enlightenment of the elect.' The denial of literal and verbal inspiration is a responsibility from which Dakin apparently shrinks, though he quotes the authority of Doumergue to this end. All he will allow himself to say is that 'it would certainly give a false impression to say that [Calvin] held by verbal infallibility'. He continues: 'At the same time he firmly insists on the fact that the Bible as a whole is both infallible and authoritative.'

At the other extreme is the view of Doumergue. He quotes[1] Seeberg: 'Calvin founded the authority of Holy Scripture, on the one hand, upon the thought that it is a dictation of God', and adds that on the other hand 'from a historical point of view, he combines the school of inspiration of the end of the Middle Ages with the thought of Luther'. Commenting, Doumergue says: 'Half a borrower of the Middle Ages; half a Lutheran—this is the habitual formula.' The denial follows: 'Calvin did not teach the theory of dictation in the sense here meant, in the sense of an inspiration verbal and literal.'[2]

What are the data that have here to be taken into account? The general situation is to be remembered first. When Luther burnt the papal bull issued against him in the square at Wittenberg, a shock was administered to the whole of Western Christendom, whose tremors were not lightly to be composed. The authority of Holy Church had been openly defied—and nothing had happened to vindicate this authority or to visit upon the defaulter the displeasure of Heaven. But to overturn authority is one thing; to deal with the resulting situation is quite another. It is often said[3] that 'the average man demands authoritative guidance in regard to unseen things', and, we are told, that the reformed attempt to set up the Bible as authoritative was a deliberate attempt at substitution—the supply of an alternative authority for that hitherto exercised by the Roman hierarchy. Thus A. F. Pollard says:[4] 'to the infallibility of the Church the Reformers and later Protestants opposed the infallibility of the Scriptures'; and Chillingworth:[5] 'The Bible alone is the religion of Protestants'. There may be something in this. But for the purpose here, the

---

[1] *Jean Calvin*, IV, 73.   [2] See Supplementary Note at end of Chapter.
[3] So A. M. Hunter: *The Teaching of Calvin*, 64.
[4] Qtd. by Albert Peel: 'The Bible and the People', in *The Interpretation of the Bible*, 49.
[5] Qtd. ibid. from *The Religion of Protestants, a Safe Way to Salvation*.

C

situation can be simplified. It is not the re-establishment of some authority that is in question; it is rather the rehabilitation in its proper authority of something which always had enjoyed some degree of reverence and respect, Holy Scripture itself. The quest is for a ground, stronger than that of the impaired and injured Church, on which the authority of Scripture could be securely based. That this ground was found to lie within Scripture itself is a tribute to the spiritual insight of the Reformers. That Scripture then came to occupy the place vacated by the stultified claims of the Pope is a consequence of the Reformers' work, not a deliberate aim. The thought is rather to do justice to Holy Scripture itself than to supply man's felt need for authoritative guidance. Seeberg,[1] whose appraisal of Luther is on the whole just, seems to suggest that even he looked round for 'an absolutely sure standard recognized by friend and foe alike, from which to criticize his opponents and defend himself'. New insight into what Scripture is and has to offer may certainly be said to be the occasion of Luther's characteristic understanding of the Christian faith and life. But it is unconvincing to represent the place which Scripture is given in his theology as dictated by tactical considerations and the desire to occupy a position of advantage against possible opponents. The case is not so clear with Calvin, who appreciated the advantages which the Bible possessed as an objective and widely recognized standard of appeal and exploited them to the full. But, though plausible, it is not correct to think of him deliberately looking for something to take the place of the fallen authority of the Church.

In fact, credence of Holy Scripture was a common possession of the undivided Church. Here the Reformers met unreformed Churchmen on ground that each claimed and valued. The quick reaction on the part of the unreformed Church at the Council of Trent to vindicate the grounds on which Scripture was to be believed is indication of this concern for Scripture. Calvin therefore does not find it necessary to argue at length the case for the authority of Holy Scripture. It is the grounds for this authority and its nature that are the substance of the dispute. That the recognition of the authority of Holy Scripture grew strong in the Church of the reformers, while in the unreformed Church it was choked by accessory growth is also

---

[1] *Lehrbuch der Dogmengeschichte*, IV/1, 409.

true. But this diverse development is to be attributed to the positions which the two sections of the Church respectively occupied at the time when the grounds and nature of the authority of Holy Scripture were under debate. The affirmation of Holy Church as the sole interpreter of Scripture, and the declaration that tradition is alongside of Scripture an 'authoritative contributor to the substance of the faith'[1] obtained (or retained) such a stranglehold, that the real living influence of Scripture was smothered.

On the reformed side, it is a necessary preliminary to distinguish what properly belongs to Calvin, from the ideas attributable to his successors. A good deal is laid at Calvin's door that is by no means rightly attributed to him. Even to place on him the responsibility for the conclusions, or some of the conclusions, in which his doctrine is said to issue, is less than fair. Doumergue gives[2] a brief account of the development of the idea of inspiration through the Confessions, which shows that much ground is covered in a short time. Thus the Dutch Confession speaks of 'a special concern' on the part of God; the prior Confessio Helvetica of 'prompted by the Holy Ghost'; the posterior says that 'God Himself spoke to the fathers'; the Confession of la Rochelle that the Scriptures 'proceed from God'; while the Westminster Confession of Faith talks of the Scriptures 'which are given by inspiration of God'. It is only in the last stages of development that one comes across such an expression as is contained in the Formula Consensus Helvetica of 1675, which speaks of the Hebrew text as 'οεόπνευστος regarding both the vowels (whether the very points or at least the power of the points) and regarding things as well as words'.[3] Yet this is the view for which Calvin is made responsible by A. M. Hunter,[4] even if he blunts the charge by adding: 'though Calvin might have disclaimed responsibility for the mode of expression, the article . . . only carries his views to their conclusion'. Such conclusions are not rightly ascribed to Calvin, who had, as will be shown, excellent grounds for stopping far short of them. What Schaff calls the 'hoarfrost of later Protestant scholasticism' must

1 The words are from A. M. Hunter: *The Teaching of Calvin*, 63.
2 *Jean Calvin*, IV, 73, n. 4.
3 *Tum quoad consonas, tum quoad vocalia, sive puncta ipsa, sive punctorum saltem potestatem, et tum quoad res, tum quoad verba theopneustos.*
4 *The Teaching of Calvin*, 73.

not be antedated to the early summer of the Reformation.

When the extreme conclusions drawn from Calvin's doctrine have been dismissed, there still remains much that can be employed to give colour to the allegation that Calvin is a literalist. Only a brief indication need be given here of the kind of phrase and expression which gives rise to ambiguity, and this must do duty for much material scattered throughout the works of Calvin. First, from the Commentaries, on 2 Tim. iii. 16, 'all scripture is given by inspiration of God', etc., Calvin writes:

'To show its authority, the writer declares that it is divinely inspired. . . . And this is the principle that distinguishes our religion from all others, namely that we know that God speaks to us, and are certainly assured that the prophets did not speak on their own, but as organs and instruments of the Holy Spirit, so that they announced only what they had received from on high.'

And further, 'the law and the prophets are not a doctrine delivered according to the will and pleasure of men, but dictated by the Holy Spirit'.[1] On 1 Pet. i. 11, he writes: 'The ancient prophecies were dictated by Christ'; while on 1 Pet. i. 25, he says: 'We ought then to believe that God desires to speak to us by the apostles and prophets, and that their mouths are no other thing than the mouth of God Himself.'

From the Sermons on Deuteronomy, the following passages are worth attention:

'What is Holy Scripture but a declaration of the will of God? And so all that is there contained is as if God opened His sacred mouth to declare to us what He demands.'

'Moses (or rather the Spirit of God speaking by His mouth).' 'Let us note that this word Scripture implies that Moses was not at all the author of Law or Psalms; but that he was only a scribe or secretary under the mouth of God. Thus, just as a secretary will write what is given him, so it is precisely declared here that Moses wrote what he received from God, and not what he fabricated in his own head.'

To this may be added another sentence from the Sermons,

[1] *A spiritu sancto dictatum.*

where on 2 Tim. Calvin says: 'All that St Paul has left us in
writing, we must consider as God speaking to us by the mouth
of mortal man, and all his teaching is to be received in authority and reverence as though God made Himself visible from
heaven.'

Exemplary of much that might be quoted from the *Institutes*
are the following. The Scriptures 'ought to have with believers
the same complete authority as though they were able to hear
the voice of God from His own mouth' (1. 7. 1); 'God's own
voice' (1. 7. 1); 'dictated by the Holy Spirit' (4. 8. 6); 'authentic amanuenses of the Holy Spirit' (4. 8. 9); the scriptural
'writings are to be received as the oracles of God' (ibid.);
Scripture is 'the school of the Holy Spirit' (3. 21. 3).

In another passage the idea of dictation comes to clear expression. Commenting on Jer. xxxvi. 4-6, Calvin suggests that
when Jeremiah has to repeat his message to Baruch, after the
destruction of the first copy—

'the greater part of so many words must have escaped
the prophet, had not God dictated them again to him.[1] . . .
Now the prophet, the Spirit being his guide and teacher,
recited what God had commanded. . . . Jeremiah repeats
again that nothing came from himself. We see hence, that
he did not dictate according to his own will what came to
his mind, but that God suggested whatever He wished to
be written by Baruch.'[2]

Of Calvin's exegesis here one may well have doubts. Indeed,
the passage can be[3] used to exactly the opposite effect. That
Jeremiah must have forgotten 'the greater part of so many
words' is pure hypothesis, designed solely to substantiate divine
dictation. It follows that Calvin is not here arguing for verbal
dictation, but rather from it.[4]

One cannot deny that out of the available material a formidable case for holding Calvin to be a literalist can be constructed.
But when this has been done, it is still possible to doubt whether
the real Calvin has been discerned or his intention rightly

[1] *Rursum illi dictasset.*
[2] *Ex sensu suo.*
[3] It is so used by W. Sanday (*Inspiration*, 238); see also Chapter V.
[4] In view of such a statement as this, it is hardly possible to concur in Wendel's
opinion (*Calvin: Sources et Évolution*, 117) that 'Calvin himself never affirmed
literal inspiration'.

construed. In fact, only one side of Calvin's view has been illustrated. It is just as easy to form a catena of passages in which Calvin seems deliberately to court ambiguity. And this points to a consideration of some importance. Let it be admitted, as is also the case with Luther, that some of Calvin's statements represent him as holding a doctrine of verbal inspiration, while some, on the other hand, at least permit of a different construction. If a balance has to be struck, what will the result be? If Calvin be represented as holding verbal inspiration, it is immensely difficult to account at all for the apparent deviations that are to be found. He allows to escape him, not only the isolated casual phrase, but the frequent reiterated statement that, while it is the Word of God that we have in the Bible, it is not so in any exclusive sense, but is at the same time also the word of man. This constitutes a veritable loophole, and the rigidity of verbal inspirationism can allow such a loophole only at the cost of virtual surrender. If, on the other hand, it be supposed that Calvin is not concerned to uphold the rigorist theory of verbal inspiration, the dual character of his expressions is much more easily accommodated. Calvin is at all times greatly concerned to maintain that Scripture is indeed the Word of God. If his view really is that there is, not an exact identity, but an 'indirect identity', it is not unnatural that expressions should be used which foreshorten the perspective and which, read in isolation, give the impression of affirming a direct identity. Two kinds of expression have to be accommodated; and the view that Calvin does not hold verbal inspiration accommodates them more easily than the view that he does. Already the lines of a *prima facie* case that Calvin is no verbal inspirationist are appearing.

The impression conveyed by these formal considerations is substantiated by an examination of the subjective or psychological side of the matter. Here Calvin's grasp of the situation is realistic enough to appreciate that two interests have to be maintained: both that the Bible is Word of God and that it is word of men. Against what is said by way of comment on 2 Tim. iii. 16, 'the prophets did not speak on their own, but as organs and instruments of the Holy Spirit; so that they announced only what they had received from on high', must be set the comment on 2 Pet. i. 20: the prophets 'obediently followed the Spirit as their guide', but were 'not bereaved of

mind (as the Gentiles imagine their prophets to have been)';
as well as that on Ezek. iii. 3: 'God's servants ought to speak
from the inmost affection of the heart.' Thus the Bible is represented as man's word. The other affirmation is of course also
repeatedly made. Thus the passage on 2 Pet. i. 20 must be
completed: the prophets and apostles 'dared not announce
anything of their own, and obediently followed the Spirit as
their guide, who ruled in their mouth as in His own sanc-
tuary'; and on Heb. iii. 7 he comments that in Scripture we
have words which 'are those of God and not of men'.

When the latter interest is dominant, Calvin is apt to deny
the humanness of the Bible. Thus Ezekiel is said to 'put off,
as it were, his human infirmities when God entrusted to him
the office of instructor' (on Ezek. i. 2); the writings of Isaiah
contain 'no human reasonings' (on Isa. i. 1); while those of
Daniel are 'free from any human delusion or invention' (on
Dan. x. 21). 'In the resultant word there is freedom from
human error and from the marks of human infirmity', says
R. S. Wallace,[1] whose account of this matter is fair and balanced. Yet this is not the whole story: even when regarded
as God's Word, there is in the Bible an element of 'accommodation' to human weakness. 'It shows', says Calvin (on
John iii. 12), 'an extraordinary degree of wickedness that we
yield less reverence to God speaking to us, because He con-
descends to our ignorance: and therefore when God prattles
to us in Scripture in a rough and popular style, let us know
that this is done on account of the love He bears us.' This
very significant statement is supported by other evidence when
Calvin is affirming the Bible as man's word and emphasizing
its humanness. 'Nor is it wonderful', he says (on Ps. lxxxviii. 6),
'that a man endued with the Spirit of God was, as it were, so
stunned and stupefied when sorrow overmastered him as to
allow unadvised words to escape from his lips.' Moreover, it
is well known that Calvin, 'while he affirms the general accuracy of Holy Scripture in historical matters, is at times careless
about details'.[2] Nor can we suppose that this would have
greatly troubled him since he notes that the apostles themselves quote Scripture with 'complete freedom'.

There is a good deal that is puzzling in the evidence cited.

[1] *Calvin's Doctrine of the Word and Sacrament*, 108.
[2] Ibid., 111.

But one or two things seem clear. That the Bible is God's Word in a sense that does not exclude it from being at the same time man's own word is certainly maintained by Calvin. That he fails to find the terms for presenting the problem as any more than a dilemma is also true. But that the problem appears in this form in his pages at all seems at least to exculpate him from the charge of verbal literalism.

Further evidence for this conclusion is obtained when the terminology Calvin uses is examined. There is much common sense in what Doumergue says, that while the terms used can be utilized to construct a literalist position, they must not be allowed to impose themselves too rigidly upon the reader. Calvin himself writes:[1] 'We assert that the Word itself, however it may be conveyed to us, is like a mirror, in which faith may behold God.' Here a metaphorical use of his terms is expressly affirmed. If it is permissible to take this metaphorical use as really normative for Calvin's thought,[2] it yields a clear indication of his view of Holy Scripture. For a mirror makes something visible, but the representation is not the thing in itself. Applying this to the case in hand, the Bible conveys the Word of God, but for this very reason is not identical with that word. Doumergue further suggests that the other familiar terms, 'scribe', 'secretary', 'mouth of God', and so on, 'are images like the expression "mirror"; they are not formulas scientific and theological, in the sense in which the seventeenth century theology took them'. Calvin himself says[3] that 'Scripture itself is an instrument by which the Lord dispenses to the faithful the illumination of His Spirit'. 'But Scripture is not identified with the Lord Himself.'[4]

Sometimes Calvin manifests indifference about the exact way in which the Word of God is conveyed, and it is difficult to regard this indifference as supporting a literalist view of the Bible. Thus:

'But whether God revealed Himself to the patriarchs by oracles and visions, or suggested by means of the ministry of men what should be handed down by tradition to their

[1] *Insts.*, 3. 2. 6.
[2] As by W. Niesel: *Die Theologie Calvins*, 29; Peter Brunner: *Vom Glauben bei Calvin*, 93; F. Wendel: *Calvin: Sources et Évolution*, 117f.
[3] *Insts.*, 1. 9. 3.
[4] F. Wendel, op. cit., 118.

posterity, it is beyond a doubt that their minds were impressed with a firm assurance of the doctrine, so that they were persuaded and convinced that what they had received came from God.'[1]

This suggests a greater degree of latitude in his use of the terms employed than is compatible with a literalist view. One thing, he says, is certain and assured; another thing is more obscure: the certain thing is the divine origin of the Holy Scriptures; the uncertain thing is the exact means their divine author employed for their communication. Calvin 'is saying that the Bible comes not from men but from God; [he] does not say how'.[2]

Doumergue further notes the care that Calvin takes to explain what is meant by the phrase 'taught by the mouth of the Lord'. 'The meaning is that they should teach nothing extraneous to or different from that system of doctrine which the Lord had comprised in the law.' This is said of the priests in the Old Testament. The principle is further extended: 'prophets and doctors are in the Church of God as the very mouth of God';[3] and, further:[4]

'to be assured and to have faith resolute and constant, we must be persuaded that God Himself speaks to us, . . . even though it be by means of men. . . . We must be able to declare that those who teach us are ministers of God, . . . and that they minister to us what they have received from His law and from His own mouth.'

And 'if one now ask how we have this certainty, it is clear it comes not at all of our own industry or prudence; but we must pray God to seal His truth in our hearts by His Spirit'. Such passages do not clearly support the view that Calvin holds literal inspiration; their tendency is rather against it. Two further passages seem to corroborate this conclusion. Speaking of the prescription of the words of the Lord's Prayer, where if anywhere dictation might be applicable, Calvin exercises great restraint and circumspection: 'to provide us', he says,[5] 'with a more certain aim (in prayer), He framed and as it were dictated a formula'. Again, when speaking of prayer in general,

[1] *Insts.*, 1. 6. 2.
[3] *1 Sam. Hom.*, xlii.
[5] *Catechism of the Church of Geneva.*

[2] Doumergue: *Jean Calvin*, IV, 74.
[4] *Hom. on 2 Tim.*

Calvin says:[1] 'Prayer depends on the Word of God. For it is just as if (St Paul) had prohibited all men from opening their mouths until such time as God put words into them.' Here the very same formula is used in dealing with a subject-matter to which the idea of literal inspiration is simply inapplicable.

So much by way of general review of the terminology employed. It has now to be asked how Calvin uses the words of Holy Scripture themselves. Théo Preiss denies that the strongest argument against verbal inspiration is the various incongruities and inaccuracies of the contents of Holy Scripture itself.[2] This is no doubt true. It seems almost endlessly possible to explain, or to explain away, even on the literalist interpretation, the familiar discrepancies of the text. They are due either to copyists' errors (the common Roman argument[3]); or they are merely apparent discrepancies; or they occur for some recondite reason which vindicates their place in the divine plan. But what must be allowed is that the way in which a writer uses the very words of Holy Scripture is bound to yield a clue whether he holds these words as divinely inerrant and infallible or not. Putting Calvin to this test reveals little ground for classing him with the literalists. Thus in a valuable passage, Doumergue shows how sensitive Calvin is to the carelessness of the scriptural writers about verbal accuracy in Holy Scripture, above all in the matter of quotations of the Old Testament by New Testament writers. The difficulty here is to credit with a theory of verbal inerrancy anyone who so candidly observes and comments on vagaries of this kind.

It may therefore be claimed that, whatever more remains to be said on either side, the charge that Calvin maintains verbal inerrancy is one that is at least not impregnable. The material for a full answer to the question is only reached by an examination of what Calvin has to say, first, about the formation of the record; secondly, about the *testimonium Spiritus Sancti internum*; and thirdly, about the content of Holy Scripture. This examination must now be undertaken.

a) *The formation of the record.* The key passage is as follows:[4]

---

[1] *The Necessity of Reforming the Church*; see *Calvin: Theological Treatises*, 195.
[2] *Das Innere Zeugnis des Heiligen Geistes*, 13, n. 7.
[3] See *The Teaching of the Catholic Church*, ed. G. D. Smith, 177.
[4] *Insts.*, 1. 6. 1, 2.

'This then is the singular favour that in the instruction of the Church,[1] God not only uses mute teachers, but even opens His own sacred mouth. . . . This method He observed towards His Church from the beginning, so that, beyond those common lessons of instruction[2] (i.e., the unapprehended lessons of the created world), He might exhibit also His Word. . . . It was undoubtedly by this assistance that Adam, Noah, Abraham, and the rest of the patriarchs attained to that familiar knowledge which distinguished them from unbelievers.'

Calvin here observes that from God's Word they obtained knowledge both of Himself as Creator and of Himself as Redeemer. He continues:

'But whether God revealed Himself to the patriarchs by oracles and visions or suggested by means of the ministry of men what should be handed down by tradition to their posterity, it is beyond doubt that they were persuaded and convinced that what they had received came from God. For God always secured to His Word an undoubted credit, superior to all human opinion. At length, that the truth might remain in the world in a continuous stream of doctrine to all ages, He determined that the same oracles which He had deposited with the patriarchs should be committed to public records. With this design the Law was promulgated, to which the prophets were afterwards annexed as its interpreters. For though the uses of the Law were many, . . . the particular intention of Moses and of all the prophets was to teach the mode of reconciliation between God and man.'

This cardinal passage yields four strands which together constitute the making of the record. First there is the impartation of God Himself to individuals. The statement is made in terms of knowledge;[3] but it is clear that Calvin has in mind no merely intellectual knowledge and no purely epistemological relation between the prophets and their Creator and Redeemer. The 'internal knowledge' that is later added to the knowledge of their Creator, he says specifically, 'vivifies dead souls'. It is revelation that is here the subject of inquiry;

[1] *Erudiendam ecclesiam.*   [2] *Communia illa documenta.*
[3] Beveridge's translation accentuates the intellectual aspect by using the words 'instruction' and even 'information'.

and revelation in the sense not of 'information' about God, but of the impartation of God Himself to named individuals —a 'familiar knowledge' distinguishing them from unbelievers, and enabling them (on the intellectual side) to distinguish this God from the gods of 'profane nations'.

With this personal impartation of God to individuals is woven a second strand, namely an implicit obligation to transmit what is here vouchsafed. There is a 'handing down by tradition to posterity'. Calvin is fond of quoting Isa. lix. 21: 'My Spirit that is upon thee and my word which I have put in thy mouth, shall not depart out of thy mouth, nor out of the mouth of thy seed, nor out of the mouth of thy seed's seed, for ever.' The obligation of transmission is already implicit in the familiar knowledge granted to selected individuals.

To this there is added the third strand: 'In the end' in order that this implicit obligation might the better be accomplished, there follows the commission of 'the oracles deposited with the patriarchs' to a written record. The oral transmission is succeeded by a written transmission. Thus emerges Holy Scripture, from which comes 'all true wisdom, when we embrace with reverence the testimony which God has been pleased to deliver concerning Himself'.

Thus we have in Scripture, as Calvin adds,[1] 'such a depository of doctrine as would secure the truth from perishing from neglect, vanishing amid error, or being corrupted by the presumptuous audacity of men'. The line of development of which the written Scriptures are the culmination is to be borne in mind. This written record is only a 'public record' of that which is deposited with individuals, the familiar knowledge of God Himself. It is 'testimony'; it is therefore not complete in and by itself, but perpetually points away and out from itself to Him of whom it is evidence. It is therefore a serious misunderstanding of the situation to allege[2] that the 'truth is regarded as fixed and static, capable of being put in the pages of a book and handed down from generation to generation'. This is to cut the nerve that leads from Scripture to Him to whom Scripture witnesses. Holy Scripture is the public written record of revelation imparted to the named individuals and at first orally transmitted. It is not revelation itself, but only the

---

[1] *Insts.*, 1. 6. 3.   [2] As does A. Dakin: *Calvinism*, 190.

attestation of revelation. It is the same revelation that is communicated through familiar knowledge, through oral witness, and through written record.

There is a fourth strand. Calvin resumes the same line of argument at 4. 8. 6: 'When it pleased God to raise up a more visible form of a Church, it was His will that His Word should be committed to writing, in order that the priests might derive from it whatever they would communicate to the people.' But now the matter is brought a further step forward.

'When at length, the Wisdom of God was manifested in the flesh, it openly declared to us, all that the human mind is capable of comprehending or ought to think concerning the heavenly Father. . . . [God] has completed all the branches of doctrine in His Son, so that this is the last and eternal testimony that we shall have from Him.'[1]

Again the continuity is to be observed: God's Word in familiar impartation to individuals, God's Word by oral transmission, God's Word in written record; and then at the last God's Word Incarnate. Calvin's emphasis and interest is placed, not on the record as such, but on the content of the record. Nowhere is it affirmed that the record itself is inspired. 'The authority of Scripture rests not upon the form of the recording, but upon its content, i.e. upon the reality of the revealed facts attested in the writing', writes H. Heppe.[2] God is the author, not of Holy Scripture, but of the 'doctrine' contained and transmitted by Holy Scripture. 'We are not established in the belief of the doctrine till we are indubitably persuaded that God is its Author.'[3] The passage continues:

'The principal proof, therefore, of the Scriptures is everywhere derived from the character of the Divine Speaker. The prophets and apostles boast not of their own genius, or of any of those talents which conciliate the faith of the hearers; nor do they insist on arguments from reason; but bring forward the sacred name of God, to compel the submission of the whole world.'

Even those committed to the belief that Calvin teaches verbal inspiration admit this. Thus A. M. Hunter writes:[4]

[1] *Insts.*, 4. 8. 7. [2] *Reformed Dogmatics*, 16.
[3] *Insts.*, 1. 7. 4. [4] *The Teaching of Calvin*, 77.

'If there is no doubt that there is something wrong with the words of Scripture as they stand, Calvin suavely reminds you that after all it is not the words but the doctrine that is of prime concern. . . . That is to impart a very far-reaching qualification into the theory of verbal inspiration.'

It is, however, unjust to construct a doctrine from the words of Calvin without consideration of this important aspect, and then to complain that this important aspect is incongruous with it. Doumergue seems to be right here:[1] 'The important thing is not the words; it is the doctrine, the spiritual doctrine, the substance.' This is, as Calvin points out,[2] the use to which the Apostles put the words of Scripture: St Paul, in quoting Deut. xxx. 12, 'does not cite word for word what is in the original, but uses a polishing whereby he applies the testimony of the original more nearly to his purpose'. And again[3] of the Psalms, he says that 'St Paul is not accustomed to cite always the very words exactly as they appear in Scripture, but is content to point out the passage in question and to regard rather the substance. . . . In short, it is not necessary to look for a scrupulously literal exposition of the Psalms.' How, asks Doumergue, is the truth of the book attested? And he replies: 'The witness concerns the *saving truth* which concerns all, and does not include the document which incorporates it. The Holy Spirit testifies with power to the truth of the Bible, the authority of the Bible, not to its inspiration or its canon.'

Doumergue, and also Heppe and Clavier, who urge similar considerations, appear to think that to demonstrate Calvin's interest in the content or 'doctrine' of Scripture disposes of the question whether or not he holds a doctrine of verbal inspiration. The same can be said of Pannier who says that Calvin distinguishes between the 'contents' (message of grace) and the 'container' (Scripture itself). They are probably right: the kind of interest that Calvin manifests in the content of Scripture is not compatible with verbal inspiration. As will be later seen, by the content of Scripture Calvin does not mean a merely intellectual system to which the counterpart would be belief rather than faith. Rather, he means Christ Himself; and this is true even if allowance has to be made for Calvin's

---

[1] *Jean Calvin*, IV, 78. [2] *Commentary* to Rom., x. 9.
[3] on Eph. iv. 8f.

insistence upon 'sound teaching'. 'Would you then be reckoned as belonging to Christ's flock? Would you remain in His fold? Do not deviate a nail's breadth from purity of doctrine.'[1] While this is true, there is a residual question that demands answer, but which Calvin, in his haste to expound what the content of Holy Scripture really is, may be said to bypass, or at least to which he gives no direct reply. Verbal inspiration raises the issue of the nature of God's operations with men. One view is that the Bible is simply a divine datum, something given directly by God to men. If this view be adopted, it is quite possible to relinquish the idea that the words are given and still retain the idea that the content is a datum of this kind. But the deeper issue has still not been faced. Indeed, if God really does simply inseminate the content of the Bible, there is little reason to hesitate to accept the thought that along with that content He prescribes the words in which it is conveyed. In either case, and whether the statement is made by reformed[2] or Roman[3] theology, the Bible is represented as God's Word in a sense which precludes its being at the same time a genuinely human word. When the matter is put in this way, it is fairly clear on which side Calvin must be held to stand. As has already been said, he often points out the humanness of the Bible, but always (or at least in general) without prejudice to the thesis that it is at the same time the Word of God.

b) *Testimonium Spiritus Sancti internum.* It is easier to state what Calvin says about the internal witness of the Holy Spirit than to know exactly what he has in mind.[4] The question is: How does Scripture have its authority? Or, in subjective terms: How does Scripture elicit from men acquiescence to its authority? The answer in general is that it obtains 'complete credit and authority with believers, when they are satisfied of its divine origin, as if they heard the very words pronounced by God Himself'. The Church is not able to induce this acquiescence. In fact, to suggest it does so is a *hysteron proteron* —the Church 'does not authenticate a thing otherwise dubious

---

[1] on Col. ii. 8; see T. H. L. Parker: *The Knowledge of God*, 46f.
[2] As in Protestant scholasticism.
[3] As *Providentissimus Deus*, xxiii and, of course, *passim*.
[4] *Insts.*, 1. 7. 1ff.

and controvertible, but knowing it to be the truth of God performs a duty of piety by treating it with immediate veneration'. But even if the Church cannot accomplish the task, it remains that Scripture, to those on whom it makes the right impression, 'exhibits as clear evidence of its truth as white and black things do of their colour or sweet and bitter things of their taste'. How is this assurance conveyed? The correct answer is not: By disputation or argument; though these have their rightful place in demolishing difficulties, they do not by themselves vindicate the authority of Scripture. Nor do arguments based on the majesty of Scripture, its excellence of style and its 'beautiful agreement of parts',[1] while all have their place, really bring the hearts of men to the point of conviction. What does this for them is the Holy Spirit: 'as God alone is a sufficient witness of Himself in His own Word, so also the Word will never gain credit in the hearts of men, till it be confirmed by the internal testimony of the Spirit'; and Isa. lix. 21 is quoted: 'My Spirit that is upon thee. . . .' Hence 'they who have been inwardly taught by the Spirit feel an entire acquiescence in the Scripture'. It is 'self-authenticating, carrying with it its own evidence; . . . but it obtains the credit which it deserves with us by the testimony of the Spirit'.[2]

It is possible for this Word of God to assail man's ears and impinge upon his hearing without reception taking place. Thus referring[3] to the incident on the road to Emmaus: 'Wherefore Christ's two disciples receive no benefit from his excellent discourse to them. . . . Though [they] were taught by His divine mouth, yet the Spirit of truth must be sent to them, to instil into their minds the doctrine which they had heard with their ears.' The work of the Spirit, alternatively, is to supply 'new eyes', for 'we are all blind by nature'. The 'human intellect . . . then begins to relish those things which pertain to the Kingdom of God, for which before it had not the smallest taste'. Alongside of this intellectual work of illumination there goes an accompanying work upon the heart. Calvin always regards the need for assurance as an important concern: 'the knowledge of faith consists more in certainty than in comprehension'.[4] Hence

---

[1] Op. cit., 1. 8. 1.   [2] Op. cit., 1. 7. 5.
[3] Op. cit., 3. 2. 34.   [4] Op. cit., 3. 2. 14.

'it remains that what the mind has imbibed, be transfused into the heart. For the Word of God is not received by faith if it floats on the surface of the brain; but when it has taken deep root in the heart, so as to become an impregnable fortress to sustain and repel all the assaults of temptation.'

Thus the removal of both blindness and distrust is the work of the Spirit. 'Right apprehension of the mind' and 'confirmation of the heart' both proceed from the operations of the Spirit.

One may sum up thus. The Word of God is authoritative because it is God speaking; the recognition of this authority is made when it is apprehended that it is God who speaks; and this recognition is not made independently of what is recognized, but consists rather in an apprehension by the mind, aroused by the Holy Spirit, of the truth of what is said and acceptance of it by the heart. When God is heard thus speaking, it is impossible to resist the overwhelming conviction that what He says is true, and impossible not to be comforted and assured by what is said.

The possibility is thus allowed and explicitly affirmed that the divine mouth can teach and yet produce no conviction, and that over and above the Word of God there is required the operation of the Holy Spirit before persuasion is achieved. Between the Word of God *simpliciter* and conviction by the Word of God there lies the work of the Holy Spirit. It is then impossible to identify the Holy Spirit with the Word of God, or for that matter lock the Holy Spirit up within Scripture. The two are not only distinguishable in thought, but separate in reality.

If this separation be recognized, it is impossible to impose upon Calvin a doctrine of verbal infallibility and inerrancy. The point to be made is not that to hold the 'accuracy of every word of the record' is incompatible with holding that the intervention of the Holy Spirit is necessary before the Word lays hold upon the mind and heart. By an application of the principle of predestination and election, it could be held that only in the case of the elect do the words have such efficacy. But while this is possible, it does not in fact appear to be what Calvin is saying. What he says is quite different: not that the locus of that inspiration by which men's minds and

D

hearts are won over to acceptance is in the words of the record, which, however, only on occasion perform this office, as in the case of the elect. Calvin is stating rather that the locus of this inspiration is the Holy Spirit, that the Holy Spirit retains this function and does not delegate it to the words of the record. That is, Calvin does not identify the Holy Spirit with the Word of God.

What Calvin writes elsewhere must be interpreted by this principle. There is apparent at times a certain foreshortening, and then it may appear that the authority and convincing power is located in the written record. 'The full authority which the Scriptures ought to possess', 'God giving utterance to them', and many other expressions allow of interpretation leading to verbal inspirationism. The case is not simple, and the charge of verbal inspiration against Calvin cannot be refuted as impossible. The refutation rests rather on Calvin's expressed view that there is no identity of Spirit and Word, and on his statement that the Word must be supplemented by the operation of the Spirit before becoming effective for faith and salvation.

Moreover, it is the same Spirit that both speaks and persuades. Calvin says:[1] 'The testimony of the Spirit is superior to all reason. . . . It is necessary therefore that the same Spirit who spoke by the mouths of the prophets should penetrate into our hearts, to convince us that they faithfully delivered the oracles which were divinely entrusted to them'; and Isa. lix. 21 is again quoted. 'God alone can properly bear witness to His own words.' It will be remembered that before there was a written record at all, inspiration was at work, and God was not only imparted to individuals, but also witnessed to by oral transmission. It now appears that this work of God does not cease with the commission of the revelation to writing: 'the same Spirit who spake . . . penetrates our hearts to persuade'. Thus there emerges the idea of a Spirit manipulating a number of instruments and discharging several functions: the Spirit revealing God in the first instance to individuals; the Spirit again in the oral transmission; the same Spirit operating with the written record to convince and persuade men's hearts.

It follows from this that the identification of Spirit and Word implied in the theory of verbal inspiration becomes less

[1] *Insts.*, 1. 7. 4.

and less likely. There is nothing in Calvin to indicate that the
Spirit, active in the ways just mentioned before the written
record emerges, becomes embedded in the written record when
it appears, or that the Spirit then divests Himself of this function and conveys it to the written words. The Spirit rather
retains a magisterial and sovereign control over the several
instruments under command, and continues to exercise His
proper functions. The same Spirit that uses the mouth of the
prophet for declaration effects entrance for the written Word
in the human soul by the appropriate illumination of heart
and mind. But mouth and written record are similarly instruments used by the Spirit and employed in the saving work;
and if either is said to be the Spirit it is in no direct or literal
sense. The Holy Spirit holds Himself aloof from identification
with the instruments employed.[1]

Examination of the term *internum* bears this out. The term
is certainly capable of misinterpretation. It should be remembered that it is a term designed in contrast to the external
authority which was all the Church could impart to Holy
Scripture. Whatever must be said about the authority of
Scripture, it did not rest on the testimony of a body external
to it, which by granting its imprimatur gave it official status.
The authority which Scripture possesses is proper to itself, and
not conceded to it by some quite external agent. In this sense
the testimony of the Holy Spirit is an internal witness.

But the door is open to misunderstanding on the other side.
Those who construe Calvin as though he held verbal inspiration are misled by the term 'internal' to think that the record
itself incorporates the testimony of the Spirit. What rightly
regarded is the work of the Holy Spirit, a work of testimony
to Holy Scripture, is regarded as the work and function of
the written Word itself: the written Word is what is inspired.
The virtue of the Holy Spirit is then alienated and drained
from the Holy Spirit Himself and emptied into the written
record, which now contains it without remainder. Authority
then no doubt belongs to Scripture. The Scriptures may be
regarded as *autopistos*. But it is no longer an authority of testimony, but an authority of petrifaction.

Théo Preiss says the right thing here:[2] 'In opposition to the

---

[1] See Wendel: *Calvin: Sources et Évolution*, 115f.
[2] *Das Innere Zeugnis des Heiligen Geistes*, 13f.

doctrine of Calvin, the conception of the *verbal inspiration* of the Bible petrified its authority, and we acquire a paper Pope, a Word of God which a man can stick in his pocket and whose master he himself fundamentally is.' The Bible then becomes a kind of talisman or totem—the locus of powers much greater than human, over which, however, by manipulation of the appropriate kind, men have jurisdiction. The Holy Spirit has become internalized by a kind of 'inscripturation', and independence is lost. As corollary to this, Preiss points out that 'when later in the nineteenth century the witness of the Holy Spirit was again spoken of, it was more or less identified with religious experience, which has its seat in feeling, in a religious capacity which man possesses, and through which he can exercise judgment over Scripture'. Yet this reduction of the *testimonium Spiritus Sancti internum* to terms of religious experience is entirely foreign to the thought and intention of the author of the doctrine. Doumergue may be right in alleging[1] that Calvin here 'precedes the modern theologians of Christian experience'. He certainly never followed the path which they pursued. There is nothing to suggest that for Calvin the *testimonium Spiritus Sancti internum* is reducible without remainder to religious experience.

There is indeed everything to deny it. For Calvin the Holy Spirit remained, though internal in its testimony, still and always the Holy Spirit of God, and quite irreducible to a succession of private states. As Doumergue puts it:[2] 'The Spirit comes into us but not out of us'; and he quotes an observation of Kuyper which is much to the point: 'The Reformers do not call the testimony of the Holy Spirit an external argument (*argumentum externum*) because it comes from outside of us, from God, and penetrates into us.'

If it be permissible to expound by a simile, the Holy Spirit testifies not by simply putting a stamp upon the Scriptures, which then and therefore have to be accepted by us. The Spirit testifies as a witness inside the court where we sit as jury, to be persuaded by the evidence adduced. While then the Spirit is and remains the testimony of the Holy Spirit of God, He works internally to produce within the hearts of men that conviction and persuasion that results in acceptance. It is an external witness exposing internally the evidence of which

[1] *Jean Calvin*, IV, 60.   [2] Op. cit., 65.

He is possessed. According to Calvin, this work of witnessing cannot be alienated from the Holy Spirit (as though the written Word itself could alone plead its own case); nor can the Holy Spirit who remains the Holy Spirit of God be identified with the written Word, however eloquently He may plead and commend the case of the written Word. It is of this that Doumergue reminds us when he observes that this internal testimony of the Holy Spirit is only one function performed by the Holy Spirit, one way in which He exercises His *Maîtrise*.

We may then speak with Calvin of three distinct though connected things: the written Word, the Holy Spirit, and the Word of the living God. Calvin is in no doubt that the end of Scripture is to vivify us. Holy Scripture contains a 'perfect rule of good and happy living'.[1] But[2] 'there is no life that is firm and stable but in God only; and this life is communicated to us by the Word. . . . What is then the Word of God which vivifies us? It is the Law and the Prophets and the Gospel.' Calvin states his doctrine here in a telescoped and foreshortened form. It is not the Law and Prophets and Gospel *simpliciter* that vivify—'new eyes'[3] must be supplied by the Holy Spirit; without this work, the Apostles remain deaf and uncomprehending on the road to Emmaus. It is Law, Prophets and Gospel accompanied by the operation of the Holy Spirit that are effective. When this contact is made, when along with the Word the Spirit operates, there comes into being (as one may say) a *tertium quid*. The Word does not become authoritative and win acceptance with men by incorporating the Holy Spirit in itself, or by receiving the stamp of the Holy Spirit upon itself. It becomes authoritative and is received, when, by the operation of the Holy Spirit, it is made the Word of the living God and the living Word of God. It is this and no other thing that vivifies.

To go thus far in interpreting Calvin is perhaps all that is possible. But one could easily go further along the path he indicates by employing terms coined long after his day.

c) One more consideration shows Calvin facing along this road. It is the examination of the content of the record, the central deposit or intention of Holy Scripture. 'All Scripture teaches nothing but the Cross', said Luther; and Calvin was

---

[1] on 2 Tim. iii. 16. [2] on 1 Pet. i. 25. [3] *Insts.*, 3. 2. 34.

in thorough sympathy. He industriously read the New Testament into the Old. 'With Christ shining through, its darkest pages became illuminated transparencies, and Calvin saw Christ everywhere.'[1] To quote his own words: 'In our reading of Scripture we shall hold simply to that which speaks clearly and definitely to our conscience and makes us feel that it leads us to Christ'; and conversely: 'Christ cannot be properly known in any other way than from the Scriptures';[2] and negatively: 'Christ is rejected when we do not embrace the pure doctrine of the Gospel.'[3]

This is sometimes alleged as an objection to Calvin's doctrine.

> 'To Calvin . . . the Old Testament could only be of value as it was regarded as bearing direct testimony to Christ. He thus makes Christ central in the whole of Scripture in a way that is scarcely possible to a modern thinker. This made it appear a unity incapable of contradicting itself, and this certainty was the strength of the theory.'[4]

But times change, and the emphasis in theology with them, and modern study of the Old and New Testaments follows just such lines. Whatever the perils of reading back the New Testament into the Old, both the Old Testament and the New have to do with the revelation of the one God and Father of our Lord Jesus Christ. It is no longer possible to read the Old Testament as though Christ were simply absent from it, awaiting an unheralded *début* in the New. If this is a realization that has in recent days been recovered, it is one already quite familiar to Calvin. It is wrong to represent Calvin as exalting the sovereignty of God at the expense of a real interest in Jesus Christ. The comprehensive principle of his theology is, of course, God's sovereignty; but when one asks concerning the content of which this is the framework, he is led by Calvin straight to Christ. Calvin's theology is theocentric in no sense that precludes Christocentricity. 'Calvinist thought is dominated wholly, not only by the *soli Deo gloria*, but also by the "life in Christ" ', writes Jean Cadier.[5] In his own words,

---

[1] A. M. Hunter: *The Teaching of Calvin*, 90f.   [2] on Jn. v. 39.
[3] on Jn. xii. 48.   [4] Dakin: *Calvinism*, 193f.
[5] Reviewing what Pierre Jourda has to say in 'La Crise du XVIe Siecle' in Vol. 16 of *L'Histoire de L'Église* (ed. by Augustin Fliche and Eugène Parry) in *Études théologiques et religieuses*, No. 4, 1950, 245.

'faith embraces Jesus Christ. . . . Faith takes up position on
the knowledge of Christ.'[1] 'The only pasture of souls is Jesus
Christ. Therefore the heavenly Father leads us to Him, in
order that being fed by His substance we may daily gather
new vigour, till we attain to heavenly immortality.'[2] 'It is unfair', Cadier continues, 'to make Calvin out to be a man of
the Old Testament, who prefers the "sombre pages of the
Apocalypse" to the sweetness of the Gospel.' Calvin's interest
in the Old Testament has a genuinely christological basis: and
yet he avoids the temptation of effacing the difference between
the Old Testament and the New. 'Though they [i.e. the men
of the Old Testament] had Christ in common with us', he
writes,[3] 'the measure of revelation was by no means equal.'
He notes[4] a certain apparent discrepancy: for while the
Psalmist praises the law ('the commandment of the Lord is
pure, enlightening the eyes'), he observes that St Paul 'over-
throws these commendations of the law'. The dilemma Calvin
resolves as follows:

'It is certain that if the Spirit of Christ does not quicken
the law, the law is not only unprofitable but also deadly to
its disciples. Without Christ there is in the law nothing but
inexorable rigour, which adjudges all mankind to the wrath
and curse of God. . . . The design of St Paul is to show what
the law can do for us, taken by itself; that is to say, what it
can do for us when, without the promise of grace, it strictly
and rigorously exacts from us the duty which we owe to
God; but David, in praising it as he here does, speaks of the
whole doctrine of the law, which includes also the Gospel,
and therefore under the law he comprehends Christ.'

It has already been pointed out that Calvin's concern is
with the 'content' or the 'doctrine' of Holy Scripture in a sense
that makes it impossible to regard him as attaching inspiration exclusively to the written word. Further, to obtain credence on the part of men, the internal testimony of the Holy
Spirit is required, for otherwise the doctrine assails the ear
without winning the acceptance of the heart. A further step
has now to be taken. Calvin associates closely the Spirit and

[1] *Insts.*, 3. 2. 8.   [2] Op. cit., 4. 17. 1.
[3] *Dilucida Explicatio, Calvin: Theological Treatises*, 289.
[4] on Ps. xix. 8.

Christ Himself. Ridiculing those who pretend to be taught by
the Spirit apart from Scripture, Calvin suggests[1] that they
may lay claim to the Spirit of Christ, and continues: 'How
ridiculous is such assurance! for that the apostles of Christ
and other believers in the primitive Church were illuminated
by no other Spirit, I think they will concede.' There is thus
established some kind of identity between the Spirit and the
Spirit of Christ. When it is contested that the Holy Spirit must
illumine, what is being said is that the Spirit of Christ must
operate.

'The letter therefore is dead and the law of the Lord
slays the readers of it, where it is separated from the grace
of Christ and only sounds on the ears without affecting the
heart. But if it be efficaciously impressed on our hearts by
the Spirit—if it exhibit Christ—it is the word of life, "con-
verting the soul, making wise the simple".'[2]

The office of the Spirit is to 'exhibit Christ'.

The demolition of the idea that Calvin teaches a verbal
inspiration is thus carried a further step. It is plausible to suggest that the written Scriptures are inspired. It has no plausibility to suppose that the written Scriptures are themselves
simply Christ. On the contrary, it is Christ that is witnessed
to by them, and it is Christ that comes breaking through them
to the believing heart.

If now the question be raised, Where for Calvin is the seat
of the authority of the Scriptures? we get a fairly clear answer.
Their authority derives from that Christ whom it is their office
to attest; but the seat of their authority is outside themselves,
in Him of whom they are the attestation. Such authority as
the Holy Scriptures possess is therefore a derivative and conceded authority, imparted to them by Him to whom they
witness.

SUPPLEMENTARY NOTE

Opinion is deeply divided concerning whether Calvin teaches verbal inspiration
and infallibility or not. It may be worth while to set forth some of the chief
authorities in the matter and the view to which they lend their support. The
following deny infallibility to be Calvin's view:

P. Barth: *Vom Glauben bei Calvin; Das Problem der natürlichen Theologie bei Calvin.*
H. Clavier: *Études sur le Calvinisme.*
E. Doumergue: *Jean Calvin.*

[1] *Insts.*, 1. 9. 1.   [2] *Insts.*, 1. 9. 3.

H. Heppe: *Reformierte Dogmatik* (Eng. trsln. *Reformed Dogmatics*); 'Die Bekenntnisschriften der reformierten Kirchen Deutschlands', in *Revue d'Histoire et de Philosophie religieuses*, Cahier 8.

W. Niesel: *Die Theologie Calvins*.

J. Pannier: *La Témoinage du Saint Esprit; Récherches sur l'Évolution religieuse de Calvin jusqu'à sa conversion*.

O. Ritschl: *Dogmengeschichte des Protestantismus*.

R. Seeberg: *Lehrbuch der Dogmengeschichte*, IV/2.

R. S. Wallace: *Calvin's Doctrine of Word and Sacrament*.

F. Wendel: *Calvin: Sources et Évolution de sa Pensée religieuse*.

The following affirm infallibility to be Calvin's view:

H. Bauke: *Das Problem der Theologie Calvins*.

R. E. Davies: *The Problem of Authority in the Continental Reformers*.

E. A. Dowey: *The Knowledge of God in Calvin's Theology*.

A. M. Hunter: *The Teaching of Calvin*.

P. Lobstein: 'La Connaissance religieuse d'après Calvin,' in *Revue de Théologie et de Philosophie*.

J. Mackinnon: *Calvin and the Reformation*.

The question is admittedly perplexing, and it is not surprising that qualifications upon the view adopted are sometimes introduced. Thus J. Mackinnon (op. cit., 217f.) says that Calvin's 'theology is the systematized expression of the religious conceptions of the sacred writings, which in virtue of the inspiration of their .authors, are absolutely authoritative and final pronouncements in matters theological. For him the fact "It is written" is sufficient to settle any point in question. His view of the Word as the infallible voice of God precluded the free exercise of the critical faculty, though he lays stress on the necessity of adequate grammatical and historical knowledge for its right understanding, and would not, like the later literalists, vouch for the accuracy of every word in the text.' H. Clavier (op. cit., 26, 81f.), while admitting that some passages in Calvin's writings seem to imply literal inspiration of the Bible, quotes others to show that he is not, as a commentator, an extreme literalist of the later type, such as Seeberg [*sic*], Wernle, Tschaekert, Viénot and O. Ritschl represent him to be. Emil Brunner occupies an intermediate position. He holds that in his 'dogmatic formulations of the authority of the Bible, Calvin was entirely under the sway of the orthodox view of literal divine inspiration', whereas 'in his exegesis the principles of the Reformation predominated' (*Revelation and Reason*, 275). E. A. Dowey (op. cit., 103) expresses a similar opinion: 'We find Calvin the theologian and Calvin the humanist scholar side by side, co-operating, but unreconciled in principle. When he writes as a theologian about the inspiration (and rarely the preservation) of Scripture, there is not the least hint that Calvin the scholar ever has found or ever may find an error in the text before him. Why is this, if not because he is writing of the original Scriptures, not as rendered by Erasmus, Jerome, the Septuagint, or even by copyists of the original manuscripts? On the other hand, when he sees an obvious error in the text before him, there is no indication that it makes any *theological* impression on him at all. It never causes him to retract or to qualify or generally even to mention his general position of verbal inerrancy. Again, why, if not because the error is a trivial copyist's blunder, not a misunderstanding of divine "dictation" by an apostle or prophet?' Calvin perceives the necessity of a 'repository of heavenly doctrine' if men are not to slide 'into forgetfulness of God' (*Insts.*, 1. 6. 3). 'This repository of doctrine is the Holy Scriptures. It is not, however, any given, specific and sacrosanct edition or translation of the Bible, but a hypothetical original document that is inerrantly inspired' (op. cit., 105). But can it really be held that this is a tenet of Calvin's?

III

Lutheran and Reformed Orthodoxy[1]

I. LUTHER

The point has already been made[2] that, when Calvin set up Holy Scripture as authoritative for true doctrine,[3] he was doing nothing quite new. The Roman Church also regarded Holy Scripture as authoritative, however much its authority had become obscured and impaired. But the ground he had in common with the Roman Church was also shared with Luther and the Lutherans. They too faithfully held to Scripture, and regarded it as the norm of doctrine and practice. The distinction commonly drawn between Calvinism and Lutheranism at this point is that, while for Lutherans all was admissible which did not contradict Scripture (which thus operated negatively, to exclude what could be shown to be in conflict with it), for the Reformed Church that alone was admissible which could be actually found in Scripture (which thus operated as the sole positive source of all that could be either held or done). This is true in a general way. But the

[1] In this chapter the following abbreviations have been used:
Luther: *Works*, Weimar Edition—*W.A.*
                 Erlangen Edition—*E.A.*
         Letters, collection by Enders—*B.*
         Disputations, edited by Drews—*D.*
         Epistle to the Romans, edited by Ficker, *Anfänge reformatorischer Bibelaus-legung*, 2 vols.—*R.*
Bekenntnisschriften der evangelisch-lutherischen Kirche, 1952—*B.S.*
Bekenntnisschriften und Kirchenordnungen, 1938—*B.S.K.*
Calvin: Theological Treatises, 1954—*T.T.*
Corpus Reformatorum—*C.R.*
[2] See Chapter II.
[3] See *Insts.*, 1. 6. 1, 2, 3; *Reply to Sadolet* (*Calvin: Theological Treatises*, 248): 'Thou didst bear before me the torch of Thy Word'; *Necessity of Reforming the Church* (op. cit., 211). 'We hold there is no legislator but God. To Him alone then let this authority be reserved, which He claimed for Himself in many passages of Scripture'; *et passim*.

difference is not perhaps so marked as it is often thought to be—and this rather because Calvin and Calvinism stood nearer to the position ascribed to Luther than the other way about. In other words, Calvin allows a real value to tradition.[1]

This common adherence to Holy Scripture lies at first in the realm of presupposition. Later it is regarded as a possible basis of the restoration of Church unity. This is realized in the disputation of Ratisbon in the controversy with the Jesuits, who, in the interests of Church and Church tradition, tended to deny the normative sufficiency of Scripture. A new consciousness of unity was felt by those who took part on the side of the Reformation: *aliam normam veram ad unitatem procurandam praeter Scripturam sanctam nescio.*[2] Since truth is one, since it is to be found in Scripture, and since it must never be sacrificed even for the sake of unity, it is therefore not true, as the Romans contended, that Christian unity is only to be achieved by submission to the Pope. Unity must be advocated and contrived only on the basis of the truth, and this, the reformers realize, can mean only the Bible. This principle, already recognized by Lutherans and Calvinists, could be used as a basis to embrace both reformed and unreformed Churches, if only it were accepted. 'O blessed schism', exclaims Gerhard,[3] 'through which we are united with Christ and the true Catholic Church!' *A fortiori* the principle applied to the relations of reformed Churches among themselves. It therefore comes to expression when, the first violence of controversy being spent, leaders in both Lutheran and Reformed Churches prepared to talk peace and a period of formulas of concord ensues. On both sides of the rift dividing the two reformed Churches, the affirmation was made that the 'essence of all Christianity' consisted, not in contested, but in common doctrine. When the question was further raised concerning the definition of the doctrine held in common, the answer on both sides was given: it consists

---

[1] Besides his unrivalled knowledge and the frequent use he makes of the Church fathers, it is worthy noting that (*The Genevan Confession*, §17) he empties the class of 'human traditions' as such, in favour of a distinction between 'perverse doctrines of Satan' and 'the ordinances that are necessary for the internal discipline of the Church, and belong solely to the maintenance of peace, honesty and good order in the assembly of Christians, . . . comprised under the general command of St Paul'.

[2] Dannhauer in a letter to John Duraeus, an ecumenically-minded Scot, 1664.

[3] *Loci Theologici* (1610), 11. 224.

in the 'absolute dominion of the Word of God'.[1] Franck[2] from the Lutheran side, who took a leading part in the negotiations for pacification between the contending Churches, propounded the eirenic rubric: *in necessariis unitas, in non necessariis libertas, in utrisque caritas,*[3] and his thought and action were governed by the proposition. Affirming that both sides have the Bible in common, he goes on to draw the negative implication that human authority for the construction of doctrine and in the formation of the cultus must be set aside in favour of the sole authority of Scripture. He suggests that theological formulations have only a relative worth.

'Luther, Zwingli, Calvin lived so that they daily learned more and more, we stand on the shoulders of these giants and see farther and clearer than they. Who knows whether after us others will not arise who will formulate all this more fruitfully for spiritual edification, more fitly, strongly, luminously, more precisely and more fundamentally.'[4]

This is excellently said. In temper it resembles the much later familiar words in which Pastor Robinson warned the Pilgrim Fathers, that Luther and Calvin were indeed 'precious and shining lights in their times, yet God did not reveal His whole will to them. I am very confident that the Lord hath more truth and light yet to break forth out of His Holy Word'.[5] For Franck it is from the Bible that new illumination is to be expected. But the point to be more particularly noted here is the freedom permitted in relation to the formulations of the Reformers, with the intention that the supreme authority of the Bible should enjoy unrivalled pre-eminence. There is a fine sense of the very principle of the Reformation which sets everything clearly under the one supreme authority, and in the name of those that fathered the Reformation affirms the relativity of what even they said.

Had reformed scholasticism remained true to this principle in its purity, there would be a different story to tell. Unhappily,

---

[1] So Hans Leube: *Kalvanismus und Luthertum*, Bd. I, Der Kampf um die Herrschaft im protestantischen Deutschland (Leipzig, 1928).

[2] Gregor Franck: *Consideratio theologica de gradibus necessitatis dogmatum Christianorum quibus fidei, spei et charitatis officia reguntur*, 1628.

[3] It is not clear that he is the author of this excellent maxim.

[4] Qtd. H. Leube: *Kalvinismus und Luthertum*, Bd. I, 2.

[5] See Daniel Neal: *The History of the Puritans*, II, 129.

at least at two points it departed from it. It failed to maintain such a high freedom over against the formulations of the Reformers; and, even more fatally, it failed to carry over the essentially dynamic view of Scripture which the Reformers held. But this is to anticipate.

In Luther the pattern of the Protestant view of Holy Scripture is outlined. When the Reformation began, Scripture was regarded as a divine law book ordaining both the constitution of the Church and its doctrine, and it is by these on the other hand guaranteed and defended. 'As ground for the binding authority of this book, there was adduced on the one hand its recognition by the Church under direction of the Holy Spirit, and on the other hand its origin in verbal inspiration by the Holy Spirit.'[1] When Luther challenged this view, he did not stand alone. It was one of the accomplishments of Occam to expose the hollowness of much of the system of legalistic authorities with which the Scriptures were tied up, and to reduce it to the Bible which alone wielded authority, though it was an authority of an external or legal and nominalistic kind. Traces of this legalistic view of Scripture are to be found in Luther, and he can speak of *sacra scriptura quae est proprie ius divinum.*[2] That these traces do not adequately represent Luther's view need perhaps hardly be said, and this will in any case later become clear. But so far as they are present, Luther makes common cause with the nominalistic simplification of authority to a single source. Authority in matters of faith does not reside in the Pope, nor in canon law and Councils. It is true that no one affirmed in its simplicity what is here denied. What was affirmed, however, was a condominium of Pope, canon law and Councils along with Scripture. In this association what the Church held as doctrine was tacitly identified with what Scripture taught, and what had the appearance of co-operative rule worked out in fact as dominance by the ecclesiastical side of the condominium. Hence it was no misunderstanding of the situation, but a

---

[1] See Seeberg: *Lehrbuch der Dogmengeschichte,* 5th edn., IV/1, 422.

[2] *W.A.,* 2. 279. Further evidence of this attitude to Scripture is to be found at another point to which P. S. Watson (*Let God Be God!,* 149ff.) has recently drawn attention. Because the Old Testament is a law and is appropriately written down, and the New Testament is essentially a gospel and appropriately spoken, Luther sometimes expressed himself as though only the Old Testament were Scripture in the strict and proper sense.

shrewd and true instinct which led Luther to strike at this tyranny, in order to set up the authority of Scripture in its rightful pre-eminence. The Scriptures alone, unobscured and unstained by the rubbishy speech of men, are to be the source of truth and as such to have validity in the Church.[1] Scripture alone is to be believed.[2] With this wine, no water is to be mixed; alongside of this sun no lantern is to be held.[3] Scripture is normative authority for all life and doctrine. It is the 'carpenter's ruler' (*Richtscheit*), the proof-stone (*Prüfstein, Streichstein*), and the standard to which Church doctrine has to conform.[4]

This standard and norm applied not only in a positive but also in a negative way. Scripture for Luther is norm 'in the negative sense, that nothing in the Church is authorized which contradicts Scripture, and in the positive sense, that only that is authorized in the Church which is inwardly in accordance with Scripture, even if its outward form is not given in Scripture'.[5] Put in this way, the position of Luther differs little from that more familiarly associated with Calvin and the Reformed tradition.

The authority which Luther recognizes Scripture to have is not a mechanical authority. This will be later seen when the essential nature of the authority accorded to Scripture is discussed. At this point it is enough to indicate the close and constant association which Luther affirms between Scripture and Spirit. Luther knew that he must defend himself on two sides and against two opponents. The Romans worked with a conception of authority that was formal, external and legalistic. Whatever was credited with this authority, therefore, was imposed mechanically from outside. Luther insisted that, whether such a conception of authority was real or not, at all events it was not the kind of authority which Scripture exercised. Word and Spirit were held by him in the closest conjunction; and the Word which obliged was never to be separated or even distinguished from the Spirit which persuaded. Against the Roman position, he affirms a real relation of Spirit and Word in place of a Word perverted and exanimated by the

---

[1] *W.A.*, 8. 103, 484f., 491.   [2] *W.A.*, 15. 118; 19. 219; 43. 145.
[3] *W.A.*, 8. 141f., 143f.
[4] Seeberg, op. cit., 413, supplies the following references: *E.A.*, 9. 207, 372; 12. 289; 13. 208; 15. 144; 18. 22. *W.A.*, 33. 276, 304; 46. 771f., 780.
[5] Op. cit., 413.

influence of canonical law.[1] If, however, the Romans wanted
the Word without the Spirit, on the other side there were
those that wanted the Spirit without the Word. The Anabaptists and the 'Enthusiasts' made frequent appeal to the
Spirit as source and authority for what they did and taught.
From them, Luther demands a scriptural authority. Thus:
'Thou must base thyself on a clear, evident and powerful saying of Scripture, whereby thou mayest firmly stand.'[2] As Seeberg says,[3] 'the appeal to Spirit satisfied him not at all. For
him Spirit and Word were inseparably united'. If the Romans
ignored the Spirit, the Anabaptists ignored the Word; and
Luther says of Karlstadt that he was full of Spirit and empty
of Scripture (*ein geistreiches und schriftloses Kopf*).[4] Yet Luther,
while attacking enemies on each side, does not merely pursue
a judicious *via media*. The fact is that the 'spiritual authority'
which he finds in Scripture opens up a new understanding of
authority and leads beyond the views he rightly finds inadequate. It is not a merely objective and external authority
credited to Scripture because of the testimony of an 'inspired'
Church; nor is it a merely subjective and internal authority,
since for him it really is a book that is 'inspired' and not
merely the individual soul. By tenaciously maintaining the
thesis that it is a book that is inspired, Luther contrives to set
the problem in a new light. The terms hitherto used will no
longer fit the case, and a new solution to the problem can be
looked for. It is also true that in so defining the problem and
its possible solution, Luther stands at a cross-roads, and from
the point he occupied at least two paths lead forward. One
is that which he himself and also Calvin followed, according
to which the Bible is a living authority making itself felt and
heard in religious experience. The other is the path followed
by Protestant scholasticism, which, holding no less that the
Bible is an inspired book, regarded it as a fixed and external
standard and textbook of what may be believed.

What kind of authority is it to which Luther conceived the
Bible to have a title? Where does it reside and what is its locus?
And in what aspect or element of Scripture is it to be sought?
The simple general answer to the inquiry is that Scripture has
claim to be authoritative because it is the Word of God. Luther

---

[1] See Seeberg, op. cit., 412. [2] *W.A.*, 10. 3. 22f.; qtd. Seeberg, op. cit., 412.
[3] Op. cit., 412. [4] Op. cit., 414.

says also more than this; for he frequently asserts that the words of Scripture are God's words. Moreover, this is corroborated when he looks at the matter, as he also often does, from the subjective side, and declares that the mouth of the prophets and apostles is the mouth of God and their writing is the writing of the Holy Spirit.[1] Seeberg assembles evidence of this kind. According to it, Luther affirms that the true God speaks in Scripture, and man ought therefore simply to accept what stands therein.[2] Whatever St Paul says is said by the Holy Spirit, and whoever speaks against St Paul speaks against the Holy Spirit.[3] According to God's decree, the apostles are to be reckoned as *infallibiles doctores*, and from this fact both apostles and prophets derive their authority.[4] They receive the Holy Spirit so that their words are the words of God.[5] Luther is aware that they are sinful and erring men; but this implies no diminution of the divine character of the Scripture for which they are responsible, since their sins and errors are corrected by the Holy Spirit.[6] By His agency the sense in which they speak is true, even if they fall into grammatical error, and when under His direction they speak with passion, the rules of grammar do not apply.[7] Hence the Scripture is not man's word, but God's Word.[8] God is the author of the Gospel,[9] and the Holy Spirit of Genesis.[10] The Bible is the Spirit's own scripture.[11]

This is an impressive list of evidence, and it could easily be enlarged. So far as it goes, it seems to demonstrate a simple identification between Scripture and the Word of God, and even between the words of Scripture and the words of God. As in the case of Calvin, so here with Luther: it is easy to bring forward evidence to show that Luther holds that what Scripture contains comes directly from God. And if this evidence stood alone, this is the conclusion that would have to be drawn. But it does not stand alone, and some way has to be found of reconciling other different evidence with what is set forth here. Reconciliation is impossible and we are left with a contradiction on our hands, if it be thought that Luther holds the simple identification of Scripture and the Word of God.

[1] *W.A.*, 40. 2. 593.   [2] *W.A.*, 10. 2. 139f.   [3] *D.*, 12. 100.
[4] *W.A.*, 40. 1. 173f.   [5] *W.A.*, 40. 1. 195f.   [6] *D.*, 598; *W.A.*, 40. 1. 170.
[7] *W.A.*, 5. 184; 8. 597.   [8] *W.A.*, 8. 584.   [9] *W.A.*, 44. 532.
[10] *W.A.*, 7. 638; 46. 545; 47. 133; *E.A.*, 52. 321, 333.
[11] *E.A.*, 57. 39f.; *W.A.*, 47. 183.

But reconciliation is possible on the supposition that when Luther declares that the words of Scripture are the words of God, he interprets the copula in some wider sense than that of simple identification.

Before gathering more impressive evidence from Luther himself, it is possible to have an indirect light thrown on what he means when he uses 'this little word "are" '. He holds[1] that the tongue of the preacher of today does not speak merely human words, but is the 'slate-pencil of a good writer'—that is, the organ of divine communication. The significant thing here is that just the same kind of language is being used of the contemporary preacher as of the prophets and apostles. Similar considerations arise in connexion with the affirmation that *predicatio verbi divini est verbum divinum*. Scripture is also said to be the *verbum divinum*. The same statement, that is to say, is made both of preaching and of prophets and apostles. The question must be asked, in what sense can the same thing be said in both instances, both of present-day preaching and of the men of the Bible? It must be a sense wide enough to accommodate both cases which the terms cover. It is this principle that is violated if simple identification between Scripture and the Word of God is insisted upon; for those who maintain identification cannot wish to make out that it also holds good between today's preaching and the Word of God. A *prima facie* case exists for denying that Luther is committed to what some of his asseverations admittedly seem to permit, if not demand—namely, a simple identification between Holy Scripture and the Word of God.

Can there be attributed to Luther any such more flexible view of the way in which Scripture *is* the Word of God than identification imposes? Three considerations have here to be given full weight.

a) Luther's theology is closely connected with his conversion. It will therefore be not surprising to discover that the authority of Scripture is for him a fundamentally religious authority. When Luther divested Scripture of its primary dependence upon the authority of the Church,[1] Scripture itself had to sustain the burden of authority. One way of conceiving this would have been to repose in Scripture itself that authoritativeness

---

[1] *Verbum Dei est verbum Dei originaliter et authoritative, non ecclesiae nisi passive at ministerialiter* (*W.A.*, 30. 2. 682).

E

which, by the withdrawal of Church authority, it seemed to have lost. Scripture would then have enjoyed an external and objective authority, and thus demanded obedience. This was not the way which Luther elected to take. The authority of Scripture was indeed objective, but it could not be understood as merely objective. Rather it carried with it a relation to the subject to whom it commended itself and upon whom it impinged by the agency of the Holy Spirit. Instead of an authority of a purely objective kind or of a purely subjective kind, Luther maintains that the authority of the Bible lies in an objective-subjective relationship.[1] Spirit and Word go always together—not the Word imposing itself upon the subject externally, but the Word commending itself to the subject and quickening in him that response of faith in which its authority is both recognized and accepted. The Christian is thus not compelled to belief in the Word, *sed verbo trahendus, ut volenter credens sponte veniat.*[2]

This is one of the key conceptions of Luther's view of the authority of Scripture. On the one hand, the objectivity of scriptural authority is modified, but by no means surrendered. It retains its objective ground in a written book. On the other hand, it is not simply submerged in subjectivity. It is probably inevitable that the term 'religious experience' should somewhere be used here. Seeberg[3] declares that for Luther the Spirit in Scripture and the experience of faith are interchangeable, and this is no doubt true. But it does not imply that 'religious experience' becomes the only court of appeal. Scriptural authority is exercised where faith is aroused, and faith is aroused where the Word of God is fittingly and effectively commended by the Spirit. In virtue of its constant association with the Holy Spirit, Scripture provides the conditions for its own exercise of authority. There is a sense in which *scriptura et ratio* work together, but it is subsequently that this takes place. Thus 'I believe that I cannot of my own understanding and strength believe in or come to Jesus Christ my Lord, but that the Holy Ghost has called me by the Gospel and illuminated me with His gifts, and sanctified me in the true faith'.[4] 'Again and again', says P. S. Watson,[5] 'Luther

---

[1] See Seeberg, op. cit., 79. [2] Seeberg, op. cit., 410, qtg. *B.*, 3. 312.
[3] Op. cit., 417. [4] In *The Shorter Catechism*.
[5] See P. S. Watson: *Let God Be God!*, 167, qtg. *E.A.* (2), 13. 320.

asserts that we can have no assurance that the promise of the Gospel is the Word of the living God to us, unless the Holy Spirit says in our heart: "that is God's Word".' 'Therefore must God say to the heart: This is God's Word, otherwise it is unconvincing.'[1] The authority which Scripture possesses is objectively grounded, spiritually commended, and subjectively acknowledged. This threefold aspect of the authority of Holy Scripture constitutes Luther's distinctive contribution to the matter. At the same time it affords the foundation for the further definition of this authority.

Luther's view of inspiration is controlled by the same principle. While the Bible is an 'inspired book', Luther is quite willing to allow that those who wrote it may also be rightly said to be inspired. Taught by 2 Pet. i. 21, he declares that the prophets were 'moved by the Holy Ghost' and compelled to deliver what they had received. The writers not only discharged themselves of what is committed to them, but 'spat it out'. Less vehemently, they become the tongue, or the pipe, or the channel of the Holy Spirit. As will be said in a later chapter,[2] if the key to the authority of the Bible be looked for in inspiration, it may be either the writer or the words that are the object of inspiration. If the writer, the conception is that he is so elated or animated by visitation of the Holy Spirit as to become God's spokesman. It is sometimes this view that Luther seems to be presenting, and it then appears as if Holy Scripture were a matter of a specially high degree of possession by the Holy Spirit.[3] He even suggests that whoever had enough Spirit could write as good a new decalogue as Moses,[4] or even a new testament: 'For then I should take Moses, the Psalter, Isaiah and even the Holy Spirit Himself, and make as good a New Testament as the apostles wrote; but because we have the Spirit in no such rich and powerful degree, we must learn from them and drink out of their stream.'[5] These are the authentic tones of Luther. Yet they are not the only tones, nor do they constitute, if reasons already given have any weight, the dominant and characteristic note. The emphasis on inspiration is, within due limits, a good thing. It draws attention to the fact that when a man is said to be inspired, the Holy Spirit really does impinge upon

[1] *W.A.*, 10. 1. 2. 335.   [2] Chapter V.
[3] See Seeberg, op. cit., 421.   [4] *D.*, 12.   [5] *E.A.*, 11. 248.

him in some specific way, and with consequences of an observable kind. The trouble begins when this admitted fact is turned into an independent and exhaustive account of inspiration. For this is to force a psychological description of the manner in which something takes place into an ontological account of its being. By selection of what he has to say on the subject, Luther can be presented as making this error. But his general position is different. The close conjunction of Holy Spirit with Scripture prevents him slipping into so subjective a view of inspiration, however emphatically he maintains that it is within the context of 'religious experience' that the authority of the inspired Word of God operates.

Neither can it with greater plausibility be affirmed that Luther, taking the other alternative, holds the very words of Scripture to be the object of inspiration. Perhaps enough has already been said to vindicate Luther from this interpretation. It is quite true, as has been said, that he uses phrases—for example, that the words of Scripture are the words of God, thus apparently equating the two—which do not make this view clearly untenable. But these isolated but frequent expressions must be offset by others which have a quite different tendency. Thus: '*es ist dem heiligen Geist ein schlecht Ding um ein Wort*'.[1] Köhler uses this to support his affirmation that 'verbal inspiration is never made a principle by Luther'. A fair judgment must hold that it is words of this kind, and not those which tend in an opposite direction, that most nearly express the mind of the Reformer.

b) The second consideration may be more briefly dealt with. Constitutive for the understanding of Luther's conception of scriptural authority is the distinction he draws between Scripture and the Word of God. Rather than say that the Scripture is *not* the Word of God, Luther will often make the bare assertion that it is the Word of God. The decisive consideration here seems to be the credence Luther gives to certain critical conclusions regarding Scripture. It is well known that he had his attention drawn by Erasmus to certain discrepancies which the contents of Scripture manifest. For example, Isaiah in chapter xiii sets in the time of Ahaz what in fact occurred in the time of Ezekiel; Jeremiah in chapter xii relates things which belong to chapter xxv;[2]

[1] W. Köhler: *Dogmengeschichte*, II, 112.   [2] *W.A.*, 25. 138.

Moses made use not only of the patriarchs, but also of the traditions of other heathen people.[1] Luther, however, is inclined to lay little emphasis on such discrepancies: 'They are not of much importance', he says.[2] 'If there occur a contradiction in Holy Scripture which cannot be composed, one must let it go'—so long as it does not affect 'the articles of the Christian faith'. The attitude here implied renders quite unlikely the suggestion that for Luther Scripture and the Word of God are identical.

Yet many have contrived at least to avoid denying the results of such criticism while maintaining a rigid biblicism. More must therefore be said and further evidence brought forward. The conclusions just considered rest upon purely literary grounds. But as W. Köhler points out,[3] Luther passes also another kind of judgment, which rests, not on literary, but on religious grounds, not, that is, upon the scriptural form, but on the very content of Scripture. Thus while the judgment that 2 Maccabees does not belong to the canon is a historical judgment, the verdict that the Epistle of James should be omitted from Holy Scripture rests on the quite different ground of religious assessment: its omission is recommended because its thesis that 'faith without works is dead' conflicts with the principle 'by faith alone'.[4] Unless it is written off as a mere momentary aberration, a judgment like this is not based on a view which equates Holy Scripture and the Word of God. On the contrary, there is some standard here at work, which enables Luther to distinguish between different portions of Scripture. What this standard is cannot be in doubt. It is the familiar Lutheran principle of *was Christum treibet.*[5] What we have here, then, is the surface appearance of a conviction that for much of the time lies hidden, that Holy Scripture and the Word of God are not to be regarded as equivalent or identical. Luther does not in fact act on the

---

[1] *W.A.*, 43. 54. A more extensive list of Luther's critical judgments is made out by Seeberg (op. cit., 419). He expresses doubt of the Mosaic authorship of the Pentateuch, the opinion that the works of the prophets are later collected into the form in which we know them, that the later prophets are of mixed quality, that there is failure in prediction as well as success, that the Book of Kings is more reliable than that of the Chronicles; and in the New Testament, he prefers the Fourth Gospel to the other Evangelists, holds Hebrews to be a composite production, throws doubt upon the value of the Revelation, and says that James in his Epistle *delirat.*

[2] *W.A.*, 46. 727.   [3] Op. cit., 106.   [4] *W.A.*, 2. 125.   [5] *R.*, 3. 21.

judgment he passes. He makes no attempt to introduce a new canon.[1] This may be attributed to the strong sense of unity which he perceived between the Old Testament and the New, and also to the recognition that a providential ordinance determines what is there given.[2] There is no more reason to suppose that Luther maintains an identity between Scripture and the Word of God than to suppose that when he affirms that Christ was incarnate he holds that the flesh of Christ is identical with Christ Himself.

Luther thus leaves room for the distinctively human characteristics of the Scriptures. 'The creaturely words, whether written or spoken, are for him rather the vehicle or media of the divine, creative Word, by which God addresses Himself directly and personally to us.'[3] The instrument is distinguished from the agent employing the instrument, and qualities of the one need not be attributed to the other. Hence Luther freely admits human characteristics and even imperfections in Scripture. For him the incarnation provides the clue, and the humanness of Jesus is a real parallel to the humanness of Holy Scripture. 'The Church', says Brunner,[4] 'must develop its doctrine of the Scriptures on the same lines as the doctrine of the two natures. The Bible shares in the glory of the divinity of Christ and in the lowliness of His humanity'; and Luther would fully agree. He is able with much frankness, as has been said, to note many of the difficult features which the critics were later to emphasize, passes adverse judgment with the greatest freedom upon certain books of the Bible, and finds the prophets capable of erroneous utterances. He has no vested interest in concealing or diminishing such features: the denial of identity between Scripture and the Word of God frees him from embarrassment. An even more notable advantage is secured for him in another direction. If the Scriptures are held to be identical with the Word of God *simpliciter*, their application to men of today occasions some perplexity. How are the words which God addresses to Abraham, Isaac and Moses, to be applied to the men of a much later date and of greatly changed circumstances? If the same words are addressed to

---

[1] See his *Deutsche Bibel*, 4. 456.

[2] Cf. the favourable judgment, *Works of Martin Luther* (Holman, Philadelphia), VI, 477 (*Let God Be God!*, 179): 'I praise it and hold it a good book, because it sets up no doctrine of men and lays great stress upon God's law.'

[3] P. S. Watson, op. cit., 152.   [4] E. Brunner, *Revelation and Reason*, 276.

those of the later age, they must nevertheless bear at least an altered meaning, since it is in a different *milieu* that they are now spoken. If they are not the self-same words, is not the identity between Scripture and the Word of God really surrendered? As will be seen later, the reformed scholastics were aware of this difficulty, and tended to take an easy way of escape. They virtually held that what was imposed upon men of all ages was some recondite meaning lying behind the words themselves. But any such means of escape is only effective at the cost of dehistorizing Scripture. Luther on the other hand, free from the supposition of identity, can retain the full historical character of Scripture. On the one hand, the faults and failings of the men of the Bible fall under the providential rule of God: the lie of Abraham in declaring his wife to be his sister (Gen. xii), the deception practised upon Isaac by Rebecca and Jacob (Gen. xxvii), as also David's adultery with Bathsheba (2 Sam. xi), are entirely real, but they are caught up into the divine intention and purpose.[1] On the other hand, as Köhler remarks,[2] he accords to historical, ethical, and psychological facts their own reality, their own place in time, and accordingly their own restricted relevance. If polygamy is permitted to Abraham, in order that the promise be fulfilled that his seed be as the sand of the sea, this is a concession special to the occasion; and if Lot gives his daughter to prostitution, Luther issues the warning: *'Du bist nicht Loth.'*[3]

c) The third consideration is even more substantial. Since Luther does make a distinction between Scripture and the Word of God, the question arises: In what does he see the distinction to consist? What is this Word of God that is distinguished from the written Scriptures? The matter can be put quite simply. The Word is Christ, and Scripture contains Christ. Both propositions can be substantiated by Luther's own words. 'Christ and the Word', says P. S. Watson,[4] 'are virtually interchangeable terms for Luther'; and he goes on to cite Luther's own statements: 'Christ is Himself the Word';[5] 'the Father through the Son, whom Moses calls the Word,

---

[1] This would alone suffice for justification. But in fact Luther goes even further. For the end sanctifies the means: 'When God requires the patriarchs and the faithful to do anything, it is beyond doubt both holy and permissible' (W.A., 43. 694). This is doubtless a trace of Luther's recurrent nominalism.

[2] W. Köhler, op. cit., 114.   [3] *W.A.*, 43. 62.

[4] Op. cit., 149.   [5] *W.A.*, 10. 1. 158. 16.

creates heaven and earth out of nothing'.[1] On the other hand, 'in all Scripture, there is nothing else than Christ, either in plain or in involved words'.[2] And again: 'The whole Scripture is about Christ alone everywhere, if we look to its inner meaning, though superficially it may sound different'.[3] This is true, as P. S. Watson goes on to say, of both Old and New Testaments. 'The entire Old Testament refers to Christ and agrees with Him.'[4] The prophets and the law are the 'swaddling clothes and manger in which He was wrapped and laid', and they truly contain Him.[5] As for the New Testament, it is the disclosure of what lies latent in the Old Testament, and the Old Testament is accordingly rightly interpreted in the light of the New. The Gospel too teaches nothing but Christ.[6] It is true that for Luther the Old Testament is primarily the law, and the New Testament primarily the Gospel; but there is a real unity underlying the differences; for in the law there are promises, and in the Gospel both commandments and interpretation of the law. Their unity consists in the fact that both contain Christ. 'If I know what I believe, then I know what stands in Scripture, for Scripture has nothing more than Christ and Christian faith in it.'[7]

'This then is the proofstone to apply to all books, that one looks to see if they treat of Christ [*ob sie Christum treiben*] or not, for all Scripture declares Christ, and St Paul will know nothing but Christ. What does not teach Christ is not apostolic,' even if St Peter and St Paul teach it. Again what preaches Christ is apostolic, even if it is Judas or Annas or Pilate or Herod that does it.'[8]

Thus again the rigid distinction between the objective and the subjective, which both before and after Luther was the fatal weakness of so much thinking about authority, is overcome. 'Christ enters by the Gospel through a man's ears into his heart and dwells there; nor does He come empty-handed, but brings with Him His life, Spirit, and all that He has and can.'[9] If Scripture contains Christ, it has something quite specific and objective to offer; but what it offers is something that takes up its residence within the subject,

---

[1] *W.A.*, 42. 8. 24f.   [2] *W.A.*, 11. 223. 1f.   [3] *R.*, 240. 1of.
[4] *W.A.*, 10. 1. 576. 12ff.   [5] *W.A.*, 10. 1. 576. 12ff.
[6] *W.A.*, 11. 30. 17f.   [7] *W.A.*, 8. 236.   [8] *R.*, 3. 21.   [9] *E.A.*, 63. 157.

who then by faith acclaims its authority and yields to it.
At times Luther puts the thing in other words. If we ask
again the question what it is in Scripture that gives it power
and authority, the answer can be given: the Gospel or doctrine is the real kernel of Scripture. Thus Seeberg says:[1] 'For
Luther there is no sacred text. God's Word is not dependent
on the letter. It lies in the sense.' From this point, it is possible
to move forward in two directions. If doctrine be interpreted
in the scholastic sense, the Bible becomes a textbook and can
possess only the authority of a textbook. We shall see that this
is the way which Protestantism later chose. For Luther, this
direction was quite precluded, and he chooses the other. The
Lehre which he found in Scripture must be interpreted in a
religious sense. It is not a series of propositions, however edify-
ingly moral or religious. Doctrine for Luther is rather what
Scripture contains; and what Scripture contains is Christ. If
there is a kernel in Scripture, it is not rightly conceived as the
teaching which Scripture no doubt contains, but rather as He
who is taught—namely, Christ Himself.

It ought now to be clearer where and in what Luther finds
the authority of Scripture. He brings subject and object into
a living relationship. Authority does not reside in the object,
with the subject obliged to play a passive role. Nor does it
reside wholly within the subject as such, so that it becomes
just what each individual cares to make of it. The charge that
he makes of Scripture a 'wax nose' Luther hotly rebuts, declaring that it is the heretics and not he who are thus guilty.[2]
The fact is, as Köhler says,[3] that for the understanding of
Scripture and the recognition of its authority object and subject have to be held together. This coming together takes place
in the stillness (*Stillehalten*) of the individual before the Word.
But this stillness is not on the one hand a 'sacred vacancy of
mind',[4] nor any ready-made equipment which the individual
must himself supply (such as for example the *ratio*, which is
indeed used by Luther in understanding Scripture, but in a
merely formal and not a substantial way). It is rather the
waiting of the believer upon God. Luther thus propounds a
new conception of authority. It is not the same authority that

---

[1] So P. S. Watson: op. cit., 167, qtg. *W.A.*, 10. 1. 48. 16ff.; 49. 1ff.

[2] Op. cit., 113.   [3] Op. cit., 120.

[4] The phrase is used by R. L. Stevenson in *Weir of Hermiston* to describe Dandie's
way of 'honouring the Sabbath'.

is now differently disposed between the possible claimants and distributed to give each a fair share. The authority which Scripture possesses is one which is objectively grounded in a book which speaks of Jesus Christ. This authority, however, it establishes within the heart into which Christ enters, or (which is much the same thing) upon which the Holy Spirit works, to create the faith in which it is both recognized and obeyed. In the last resort, the authority of Scripture is not its own possession held by independent right. For Luther, Scripture is not the Word, but only witness to the Word, and it is from Him whom it conveys that it derives the authority it enjoys.[1]

II. RIGOR SCHOLASTICUS

At first glance, there seems to be a gratifying resemblance between Luther and Calvin and the later reformed theologians in the place respectively assigned to Scripture. The period that follows a time of revolution and the rapid and vigorous emergence of new ways and categories of thought is usually and perhaps inevitably a time of consolidation. In this succeeding period, much from the earlier revolutionary age may perhaps be lost, but certainly without it little or nothing would remain. The new growth must equip and arm itself in order to survive. One of the things that was retained in the age that succeeds that of the Reformers is respect for Holy Scripture. Whether the respect accorded is quite the same as is found in the Reformers is another question, to which a less satisfactory answer must be given. The importance of the Bible was undiminished, but it was a changed importance.

There are two sources for discovering what those who followed the Reformers held concerning Scripture and its authority. The first is the confessional documents of the Lutheran and Reformed Churches, including the various articles, catechisms, and formulas of concord; the second is the writings of the individual theologians themselves. In the confessional documents on the Lutheran side, surprisingly little space is occupied by explicit definition of Scripture and its proper place. What is set forth is fully documented by passages from Holy Scripture, and it is clear that the standard of reference is Scripture; but only occasionally is this presupposition

[1] So P. S. Watson: *Let God Be God!*, 179, note 30.

brought explicitly forward. Thus the *Augsburg Confession* has no paragraph dealing with Scripture as such, and its references to Scripture are infrequent. It is mentioned in Article 27, Of Cloister Vows, but only in passing: men dedicated to the monastic life agreed that they must learn Scripture. Hutter remarks that, though there is no treatment of Scripture in the Augsburg Confession, its presupposition is that Scripture is the inspired Word of God.[1] The *Apostolica Confessio Augustana* says:

> 'This proposition, in which is comprised the cardinal point of the whole Epistle [to the Romans], indeed of the whole of Scripture, [St Paul] sets forth in the third chapter in words that are terse and clear: Therefore we conclude that a man is justified by faith without the deeds of the law.'[2]

The *Solida Declaratio* contains the express statement: 'the Word of God alone is and should remain the sole standard and rule of all doctrine.'[3] On the other hand, we find the confessional documents put virtually on an equality with Holy Scripture, as when it is stated[4] that, 'since these things concern the common laity and their soul's salvation, we confess also the Lesser and Greater Catechisms of Doctor Luther . . . as a Bible for laymen, wherein all is comprised that is treated of throughout Scripture and is necessary that a Christian man know for salvation'. The priority of Scripture over the Confessions is affirmed more explicitly in the *Solida Declaratio*, which declares[5] that all the summary doctrine of the Christian religion is drawn from the Word of God, that confession is to be made of no new doctrine, but only of Scripture, and that Churches adhering to the Augsburg Confession do so in the sense that they remain by the pure doctrine of the Word of God, as expounded by the blessed Lord. So too, and clearest of all, there stands the passage with which the *Epitome Articulorum* opens:

> 'We believe, teach and confess that the sole rule and standard, by which both teaching and teachers are to be assessed and judged, is the prophetic and apostolic Scrip-

---

[1] Preface to *Libri Christianae Concordiae* (1609), 2.
[2] *Ap. Conf. Aug.*, §87; *Bekenntnisschriften der evangelisch-lutherischen Kirche* (referred to subsequently as *B.S.*), 178.
[3] *Solida Declaratio*, §6; *B.S.*, 836.   [4] *Epit. Artic.*, §3; *B.S.*, 769.
[5] Op. cit., opening words of *de Compendiora Doctrinae Forma*, *B.S.*, 833.

tures of the Old and New Testaments. . . . Other writings, whether of old or new teachers, are not to be held as equal, are one and all to be placed under Scripture, and are not to be otherwise or further accepted than as witnesses.'[1]

From this it appears that the place of Scripture in Lutheran doctrine is assured. The expressions used, however, are formal and lack detail and distinctness. To what has been said, both Luther and those who follow him are parties; nor would it strain the Reformed tradition to give agreement.

In the confessional documents of the Reformed Church, there is found the explicit and repeated exposition of the place of Holy Scripture in the Christian faith for which one looks in vain in the documents of Lutheranism. The Genevan Confession of Faith (1536) has 'The Word of God' as its first article, and affirms that

'we desire to follow Scripture alone as rule of faith and religion, without mixing it with any other thing which might be devised by the opinion of men, apart from the Word of God, and without wishing to accept for our spiritual government any other doctrine than what is conveyed to us by the same Word without addition or diminution, according to the command of our Lord.'[2]

The other articles are then expounded, 'following the lines laid down in Holy Scripture'. Holy Scripture is the standard of 'true faith', which is 'not only a certain knowledge by which I hold everything for true which God has revealed in His Word, but also a hearty confidence which the Holy Spirit works in me through the Gospel'.[3] The *Scots Confession* (1560) declares that 'the doctrine, taught in our Churches, is contained in the written Word of God'.[4] Moreover, it contains[5] a section devoted to the 'Authority of the Scriptures' in the following terms:

'As we believe and confess the Scriptures of God sufficient to instruct and make the man of God perfect, so do we affirm and avow the authority of the same to be of God

---

[1] Op. cit., §1; *B.S.*, 767f.   [2] See *Calvin: Theological Treatises*, 26.
[3] *Kirchenordnung der Kurpfalz*: Katechismus Q. and A. 21, *Bekenntnisschriften und Kirchenordnung* (subsequently *B.S.K.*), 1938.
[4] Op. cit., Art. 18.   [5] Op. cit., Art. 19.

and neither to depend (on) men or angels. We affirm therefore that such as alleged the Scripture to have no authority
but that which it receives from the Church, to be blas-
phemous against God and injurious to the true Church,
which always hears and obeys the voice of her own Spouse
and Pastor, but takes not upon her to be mistress over the
same.'

The *Confession de Foy discipline ecclesiastique* (1559), the 'clearest
expression of the Calvinistic doctrine of Scripture',[1] declares
Scripture to be the second and clearest way in which God
manifests Himself, the revelation being at first by oracle and
then by written books. Scripture, canonically defined, is the
'very certain rule of our faith, not so much by the common
accord and consent of the Church, as by the internal witness
and persuasion of the Holy Spirit'.[2] Its authority proceeds
from God and not from men; and, because of their conformity
to it, the Apostles' Creed, the Nicene and the Athanasian
Creeds are to be acknowledged. The doctrine of the Trinity
and other articles of faith are confessed as taught in Scripture.
The *Confessio et Expositio simplex orthodoxae Fidei*[3] similarly de-
votes an opening paragraph to '*de Scriptura sancta, vero Dei
Verbo*', in which scriptural authority is declared to be sufficient and derived from Scripture itself. 'For God Himself
spoke to the fathers, prophets, and apostles, and speaks now
to us through the Holy Scriptures', in which everything per-
taining to salvation is most clearly set forth. In Scripture is
to be found the rule for all true wisdom and piety, for the
reform and government of the Church, for the institution of
all offices of religion, and for all necessary admonitions. In
the lesser-known document, *The Ministry of Word and Sacraments*,[4] the Holy Spirit is said to make use of an external
minister. He 'holds forth the vocal word, and it is received
by the ears. The internal minister, the Holy Spirit, truly communicates the thing proclaimed through the Word, that is
Christ, to the souls of all who will'.

A much fuller account of the place of Holy Scripture is
given in the later *Westminster Confession of Faith* (1649). This
exposition reiterates the affirmations already exemplified, and

[1] So Dr Wilhelm Boudriot in *B.S.K.*, 65.   [2] Op. cit., §2; *B.S.K.*, 66.
[3] *B.S.K.*, 222f.   [4] Op. cit., §vi; *T.T.*, 173.

goes on to state that the Old Testament in Hebrew and the New Testament in Greek, 'being immediately inspired by God, and by His singular care and providence kept pure in all ages, are therefore authentical'.[1] But the command that all the people read and search the Scriptures is the warrant for translation into the vulgar language. The relation of such translation to the original texts is not expounded. Further, 'the infallible rule of interpretation of Scripture is the Scripture itself': while the 'supreme Judge' in all controversies, plainly denying the right of merely individual interpretation, is said to be 'no other than the Holy Spirit speaking in the Scripture'.[2]

This summary examination of the two Reformation strands is enough to reveal a difference between them. The Calvinistic tradition gives Holy Scripture a more explicitly prominent place; the treatment of Scripture is more detailed; and it is possible to trace some development towards greater literal rigidity. This development is already noticeable in the *Westminster Confession of Faith*, and certain features become even more pronounced in the later *Formula Consensus Helvetica* (1675). It would be easy to make too much of the difference. Two mitigating features diminish its importance. The first is that fundamentally the two reformed Churches profess and maintain an adherence to Scripture which is at least in general principles the same. As already said, when the gulf widened between them, the attempt is made to attain agreement and concord, and the common basis found is Holy Scripture. The only difference is in explicitness. The second factor corroborates this conclusion. On the common ground of adherence to Holy Scripture, the later theologians of the two reformed Churches did in fact come together, and from it they went forward more or less together to develop and define the place Holy Scripture should occupy. Lutheranism and Calvinism divide over matters other than Scripture; but in the Orthodoxy that follows the two strands come and remain together as the doctrine of Scripture is unfolded and systematized. This having been said, it is time to see how Orthodoxy developed the reformed view of Scripture.

That differences should have manifested themselves in the course of Protestant theology after the great Reformers is what one might expect. As in the case of the leaders of all great

[1] Op. cit., Ch. 1, §viii.   [2] Op. cit., Ch. 1, §§ix, x.

movements in history, Luther is as much mouthpiece as creator
of reformation. He sets himself at the head of forces already
present, and these forces by his action and work receive expression and direction and thereby increased power. However
private, pure and specific the motives of Luther may have
been when he nailed the Ninety-Five Theses to the door of
the Church at Wittenberg, these forces saw the banner of
general revolt unfurled and rallied behind it. It thus happened
that all too soon this banner waved over a diversity of people
variously dissatisfied with the ecclesiastical or political conditions of the time.[1] 'The religious individualist and the revolutionary communalist, the sceptical humanist and the German
nationalist—all these joined in dislike of the ecclesiastical and
political situation they had inherited.'[2] This helped to swell
the numbers and even at the beginning the strength of the
reformers. But the ways of these different elements had almost
necessarily to part, whenever the time of destruction came to
an end and that of construction began. Even among those
who had and retained a primarily theological interest, the
strain of reconstruction gave opportunity to centrifugal tendencies already present, and wide and bitter differences of
opinion ensued, which have in certain cardinal instances
proved irreconcilable up to the present day.

On the other hand, the matter of Scripture and the views
entertained concerning its authority and position in the Christian faith remained much less contentious. Here too there
were differences of opinion, but the lines of division were not
'party lines', and the divergences were thus deprived of the
violence and bitterness which sectarianism would have inevitably imparted to them. Moreover, through the differences
there may be observed certain identical features, which distinguish the time of Orthodoxy from that of the Reformers.
There is a regrettable similarity in the way in which those
who succeeded to the Reformers lost the living reality with
which Luther and Calvin had invested Scripture, so that in
their hands Scripture became an external authority legalistic-
ally conceived, and adherence to Scripture rigid biblicism.
'The age of Orthodoxy', says E. Brunner,[3] 'appears like
a frozen waterfall—mighty shapes of movement, but no

---

[1] So Hans Leube: *Kalvinismus und Luthertum*, 5.   [2] Loc. cit.
[3] *The Divine-Human Encounter*, 22.

movement': and this recalls Schaff's phrase, 'the hoar-frost of Protestant scholasticism'. Putting the matter in other words, Luther especially,[1] and Calvin to a lesser extent, left doors open which they did not enter. It is these alternative doors that are now used. The paths to which they lead are followed to very different conclusions.

Melanchthon may be said to act as the link between Luther and Orthodoxy. This is not only because he occupied a position intermediate between the two, sharing some opinions with both sides, but because in his own work it is possible to see a change coming over reformed theology. The first (1521) edition of the *Loci Communes*, itself a reversion to a scholastic method of theological exposition, expressed 'with extraordinary clearness the rediscovery of Christianity which marked the first years of the Reformation, and the concentration at that period on the practical issues on religion'.[2] But in later editions, the marks of scholasticism are increasingly apparent. The original emphasis never quite dies out. Even in the edition of 1535, Melanchthon can say that:

> 'Scripture teaches us concerning the divinity of the Son not speculatively but practically; that it bids us invoke Christ and confide in Christ, for this is to accord Him the honour of divinity. Similarly it wishes us to acknowledge the divinity of the Holy Spirit in its own comforting and vivifying power.'[3]

But it remains true that the first force of the new reformed understanding of Christianity is already spent, and Christianity becomes increasingly intellectualized. Melanchthon primarily plays the role of apologist,[4] with its attendant dangers. He first appreciates the problem, which the authority of Scripture raises, of revelation and reason.[5] It was not the intention of Melanchthon to rationalize the Christian faith. But he did feel that the Christian faith could not be left isolated and

---

[1] Cf. A. L. Drummond: *German Protestantism since Luther*, 14: 'Luther's words were "half-battles". There lay their strength while he lived and uttered them; their weakness too, when exposed to the static silence of the printed page' (qtg. *Times Literary Supplement*, 23 September 1946).

[2] S. Cave: *The Doctrine of the Person of Christ*, 143.

[3] *Corpus Reformatorum*, XXI, 366.

[4] Cf. A. L. Drummond: *German Protestantism since Luther*, 14: Luther, 'I hew trees. Philip [Melanchthon] planes them.'

[5] So Köhler, op. cit., 124.

unrelated as truth emanating from a supernatural source without real contact with truth apparent elsewhere. 'Could [the Christian self-consciousness] be content in the long run with the severance of all ties from below?'[1] Another factor from within the Christian faith moved him in the same direction. He is much more acutely aware than Luther ever allowed himself to appear of the possibility of Scripture being read in different ways. Once the authoritative guidance of the Church for the interpretation of what Scripture is saying is repudiated, how are the vagaries of individual interpretation to be effectively guarded against? And where ambiguities give rise to differences of opinion, how are they to be resolved? Melanchthon has resort to right understanding as the required standard. 'God', he says,[2] 'reveals Himself in the prophetic and apostolic Scriptures, and in the symbols.' Once this road is taken, and the three Creeds accorded this important place, it is impossible to stop: he must add also the confessions. Thus alongside the Creeds are placed the Augsburg Confession, the Apology to this Confession, and the Schmalkald Articles.

Luther had not himself dispensed with the formula, *scriptura et ratio*.[3] Positively reason had nothing to offer to faith, and it never becomes for him a second source of doctrine. But negatively it did have a function to perform. Nothing contrary to logic could be true, and reason had the duty of showing what is biblical and true. This, however, is a different responsibility from that which Melanchthon accords to reason. It is one thing for reason to be given the duty of declaring what Scripture says; it is quite another to allot to it the function of discerning between different views of what Scripture is saying. For Luther no such problem really presented itself. Melanchthon does not quite share Luther's confidence that the Scripture itself by the illumination of the Holy Spirit will say the same thing to all. Hence his resort to reason at the point where divergence of opinion is apparent.

Two consequences follow. The authority of Holy Scripture is not surrendered, but it suffers change. Scripture and the theology founded upon it, if not exactly rational in the sense that it all arises from reason, is regarded as understandable and openly intelligible. It lies open to the judgment of reason

---

[1] Op. cit., 125.   [2] *C.R.*, IX, 733.
[3] *W.A.*, 7. 101, 135, 849; 6. 371; 8. 484, 668.

F

in a sense in which it never was with Luther. It follows that the distinction, always so clear with Luther, between the faith and the statements in which the faith is comprised, between Scripture and doctrine, becomes blurred or even obliterated. The element of knowledge (*notitia*), always recognized as present in faith, now attains an importance hitherto denied it. Faith itself is determined less in terms of quality and more in terms of quantity. The principle of authority is regarded doctrinally. God has planted wisdom in the spirit of man. It is therefore not an accident that 'with Melanchthon Aristotle accompanied all dogmatics, and dominated all Protestant theology until the *Aufklärung*'.[1] Melanchthon's aim is thus achieved: he has indeed given Christian faith roots in the world in which it operates, and its isolation is overcome. It now stands securely within the *orbis artium*.[2] But the cost of this security was high, and its consequences had still to be worked out.

The other consequence runs parallel with what has just been said. When reason is given this place of importance alongside authoritative Scripture, it naturally furnishes itself with a rule of thumb which it can apply to matters scriptural and doctrinal. This rule is found in the Creeds together with the confessions in which they find more detailed expression. The Reformers agree in emphasizing the importance of the Creeds, but it is an importance not of this kind, and they are not placed alongside Holy Scripture. When this is done, there inevitably results an assimilation of Scripture with Creed. Under this influence, Melanchthon conceives of a *corpus doctrinae*, and variously defines it as the cardinal points of Romans, together with the doctrine of the Trinity as found in the Fourth Gospel, or with the Nicene Creed, or the Augsburg Confession.[3]

It is evident that under this rigorous systematization, much of Luther's insight into the meaning of scriptural authority has been, if not surrendered, at least obscured. An intellectual view of Holy Scripture is taking the place of the essentially religious view which Luther maintained. In other words,[4] the existential point of view has been replaced by the point of view of the spectator. It was seen earlier that, when Scripture was divested of the authoritative co-operation of the Church,

[1] So Köhler: op. cit., 127.
[2] Loc. cit.
[3] Op. cit., 125f.
[4] Op. cit., 128.

the way lay open in two directions. Either the lost authority must be made good by an accession of authority to Holy Scripture itself, or a new conception of authority had to be worked out in which the locus of authority could not be so simply defined. It was the second way that Luther adopted and followed. Melanchthon went the other road. Rightly aware as he was of the imminent danger that individual interpretation might be given occasion and free rein, and lead eventually to chaos, he allowed this awareness to deepen into distrust. This apprehension led him to diminish the part in authority which Luther was courageous enough, but with the greatest of circumspection, to allot to the subject. The object then retracted to itself the entire exercise of authority. But this involved the surrender of what was new in Luther's conception of authority, and a reversion to that from which he saw the need to depart, once the authority of the Church had been dismantled. It is an astonishing commentary upon what is taking place here to observe that, just as the Roman Church at Trent was putting two books upon the altar, the Bible and the *Summa Theologica*, Lutheranism and the reformers are to be found setting the authoritative confession alongside the Bible.[1]

It is from this point that Protestant Orthodoxy advances. For the understanding of scriptural authority, Luther's work constitutes a watershed. Luther confidently placed himself on one side; Melanchthon pioneered the other side without penetrating deeply or going beyond recall. It was left to Protestant Orthodoxy to do this.

a) *Scripture as an inspired book*. The prime motive for the emphasis which both Luther and Calvin laid upon Scripture is not the need for some authority to take the place of the discredited Church, but rather the renewed insight that the Bible is itself authoritative. But when controversy broke out, both between the reformed faith and Rome and also between exponents of the reformed faith themselves, an authority to which appeal could be made was uncommonly useful. As the Orthodoxy of Protestantism develops, Scripture was increasingly used in this way, and so came to be credited with an authority of the same kind as the Church had formerly wielded. If the works of the Reformers could be elevated into a place of

[1] See A. L. Drummond: *German Protestantism since Luther*, 18.

authority, as was (and in some degree still is) the case with the
Augsburg Confession in Lutheranism, much more so with the
Scriptures. It is nevertheless a betrayal of the Reformers' insight, and the authority credited to Scripture is of an external
and objective kind. It is the development in this direction that
has now to be briefly traced.

The principle of *sola scriptura* takes its rise from the repudia-
tion of the idea that Scripture needs any other authority than
its own. Compliance with this rubric and the desire to enhance
its prestige and conserve its security are the dominant motives
behind the developments that follow. The Scriptures more
and more come to occupy a place of unique isolation. The distinction between Scripture and the Word of God, which Luther
maintained but so often by his own utterances imperilled, is
now lost, and the two are regarded as identical. This lack of
distinction between Scripture and the Word of God is a cardinal point of difference between the theology of Orthodoxy
and that of the Reformers. Thus Gerhard[1] *inter verbum Dei et
scripturam sacram, materialiter acceptam, non esse reale aliquod discrimen.* Two qualifications are sometimes made. The first is that
it is generally the meaning and not the word that is regarded
as inspired. Thus Gerhard:[2]

> 'By the term Scripture, we do not mean the outer form or
> sign, that is the particular letters, the act of writing and the
> words with which the divine revelation has been written
> down, so much as the matter itself and the thing signified,
> that which is meant and designated by the writing, namely
> the Word of God which informs us about His essence and will'

and similarly Calov.[3] The other qualification is that an occasional attempt is made to distinguish between Scripture and
the Word of God. It is recognized that the written word is
not the same as the everlasting hypostatic Word who is the
second person of the Trinity. These two qualifications may
seem to restore the position and bring Orthodoxy into something like harmony with its predecessors, the great Reformers.
It is not in fact so. In general, Orthodoxy holds that there is
'no real difference between Scripture and God's Word'.[4]

[1] *Loci Theologica* (1610), 2. 15.   [2] Op. cit., 2. 14.
[3] *Systema Locorum Theologicorum* (1655), 1. 707.
[4] R. Preus: *The Inspiration of Scripture*—a Study of the Theology of the
Seventeenth-century Lutheran Dogmaticians, 14.

Verbum Dei hodie non est nisi scriptum.[1] It is true that this admission is formulated by Orthodoxy in criticism of the Roman position and in order to deny any normative Word of God apart from Scripture; but this does not mitigate its importance. So too it is repeatedly asserted that Scripture is never uninspired. Thus Calov:[2] *At Scriptura sancta intrinsece, ac per se nunquam non θεόπνευστος, nec citra inspirationem divinam, ut pote, quae ad formale eius pertinet, nusquam datur, aut dari potest: quando quidem per eandem a verbo humano discriminetur verbum Dei quatenus quale.* Hutter[3] says the same thing. Here too the Orthodox theologians are defending themselves, both against the thought that it is by sanction of the Church that Scripture enjoys its inspiration, and against the idea that subjective considerations are necessary for its operation. But to do so they propound the doctrine that Scripture has locked up within it the virtue it possesses. Orthodoxy, attempting with right to exclude the dependence of the inspiration of Scripture upon the Church or upon the individual believer, falls into the trap of making Scripture self-contained. The sovereign action of God in making Scripture the vehicle and occasion of His Word is excluded. If the Word of God is in any sense free of Scripture—a *verbum diversum*—it is only in so far as a hiddenness belongs to it which in any case we cannot probe—so Calov.[4]

Thus one of the sheet anchors of Luther's treatment of the meaning and authority of Holy Scripture is slipped. On the Reformed side, Calvin made a parallel distinction between the Word of God and the Holy Spirit, and the communication of God through the Holy Spirit is held to be something separable and in fact frequently separated from His communication through Scripture. The mark of Protestant Orthodoxy is the identification of the two concepts. Calvin holds that the primary function of the Holy Spirit is revelation, and that Scripture transmits this revelation through the agency of the Holy Spirit. But Cocceius is typical of Orthodoxy in amalgamating the revelation and its written record and holding the Holy Spirit as directly responsible for both. Thus[5] the men of the Bible 'wrote exactly as they spoke, not by their own will but driven by the Holy Spirit'. As Tertullian earlier

[1] Huelsemann: *Calvinismus Irreconcilabilis* (1667), 423; so also Calov.
[2] *Systema*, 1. 711.   [3] *Loci Communes Theologici* (1619), 31.
[4] *Systema*, 1. 451.
[5] Johannes Cocceius: *Summa Theologica ex Scriptura repetita* (1665), 4. 40.

said, the Spirit of God is imprisoned within the covers of a book.

The identity of Holy Scripture with the Word of God or with the Spirit requires the closest conjunction of the spoken and the written word. This is because, however they came to write the books attributed to them, the prophets certainly also spoke what came to them as Word of God; nor is the influence of Luther quite forgotten, which tended to regard the New Testament as primarily a spoken Gospel, and only secondarily a written document. This accounts for the importance which is attached to demonstrating the coincidence of spoken and written word. Thus Quenstedt says[1] that

'what the prophets and apostles taught by the divine inspiration, preached with the living voice, and what they signified and expressed on paper through letters and characters, is one and the same Word of God. Diversity of setting forth and communicating, i.e. between writing and oral tradition, implies no diversity of object or of the material contained in written or communicated word.'

On the Lutheran side, Schmidt writes similarly:[2] *Inter verbum Dei et Scripturam sanctam materialiter consideratam nullum est discrimen. Idem est, quod Christus ore suo dixit autoribus eius, . . . et quod prophetae scripserunt, idem est quod et locuti sunt.* Statements from Flacius could also be cited here which maintain the close association of the written and the spoken word; but in view of their different and almost opposite intention, and the special place it seems now necessary to allot him (see later), it would be misleading to quote them here. The intention of Quenstedt is the assimilation of the written to the spoken word, so that the written word may share with the spoken word a direct relation with the Holy Spirit and all the prestige this gives.

The next step seems to follow unavoidably. If the written word is thus directly related to the Holy Spirit, it is credited with a direct divine origin of a singular kind, and the way immediately opens out to a full doctrine of inspiration, which is subsequently buttressed by the ascription to Scripture of other remarkable attributes. Thus Brenz speaks for Orthodoxy in general when he declares[3] that 'the Holy Scripture is the

---

[1] *Theologia didactico-polemica* (1685), 1. 4. 1, Thesis 1, note 2.
[2] *Sacrum Compendium Theologias* (1697), 15. [3] Köhler, op. cit., 130.

oracle of the Holy Spirit'; and so Gerhard:[1] 'the Holy Scripture has God for author, through whose direct inspiration the prophets, evangelists and apostles wrote. So on this ground it possesses authority. Since it is inspired (*theopneustos*), it is in and of itself worthy of belief (*autopistos*).' Inspiration is soon found to imply verbal dictation and verbal infallibility. Thus Hutter[2] holds that 'Holy Scripture is accordingly verbally dictated by the Holy Spirit, in such a way that no iota set down by the prophets and apostles in their books is not God-given'. Calov[3] similarly states that 'no error even in the smallest detail, no failure of memory, let alone any untruths, can find any place in the whole of Scripture'. Quenstedt[4] raises the question whether in Scripture even the single words are inspired and dictated by the Holy Spirit. His answer is unambiguous:

'The Holy Spirit not only inspired in the prophets and apostles the content and sense contained in Scripture, or the meaning of the words, so that they might of their own free will clothe and furnish these thoughts with their own style and words, but the Holy Spirit actually supplied, inspired and dictated the very words and each and every term individually.'

So too Calov.[5] Inspiration is an 'absolutely unique and extraordinary action' of God, according to Quenstedt.[6] It applies to the writers by inciting their minds to the writing, the moving of the pens by their hands, their inward enlightenment, and by supplying them both with the content and the words. 'Even the things known already to the writers are communicated to them afresh by inspiration.'[7] What can by such means be transmitted is necessarily intellectually conceived. The idea of revelation as an action in which God communicates Himself is foreign to the theology of Orthodoxy, though it is sometimes maintained that God in Scripture reveals not only doctrine but also Himself (Calov). E. Brunner[8] speaks of the 'fatal equation of revelation with the inspiration of the Scriptures', and quotes Calov:[9] *Forma revelationis divinae est theopneustia per quam revelatio divina est quod est.* So engrossed are the

[1] *Loci Theol.*, 2. 36.   [2] *Loci Comm. Theol.*   [3] *Sys. Loc. Theol.*, 1.551.
[4] *Theol. did-pol.*, 1. 72.   [5] *Biblia Novi Testamenti*, 2. 1034.
[6] *Theol. did-pol.*, 1. 69.   [7] *Op. cit.*, 1. 68.   [8] *Revelation and Reason*, 7.
[9] *Syst. Loc. Theol.*, 1. 280.

theologians of Orthodoxy with inspiration that they tend to neglect the idea of revelation. 'They believed that they had dealt adequately with their task when they had developed a doctrine of the divine authority of Holy Scripture.' 'They did not understand that the inspiration of the Holy Scriptures is not *the* revelation, but one of the forms of revelation, namely, the incarnation in written form of the living personal revelation of the Living God in the history of revelation and salvation.'[1] In reply to the question 'whether Holy Scripture is possessed of infallible truth and devoid of all error', the answer given by Quenstedt is plain:[2] there is in Scripture

> 'no mendacity, no falsity, no slightest error, whether in matters or words; but every single thing whatsoever that is transmitted in it, whether it be dogmatic, or moral, of history, chronology, typography or names,[3] is most true; nor can or ought there to be attributed to Scripture as transmitted in the sacred letters any ignorance, or forgetfulness, or lack of knowledge, or lapse of memory by the Holy Spirit.'

We have on our hands the classical form of the doctrine of the verbal inspiration of Holy Scripture.

Still other measures can be taken to support the forbidding view of verbal inspiration. On such presuppositions little place can be found either for the historically contingent or for individual character or idiosyncrasy. Thus, as Gerhard holds,[4] 'God's handymen, Christ's "hands", the secretaries and notaries of the Holy Spirit, write not as men, but as God-men'. Quenstedt says[5] that the writers contribute *nihil praeter linguam et calamum*. The whole matter is so conceived in Orthodoxy as to make a right view impossible. The field is regarded as divided, so that what God does man does not do, and what is reserved to man is *ipso facto* stolen from God. Yet the writers are not necessarily held to be quite dehumanized. Quenstedt, for example,[6] distinguishes the writers of Scripture from men in a trance who do not know what they are about; and Calov allows a certain συγκατάβασις or condescension on the part of God, which explains differences in style which must have

---

[1] Brunner, op. cit., 12.　　　　　　　　　[2] *Theol. did-pol.*, Q. v.
[3] *Onomastica*, including both personal and place-names.
[4] *Loc. Theol.*, 2. 15.　　　　[5] *Theol. did-pol.*, 1. 72.　　　　[6] Op. cit., 1. 64.

their ground in the individual writers. This is a necessary implication on the subjective side. It is, however, the objective side that is the concern here. The Holy Scriptures themselves are equipped with other qualities in order to play their part as such divine oracles. The original text of a book of this order, a book for whose every word God is responsible, must enjoy perfection and entire freedom from error. So far from being, as for Luther, acceptable evidence of their humanness, as the tears of our Lord were evidence of His humanity, imperfections in Scripture are embarrássments which must be deleted. The hypothesis of a perfect original text is a hypothesis designed to safeguard the infallibility of what is divinely written, and to explain the imperfections of the text in our hands. Further, not only is the content of Holy Scripture unique and the text which contains it perfect. The very materials of which the text is composed are accorded a unique quality: it is suggested that there is a special Hebrew for the Old Testament and a special Greek for the New. But the interest rests rather on the Old Testament than on the New, since Hebrew is the speech of God Himself and represents the original speech before linguistic mischief was done at the Tower of Babel. Finally, this line of thought leads to accrediting a divine origin to the vowel points and the consonants. Flacius is usually cited as the first to make this suggestion. There is reason to doubt that this is so, as will be noted immediately. But if he is not primarily responsible, others take it upon themselves to make the proposal. Gerhard committed himself to the hypothesis, and Polanus is quoted[1] as vindicating it by the citation of Matt. v. 18, 'one jot or one tittle shall in no wise pass from the law'. The equal originality of Hebrew points and consonants with the text itself finds its way at last into the confessional documents. While Gerhard asserts their originality in a purely *a priori* argument, which quite disregards factual probability in the interests of defending their authenticity, Hutter is among those that decline to draw the conclusion. But the *Formula Consensus Helvetica* of 1675 declares of the Hebrew text of the Old Testament that it is 'θεόπνευστος regarding the vowels, whether the very points themselves or at least the power of the points, and regarding things as well as words'. On the Lutheran side, it also reached expression

[1] *Loc. Theol.*, 2. 15.

in the *Consensus repetitus fidei verae Lutheranae* (1666), which is
a work of Calov. The inerrancy of Scripture follows as a
matter of course. Quenstedt[1] declares that 'the apostles could
never err after receiving the gift of the Holy Spirit'; and again:
'whatever fault or untruth, whatever error or lapse of memory,
is attributed to the prophets and apostles is not imputed to
them without blaspheming the Holy Spirit who spoke and
wrote through them'. A far road has been travelled since
Luther rejoiced in the humanness of Holy Scripture, and was
content to catch up the ascertainable lapses into the divine
providential plan. But the theologians of Orthodoxy do not
have Luther in mind, but rather the Socinians who taught
that Scripture was reliable only in the parts that pertain to
doctrine. Calov's retort is abrupt: there are, he says, no *levicula*
(trivialities) in Scripture, but all pertains to doctrine.

Thus the doctrine of the plenary inspiration of Scripture
reaches its fullest and most formidable expression, and Scripture is equipped with all the apparatus designed to vindicate
its sovereign authority. Protestant Orthodoxy arms Scripture
cap-à-pie—but that which is armoured is a very different thing
from that which Luther and Calvin commend.

The matter of translations provided some difficulty for those
who propounded so uncompromising a doctrine of scriptural
authority, and it is not separable from the allied question of
versions. What was their relation to that infallible text which
remained the sheet anchor of verbal inspiration in the face of
all the assaults of criticism? The Romans were concerned here,
since they had a vested interest in defending the Vulgate translation.[2] On the side of the reformers, it was possible to distinguish between the apographa as authentic and the translations,
the first retaining the very words, the second only the meaning,
of the original. Quenstedt holds[3] that, as Scripture is inspired
quoad formale et quoad materiale, only the original text, and not
any of the versions, is inspired: inspiration applies to original
manuscripts or autographa, not properly to the apographa.
Yet there is a difference between the apographa and the versions. Versions of the Bible, he says,[4] are the Word of God in

---

[1] *Theol. did-pol.*, 1. 80.
[2] See Tridentine Canons and Decrees, Sess. 4, Decretum de editione et usu
sacrorum librorum.
[3] *Theol. did-pol.*, 1. 73.   [4] Op. cit., 1. 207.

content and words, but the apographa are the Word of God in content, words and idiom. Hence:[1]

'We believe, as is our duty, that the providential care of God always watched over the original and primitive texts of the canonical Scriptures in such a way that we can be certain that the sacred codices which we now have in our hands are those which existed at the time of Jerome and Augustine, nay, at the time of Christ Himself and His apostles.'

That is, a good copy is inspired like the original writing. Gerhard,[2] on the other hand, is rather stricter, holding that only the original Hebrew and Greek manuscripts are authentic.

Another line of defence, following the suggestion thrown out by Quenstedt, maintained that there is no general corruption of the Scriptures in the course of transmission: 'by divine providence they have been preserved intact and incorrupt'. Thus Calov[3] says: *Distinguo inter lectionis varietatem et diversitatem, et textus originalis falsationem universalem.* Starting, that is, from the fact of imperfection in the texts in our hands, it is denied that this implies either the corruption of the originals or the distortion of what we now possess. Hollaz ventures a more general judgment in the matter when he says that the illuminating power of the Holy Scripture belongs not to the original text alone, but also to such reputable translations of the original text as Luther's own, which might therefore be said to enjoy a mediated authority.

A word should be said about Flacius (b. 1573), who is usually credited[4] with playing a leading part in the movement that has just been described, and in particular with first propounding the idea of the originality of the Hebrew points. A recent detailed study by Günther Moldaenke[5] throws doubt upon the fairness of this judgment. A strong case can be made out to show that, at a number of points at least, Flacius opposes the general tendency of Orthodoxy. For one thing,

---

[1] *Op. cit.*, 1. 206.   [2] *Loc. Theol.*, 2. 251ff.
[3] *Criticus Sacer.* (1646), 1. 430.
[4] For example, by W. Köhler and O. Ritschl.
[5] Günther Moldaenke: *Schriftverständnis und Schriftdeutung im Zeitalter der Reformation*—Teil 1: Matthias Flacius Illyricus—Forschungen zur Kirchen- und Geistesgeschichte, 9ter Bd.

he utters phrases which make it impossible to assign to him
a bare identity of Holy Scripture and the Word of God. He
clearly differentiates and defines a *Sache* for whose sake Scripture is and which in fact constitutes its heart and centre. More
exactly, the Scripture is more concerned with Him who speaks
than with what is spoken.[1] In a word, the Scripture has as
theme *non quid sed quis*. It is thus easy for Flacius to resist the
form of inspiration which did so much harm in Protestant
Orthodoxy. It is true that he is frequently concerned to make
clear the continuity which exists between the spoken and the
written word, and at this point he might seem to have something in common with other orthodox theologians. Moldaenke
cites a long list of examples in which the two sides of the relation
are held together, and the written and the oral correlated:
loqui and *conscribere*, *dicta* and *scripta*, *vocalis* and *scriptoria insti-
tutio*, *os* and *manus* or *calamus*, *Buch* and *Lehre*, and so on. And
yet he advocates the principle from a different angle and for
a different purpose. So far from thus facilitating the assimilation of the written word to the inspired status of the spoken
word, Flacius' aim is to show that both words, written and
spoken, in fact testify to the same thing. This thing is thus
different from either, and *a fortiori* different from Scripture:
the Word of God is held to be distinct from Scripture. Since
again inspiration is certainly at work where the word is written
or spoken, it becomes impossible simply to identify Holy Scripture with the Holy Spirit. Flacius repudiates the idea that
inspiration is to be limited to the mere *actus scribendi*. The
scriptural word is not the event for which inspiration is primarily responsible; it is connected with the oral word, and
inspiration lies behind and within both. It is a relief to win
clear of a doctrine of inspiration which reduces the operation
of the Holy Spirit to a merely psychological account of how
the words got written.

Flacius similarly sets his face against the limitation of Holy
Scripture to a verbal concept.

'When one says Holy Scripture [he says roundly] one
does not mean that letters A B C D , or the syllables Ba Be
Bi Bo Bu, or the word, or the pattern of lines, or the paper
or the ink, or the books in which they are comprised. The

[1] For references in the works of Flacius, see Moldaenke op. cit. 259-319.

meaning is rather the instruction or teaching which is contained by the Bible and signified by letters, syllables, and words on the paper.'

Along with this more pliant conception of what the meaning of Holy Scripture really is, Flacius maintains a dynamic view of how Scripture operates. Scripture is indeed a living effective thing, but this is only in virtue of the fact that it has that within it which it is not, and has not, in and by itself: it is God who works through Scripture, or alternatively the Holy Spirit. With truly Lutheran zeal, Flacius holds the Scripture and the Spirit together: without this conjunction, the Word remains unspoken. When it is maintained, it becomes effective: God is not to be sought without Scripture, nor is Scripture to be sought without God. Similarly it is God who saves, though He does it through Scripture: salvation is not in the Word like provisions in a sack which one can sling on his shoulder and take home.

What then of the allegation that Flacius is the first to give expression to the epitome of verbal inspirationism concerning the Hebrew vowel points? What he actually says is: 'Scripture as written by God contains not a syllable or a particle which does not conceal deep within itself a large treasure.' It is difficult without malice to make of this a reference to the originality of the Hebrew points, and Moldaenke must be given credit for firmly maintaining that such a phrase as this is no more than a hyperbolic expression of the inexhaustible riches of Scripture, a sentiment which on any showing is both true and admirable.

In fact, Flacius clings tenaciously to a conception which saved him from many of the pitfalls of Orthodoxy. He held a robust and healthy conception of the means whereby the Scriptures are in fact written. Inspiration for him is less a psychological theory of how the words of Scripture reach the page, than a divine calling by which appropriate instruments are summoned to divinely appointed work. These means do not with him degenerate to the level of mere amanuenses (as with Gerhard and many other Orthodox theologians); they remain (as for Rivet) at least *calami viventes et scribentes*—organs which have their own independence accorded to them in virtue of their being called. No doubt Flacius speaks of Scripture itself being inspired—as who does not and must not in this controversy? No doubt also Flacius sometimes holds that the writers themselves are inspired—as again in some sense they must certainly have been. But his steady affirmation is that it is God who spoke *through* the mouths of the prophets and apostles as His called organs, and that He *conscripsit* the Scriptures with them. The men of the Bible are maintained in a real *Nebeneinander* alongside God who uses them, and in a real *co-operatio cum Deo*; they are not permitted to slide down the slippery slope at the foot of which lies complete suppression of individuality.

The importance of rehabilitating Flacius from the fate that perhaps too many writers each copying the others have allotted to him should not be exaggerated. He stands out distinctively from the orthodox world around him. But his example is not enough to reverse the general judgment to be passed upon Protestant Orthodoxy. Flacius may have staved off the prevalent *rigor scholasticus*; but this is no proof that there is no *rigor* at all.

b) *The place of reason.* When the co-operation of the Church in establishing the authority of Scripture is repudiated, Holy Scripture is left on its own, and it becomes urgently necessary to enquire concerning the ground or sanction of its authority. Orthodoxy found the answer, as Luther and Calvin did not, in crediting Scripture independently with much the same kind of external authority as it had formerly derived from the sanction of the Church. Scripture regarded as in this sense authoritative is then equipped with various other attributes by which its authority is exalted, but at the same time also stiffened and hardened. It might seem not only possible but even probable that those who thought of scriptural authority in this way would have, when the problem of the relations of revelation and reason was raised, adopted the obscurantist side. A system of truth duly sanctioned by Scripture would then have been set up. Over against it, reason would claim to offer another road to truth or to yield another aspect of truth. Little or no attempt would then have been made to bring the two systems, the biblical and the rational, into effective harmony with each other. We are in our own day familiar with this method of dealing with the problem, though it rather shelves than solves it. This, however, is not the way adopted by Protestant Ortho-doxy. Another method offers a solution, if only it can succeed. The truth that is contained in Scripture and warranted by scriptural authority is related directly to reason and the truth which reason yields. It is, perhaps a little surprisingly, this alternative which Protestant Orthodoxy chooses.

No doubt the reasons for its choice are various. Two at least may be mentioned. *Scriptura et ratio* had a far fuller meaning for Melanchthon than Luther had ever allowed; and it is Melanchthon rather than Luther that the orthodox theolo-gians follow here. The other reason is more general but not fundamentally different. The importance of the parallel move-ment of the Renaissance in instigating the Reformation has often been exaggerated. The Reformers, with their insistence upon the incapacity of man in things spiritual, were moved by reaction to Renaissance thought rather than by sympathy with it. In the period of Orthodoxy which succeeds, however, it is the opposite judgment that must be passed. To its credit, Protestant Orthodoxy declined to lapse into obscurantism, and a serious attempt was made to relate the Christian faith to reason. But it did not avoid the dangers besetting this path.

Even Calvin, to the clarity and persuasiveness of Scripture itself, was constrained to add certain other sanctions, such as the fulfilment of prophecy and the presence of miracles, which supply some kind of rational basis or commendation for the authority of Scripture. Luther too subscribed within strict limits to the formula *scriptura et ratio*. The entry of rational aids is thus sanctioned by both Reformers. The question now raised is: up to what limits could the faith come to terms with reason, and admit its help for its own defence and under-standing?

The apologetic attempt is made to show that the dichotomy between faith and reason is more apparent than real. Melanch-thon had made use of Aristotle in the formulation of his Chris-tian ethic; and Köhler points out[1] that an attempt was made by Venatorius to work out a biblical ethic, though it found little success and no followers. The justification for appeal to Aristotle was that philosophy had its roots in the wisdom of the fathers of the Old Testament, and had come to the Greeks by way of Egypt. Köhler declares that Gerhard 'smuggled in'

[1] *Op. cit.*, 133.

Aristotle's view of the world and of man under cover of biblical terminology, as the ground on which the salvation drama then unfolded. In direct contradiction of the contention of Luther that philosophy is incapable of assisting the Gospel, a landslide takes place towards rationalism and rationalization of the faith. Christian dogma is found in Aristotle; its independence is weakened; we have a *theologia naturalis* on our hands. Taurellus[1] was aware that the question of faith and reason is here being raised in an acute form. While affirming in brave style that 'rational grounds are false, and there are no philosophical conclusions through which anything can come into conflict with theology', he wavered in applying the principle, and in the end sought some kind of harmony in a 'system of true philosophy'.

Sometimes indeed the solution to the problem is put in obverse form. Calov[2] asserts that 'sound reason is never in conflict with Scripture'. But there is little doubt that apparent conflicts between Scripture and reason are resolved in favour rather of reason than of Scripture. The comment of Köhler seems justified:[3] 'Reason in theology has always had the tendency to change from *minister* to *magister*.'

What is happening here? It is certainly not that for the first time faith and reason are brought into contact and that the only possible solution to the conflict is being expressed. In one form or another, the problem has been recurrent in theology. The *credo ut intelligam* is one solution, and the Reformers inclined towards it. Luther out of a profound religious experience which shaped not only his life, but also his thought, could not do otherwise than accord primacy to faith. Calvin reached a similar conclusion on the quite different grounds that man is *non capax infiniti* and must therefore wait upon the initiative of the sovereign God. It is this order of things that is gradually reversed in Protestant Orthodoxy. The primacy of faith gives way, first to an equality of faith with reason: faith must at least be intelligible. But the equality is difficult to maintain. The faith is intellectually conceived, and then it is reason and not faith that moves up into the dominant position. The authority of Scripture is compromised and made equivocal.

When faith is thus intellectually conceived, the Creeds come to be regarded in a new light and with a fresh importance.

---

[1] Nikolaus Taurellus (1547-1606). [2] Qtd. op. cit., 135. [3] Loc. cit.

They comprise conveniently what Scripture, intellectually conceived, says at greater length and with less clarity. But they come, not only to expound what Scripture is saying, but also to define it. Thus the Creeds, which set out upon their course in history as defenders of heavenly doctrine (so Georg Major[1]) against attacks from outside, become their own inner justification. They have achieved a standing alongside of Holy Scripture. It is subscription to the Creeds and confessional documents that more and more makes the Christian. Thus Hutter forbids deviation from the Augsburg Confession by so much as a finger's breadth. The brave affirmation of the confessions which set Holy Scripture as the only standard and judge for doctrinal matters, is practically repudiated by the obligation to confess the formulae. Köhler says[2] that the Mecklenburg Order for Churches of 1552 is the first document specifically to bind Holy Scripture to the three classical Creeds, together with Luther's Catechism, the Schmalkald Articles of 1557 and the Augsburg Confession. He continues: 'The Waldeck Order for Churches of 1556 added the Apologia for the Augsburg Confession. Further orders followed. The choice from the Protestant collection of confessions varied, and sometimes the Saxon Confession of 1552, sometimes Melanchthon's *Loci*, and sometimes others are accepted.' Hollaz accords to the articles of faith an impregnable authority[3] and the office of the ministry is to expound them.

The course of rationalization is not without its deviations; but they are deviations to an otherwise general rule. Flacius, as already said, insisting that the core of Scripture is *non quid sed quis*, strikes a different note. Quenstedt[4] says that 'all things divine and sacred are comprised in the Word of God, and of these the law and the Gospel are the summary of what it is necessary to do and to believe. But the nucleus, marrow, *scopus* and centre to which all Scripture refers, is Christ Jesus.' But on the whole, these are lonely voices of protest against the prevailing tendency. The testimony of Wigand[5] is more ambiguous: 'Whenever the same doctrine of God is repeated by men, whether in thought or reading, in writing or preaching or singing or in any other way, it still remains God's Word,

---

[1] Georg Major (1502-74). [2] Op. cit., 136.
[3] Köhler: op. cit., 137. [4] *Theol. did-pol.*, 1. 4, Thesis 4.
[5] Johannes Wigand: *Syntagma seu Corpus Doctrinae Christi* (1560), 409ff.

G

and God through it is effective in those who will be saved.'
The truth of this is incontestable. But it is no more than part
of the truth. The unique position of authority which Scripture
occupies as God's appointed instrument and organ, and the
covenanted place where God thus works, does not come to
expression.

c) *Subjective-objective relations.* The same tendency may be
observed from the different angle of subjective-objective relations. It has already been seen that when authority is accorded
to *sola scriptura*, Scripture attaches to itself the armour of inspiration, and at the same time understands itself in such intellectual terms as tend to destroy its uniqueness. What now takes
place may be regarded as the nemesis of this unhappy tendency.

On both counts the authority of Scripture is accorded a
formidable and imposing appearance; but it is an authority
which is remote and formal. Luther's insight that Scripture
was to be made authoritative in an event is ignored. Karl
Barth[1] points out that Lutheran Orthodoxy built into the very
idea of Scripture itself an *efficacia verbi divini etiam ante et extra
usum*, 'to the effect that a divine power belonged to the Word
of God proclaimed and written, whatever its effects upon the
hearer or reader might be'. 'Quenstedt denied specifically that
the Bible is an *instrumentum* which requires *novo motu et elevatione
nova ad effectum novum ultra propriam suam naturalem virtutem producendum.* The Bible and preaching were rather media, in
which *summa vis et efficacia* were inherent in themselves and
permanently.'[2] So too Hollaz[3] contends that the Word of God
is not an *actio* but a *vis* and *potentia*, which as such has *efficacia*
—even *extra usum.* 'A power comparable with sunshine or the
germinative power of a seed of course does not require a *nova
elevatio.* It is there, just as the powers of nature are there.'
But this really denies that the Word is the Word of a Person.
The dignity scriptural authority now possesses is compatible
only with objectivity and externality. The role of the subject
in matters of faith and Scripture is reduced to pure passivity.
The object, that is objective Scripture, is so dominant that at
the subjective end there is nothing demanded except compliance. The sense in which Luther had held Scripture to operate,

[1] *Kirchliche Dogmatik*, I/1, 124.   [2] *Theol. did-pol.*, 1. 4. 2, ekth. 7.
[3] *Examen Theologicum Acroamaticum* (1707), 3. 2. 1, qu. 4.

by evoking a real hearing and responding on the part of the subject, has been lost. As Köhler says:[1]

'the failure here consists in the misunderstanding of the subject's right to respond. To understanding there always belongs two things, a giver and a receiver. If the giver alone operates, only compulsion is possible. The speaking on the part of the subject which Luther had maintained is stifled by his successors, since for him it operated as the speaking of the object itself.'

Gerhard exemplifies this view:[2] *Homines qui intra ecclesiae pomeria* (the open spaces round a fortified town) *sunt, de scripturae auctoritate non quaerunt; est enim principium.* Brunner, who quotes this,[3] goes on to say that 'this authority of the Scriptures, which precedes all faith, and is above all questions, is the orthodox theory of the Scriptures, of the Reformed as well as of the Lutheran Churches'.

This doctrine in which a passive subject is confronted by an impregnable authoritativeness does not stand alone: the 'Spiritualists' or Pietists who were contemporary with Luther himself had already been providing an alternative view. Köhler collects citations to show the direction being taken.[4] The role of the subject has a position alongside that of the object—a position of co-ordination, not, as with Luther, of interrelation. 'Heaven's gate swings on two hinges: knowledge of God and knowledge of self.' 'The heart of the believer is a living agent of the Holy Spirit and a veritable library or Bible from which all true books are written and certified' (Franck.)[5] Schwenckfeld writes that 'God deals with the new man in a double way, inwardly and outwardly.'[6] But increasingly predominance is given to the active subject. Thus again Schwenckfeld declares:[7] 'If the man is to understand or rightly recognize or judge spiritual things, he must bring divine light to Scripture, spirit to letter, truth to the picture, and the master to his work.' This is indeed to accord the subject an active and important role. But it is a role which Luther with better judgment accords to Holy Scripture operating upon the subject. So far from being illuminated, Scripture now stands itself in need of illumination by

[1] Op. cit., 137. [2] *Loc. Theol.*, 1. 9. [3] *Revelation and Reason*, 11, n. 15.
[4] Op. cit., 137f. [5] Sebastian Franck (1499–1542).
[6] Caspar Schwenckfeld: *Decursu verbi Dei* (1527), 16. [7] *Von der heiligen Schrift*, 6. 5.

what the subject can bring to bear upon it. 'All knowledge comes from self-knowledge', writes Weigel,[1] and continues: the Scripture is 'a dark lantern, unless you have faith or the Spirit of God'. Unhappily, this is just the contribution that the individual by himself cannot make, for all the pretentious protestations of Thamer:[2] 'Scripture is Scripture, write it who will; we, each in our own way, make something of it through the Spirit.'

The ground underlying opinions so different from those of the Reformers is the difficulty of ascribing absolute authority to a book containing admitted contradictions. This seems necessarily to lead to the destruction of the authority of Scripture and its dispersal among individual opinions. Franck gave repeated expression to this felt danger. One makes Scripture into an idol, he says, 'and finds in it what he will: it offers a cushion for every elbow'; and again: 'no sentence in all Scripture is so firm and certain, as to make a universal judgment or to conclude anything'; or again: the Bible even in the letter lacks unity: it has 'spread claws'. The gravest problems thus arise: Where is the certainty of Scripture to be sought? What value is there in its alleged inspiration? And, above all, how can its authority be preserved from collapse?

The solution proposed by the Spiritualists is that what is required must be supplied from the subjective side of the relationship. As Köhler puts it:[3] 'Spirit and faith are not attained by the reading of Scripture; rather Spirit and faith must be brought to it. Scripture does not lead to God, rather God leads to Scripture.' This involves a disruption of the close connexion between Spirit and Scripture which Luther maintained. Yet even this solution did not explain or settle everything, in this simple form. The danger of pure relativity and of arbitrariness is still present, unless and until the Spirit which must be supplied by the subject and brought to the understanding of Holy Scripture can be more exactly defined. This further definition cannot be offered from the side of the object: the limits to which the object can here assist are reached when it is regarded as the 'means of solicitation' (Franck, Weigel and others[4]), in response to which the subject supplies the required spirit of understanding. This spirit itself, loosed from

---

[1] Valentin Weigel (1533-88).
[2] Theobald Thamer (*obiit* 1569).
[3] Op. cit., 139.
[4] Op. cit., 139.

its tie with Holy Scripture, may be characterized in either of two ways: either it comes to be defined as a general principle of truth, which leads immediately to Rationalism; or it is located more specifically within the soul of man himself and takes on the character of a splinter of divinity or a spark of the divine as is the contention of the Pietists.

It may be well to follow for a very short way each of these two possible courses. The Spirit which men must bring to the reading of the Bible is easily identified with that which is operative in all the dealings men have with truth. It is that by which men are distinguished from the rest of creation. It is identical with reason. This step is taken by Castellio, when he declares[1] that 'in men, reason reigns as king'; and 'where knowledge begins, faith ends'. The final court of appeal in matters of truth is reason and with it lies final judgment. It is even suggested that the many difficulties in Scripture are left intentionally by God, in order that reason may sharpen itself upon them. Once reason is accorded a place of this kind, it can be used for apologetic purposes. Reason is after all a venerable principle, reaching back to Adam, Enoch and Noah, before the time of Abraham and the establishment of the covenant; for even in these days the finger of God had already written human duties on the hearts of men. Indeed, Jesus Himself lived by this same reason, or rather He was it. Thus reason comes to be indistinguishable from the divine Logos. Innate understanding is the equivalent of the divine Spirit. Separated as it is from Holy Scripture, as a different and higher principle, reason thus defined marks the end of the process: the attempt to restore to the subjective side a reality of existence and operation over against Scripture finally loses itself in Rationalism.

On the other hand, Franck is representative of a line of thought in which the spirit men have to supply for understanding Scripture is not identified with reason. Permitted to retain a character of its own, it is described as a divine spark which burns in all men. It is this inner possession that among the Pietists does duty for Luther's faith. But as the natural possession of man, and not the creation of the Word of God acting through Scripture illuminated by the Holy Spirit, it is

[1] Köhler: op. cit., 140. Sebastian Castellio (1515-63): *de Arte dubitandi et confidendi, ignorandi et sciendi*, 349.

in itself something quite different from Luther's faith. This difference may be exemplified in the nature and intention of the spiritual exercises that are advocated. For Luther meditation was a steady reflection and waiting upon the given and objective Word of God 'in the stillness'. For Franck the spiritual exercises required partake of the nature of preparation of the soul for the right understanding of whatever is offered by Scripture.

It cannot be denied that Schwenckfeld and Franck made a real contribution. The line which they initiated and which such thinkers as Weigel and Thamer pursued may have rendered the Bible as religiously effective as in the case of Luther and Calvin. But it could lead in the end only to an understanding of the meaning and authority of Holy Scripture which is clearly an impoverishment. In place of an authoritative object working in and upon the subject and yielding an 'objective subjectivity', we have offered to us a subject in whom reside already sufficient spiritual capacities and powers which he is required to bring to the apprehension of Holy Scripture, and this yields at best a 'subjective objectivity'. When this is not even supported on the objective side by a regard and respect for the creeds and confessional statements, the faith is delivered over to the subjectivity of the believing I. It is within the believer and not in Holy Scripture that there is to be found the norm and standard for what a Christian must believe.

It is summarily correct to ascribe to Luther the principle of *sola fide* and to Calvin that of *sola scriptura*. But neither Luther nor Calvin incur the disadvantages of exclusive concentration upon either aspect of the full truth. Luther understood faith as livingly and objectively determined by an authoritative Scripture to which it owed its creation and existence. Calvin understood Scripture in such a way that it pled through the Holy Spirit its own cause in the heart of the believer and secured the conviction of faith and obedience. To see the disadvantages and inadequacies of the two principles manifested, one must turn to those who succeed the great Reformers. Here *sola scriptura* works out balefully in a rigid scriptural authoritarianism in which it is not unjust to see bibliolatry superseding the Roman ecclesiolatry. Here too adherence to the principle of *sola fide* leads to a subjectivism which either attempts its own redemption by alliance with the rational capacity of man, or relapses into the desperate expedient of incorporating portions of divinity within the soul.

One may regret the course of thought which has been traced. But it will not do to suppose that something unique is happening. On the contrary, the pattern that is evident is one which is traceable elsewhere. Men, when they tire of independence and take fright at the lonely way ahead, will readily turn to and accept authority. Moreover, it is found easier to credit authority with an external and autocratic authoritarianism than to live permanently under the authority of a more persuasive and less peremptory but no less categorical kind. Hence the living voice of God that sounded through the prophets is recorded in written Scripture. Then it is only too possible to turn to the record of that living voice as though it possessed the same entire authority as the voice itself; the age of the rabbi succeeds the age of the prophet. Thus too when the Word Himself has become incarnate, it is the task of the apostles first to witness orally to what has happened, and then, committing the gospel to writing, to continue that same witness scripturally. But a later generation succeeds which finds the record of the Word more easy to manipulate and to live under than the Word of Him of whom it is the record, and the age of Christian rabbinism begins. This pattern repeats itself at the time of the Reformation. The new insight into the living truth of the Gospel fades; the living Word of God which Scripture communicates becomes stereotyped in the pages of Scripture. Behind the armoured strength of verbal infallibility, the living authority of the Word of God withdraws and its place is taken by the rigid authoritarianism of a printed word. That those who follow this line are contending for something real ought not to be denied, even if the contention is wrongly formulated. Doumergue[1] quotes J. Müller as follows:

'An inevitable consequence of the separation of the Holy Spirit and the Word is that, in place of the Holy Spirit truly satisfying to men, there comes, under various disguises, the tyranny of reason or of natural fancy, and in place of the historical Christ the ideal Christ fabricated by

[1] *Jean Calvin*, IV, 65, n. 3.

the human spirit, from whom the human spirit cannot look for life and salvation, since it itself gives to this Christ all the life He enjoys.'

When the Holy Spirit is locked up in Scripture by a kind of inscripturation, what really occurs is the denial that the Holy Spirit has any independent virtue. It is then immaterial whether the Spirit is regarded as dead, or as absent, or as replaced by something natural and inherent to the spirit of man. For the Spirit can be dissociated from the Word either by separation, and in this case men have themselves to bring the spirit of illumination, or by inclusion in the Holy Scripture, in which case the Holy Scripture itself defines and delimits His operations and so usurps them. This is the conclusion to which Orthodoxy comes.

IV

The Roman View

The Roman Church stedfastly adheres to the doctrine of the infallibility and inerrancy of Holy Scripture.

'All the books which the Church receives as sacred and canonical, are written wholly and entirely, with all their parts, at the dictation of the Holy Ghost; and so far is it from being possible that any error can co-exist with inspiration, that inspiration not only is essentially incompatible with error, but excludes and rejects it as absolutely and necessarily as it is impossible that God Himself, the supreme Truth, can utter that which is not true.'[1]

Not much is added to the honour and dignity of the Bible when it is stated[2] that 'nowhere is there anything more full or more express on the subject of the Saviour of the world than is to be found in the whole range of the Bible'. The latest relevant encyclical, *Divino Afflante Spiritu*,[3] shows its concurrence by quoting the same words in a different version.

That authority is then ascribed to Holy Scripture by the Roman Church does not, however, mean that it is ascribed in just the same sense as in the reformed Churches. In Luther and Calvin we see the idea of the authority of Scripture loosed from connexion with inerrancy and infallibility, before the recession of Protestant Orthodoxy relinquishes this not wholly assimilated insight. But even if the Reformers be credited with

[1] *Providentissimus Deus*, xxiii. Quotations from this document (subsequently referred to as *P.D.*) are cited from the English translation prefaced, with several misprints, to the 1914 edition of the Douai Bible.

[2] *P.D.*, x.

[3] *Divino Afflante Spiritu*, 5. Quotations from this document, issued in 1943 (subsequently referred to as *D.A.S.*), are cited from the English translation in *Selected Letters and Addresses of Pius XII*.

holding scriptural inerrancy, the difference between the views of unreformed and reformed Churches at this point is clear enough. The Protestant scholastic Gerhard[1] is found declaring that the *status controversiae* between Lutheranism and Rome lies not in the authority of Scripture, but in the question whence Scripture derives this authority. Protestant Orthodoxy holds that its authority is intrinsic; the Roman view is that it has authority from the Church, and the Jesuit interpretation (for example, of Bellarmine) is that it never had any authority until the Church added its testimony. This distinction is one which still divides the Roman from the reformed fundamentalist.

Inerrancy and infallibility is, then, the form in which the Roman Church represents and maintains the authority of Scriptures. From the time of Trent, the Roman Church has defended this position and maintained it unaltered in the midst of swiftly changing circumstances. It has therefore found it necessary to condemn those both within and outside its membership who have in various forms advocated that the Bible be allowed to make an impression and convey its truth unlimited by certain restrictive *a priori* assumptions. Sometimes the Roman Church in official pronouncements has not taken care to avoid misrepresenting their statements or traducing their motives. For example, the view is repeatedly expressed, in Roman documents of various degrees of authority, that the disparagement of the Bible was and is a deliberate aim of biblical criticism. The story of the attitude and action of the Roman Church in these matters cannot be told here. Nor is there any need, since it has already been related at length in at least two well-known works: C. J. Cadoux's *Catholicism and Christianity* and A. R. Vidler's *The Modernist Movement in the Roman Church*. In the first, the facts are recorded of how the Roman Church has opposed the critical study of the Scriptures, as well as the general practice of Bible reading on the part of the rank and file of the Church.[2] The other book recounts the story of how Rome, when faced with the efforts of such scholars as Loisy and Tyrrell to induce it to

[1] *Loc. Theol.*, 2. 36.
[2] Cf. Lattey: *The Bible: Its History, Authenticity, and Authority*, 12, 17 (qtd. C. J. Cadoux, op. cit., 267, n. 10): 'The Church cannot be for "the open Bible" at any price.'

reckon with the critical study of the Bible, construed the venture as a well-organized system of speculation and tried with a large measure of success to disparage it. Underlying the judgments of these books, there is a large body of facts which throw a disquieting light upon Roman practice and action with respect to Holy Scripture.

Behind this official attitude, however, a good deal has gone on and still goes on which is at least difficult to reconcile with the declared position. Mention will later be made of the change in attitude manifest in *Divino Afflante Spiritu*. This encyclical may be regarded as some kind of encouragement to such unofficial activities, while at the same time no doubt attempting to control them. Before and after the appearance of this encyclical, there is much of importance which could be recorded. H. J. T. Johnson, in an article of more than usual interest,[1] frankly records that 'the undercurrent of dissatisfaction with the encyclical (*P.D.*) was indeed widespread', and one archbishop found it 'not up to the height' of Leo XIII's other apostolic letters.[2] A Jesuit called Clarke, writing in *The Contemporary Review* for July 1894, the year after the appearance of the encyclical, in an article purporting to commend it, maintained that 'there is a human element in the Bible pre-calculated for by the Divine'.[3] A good deal of discussion has taken place about the meaning of the encyclical. Did it constitute, for example, a condemnation of Newman's view of inspiration? An even more fundamental question was raised: 'whether or no it contains a dogmatic definition on the subject of scriptural inerrancy or should be regarded merely as a disciplinary measure by which Catholics are forbidden to make use of the hypothesis that Scripture contains error till such time as the opposite view has been made clearly untenable'.[4] Rome itself does not find it easy to determine when papal infallibility is being exercised and when it is not.

It is not, however, the present intention to give an account of the unrest evident behind the rigidity of the official front, nor of the attempts made to establish some kind of compatibility

[1] In *The Downside Review*, 1951, 411ff., under the title 'Leo XIII, Cardinal Newman, and the Inerrancy of Scripture'.

[2] Op. cit., 415.

[3] See A. D. White: *The History of the Warfare of Science with Theology in Christendom*, Vol. II, 364.

[4] *The Downside Review*, 1951, loc. cit.

between discordant elements. Here attention will be drawn to three issues of importance where the Roman attitude to Holy Scripture and its authority seems not only to be different from that of the reformed Churches, but also to be chargeable with error. These issues, which will be taken in turn, are the Church as interpreter of Scripture, the relation of tradition to Scripture, and the Roman attitude to the critical study of Scripture.

a) *The Church as interpreter of Scripture.* The Roman Church constitutes itself as the sole authoritative and effective interpreter of the Scriptures. This statement has to be read in the Roman way. Churches of the reformed tradition could say the same thing, but mean by it something quite different. For them, the statement would mean that, the Bible being the Church's book, it is the right and also the duty, the privilege and the responsibility of believers to expound this book for their own and others' profit. It is idle to think that the work of interpretation can reasonably pertain to unbelievers, or to regard as final the uncorroborated explanations of individuals. Interpretation is the *proprium* of the Church as a whole. But the Church of Rome construes the statement in a different sense. This sense is exemplified by the restrictions it imposed upon the use of the Scriptures by ordinary believers. It is true that the Roman Church appears recently to have modified and relaxed its attitude at this point. *Providentissimus Deus*, after recounting the study expended upon the Scriptures down the ages by scholars among the clergy from Clement of Rome to the time of the Councils of Vienna and of Trent, concludes (rather surprisingly) that 'the calm and fair consideration of what has been said will clearly show that the Church has never failed in taking due measures to bring the Scriptures within reach of her children', and for this end 'never required, nor does she now require, any stimulus from without'.[1] Whatever we may think of the historical accuracy of these statements, they do show the interest which the Roman Church now manifests in making the Scriptures really available for the ordinary Christian, and at least look like a withdrawal from a position now regretted. But that the Church is sole interpreter of Scripture had a hierarchical character imprinted upon it long

[1] *P.D.*, xiv.

before this present-day change took place, nor has it since lost this character. The Church is interpreter of the Scriptures in the sense that holds the Pope to be the ultimate interpreter, and under him the Roman hierarchy in their order, each rank having its appropriate degree of interpretative authority. The part that 'the masses'[1] play is still negligible.

Behind this understanding of the Church as interpreter, there lie two considerations. To suppose that the understanding arises out of these considerations is difficult; to suppose that they are designed simply to support this understanding would be uncharitable. The Roman Church emphasizes that (i) the Bible by itself is very obscure, and that (ii) any principle of interpretation other than the Roman leads immediately to a chaos of individualism. Neither consideration is wholly justified.

> 'Catholic critics often write [says C. J. Cadoux[2]] as if not a small part only, but virtually the whole, of Scripture were so obscure and ambiguous that an individual reader could not of himself properly understand it, and—further than that—as if the Protestant, when he encountered an obscure passage, scrupulously avoided consulting anyone else (any expert, for example—linguist, exegete, Church-teacher, or early Father) and insisted on interpreting the passage solely by virtue of his own unaided insight, even if that must mean nothing better than an ignorant guess.'

These considerations receive official expression in *Providentissimus Deus*:[3]

> 'Wherefore, it must be recognized that the sacred writings are wrapt in a certain religious obscurity, and that no one can enter into their interior without a guide; God so disposing, as the Holy Fathers commonly teach, in order that men may investigate them with greater ardour and earnestness, and that what is attained with difficulty may sink more deeply into the mind and heart; and, most of all, that they may understand that God has delivered the Holy Scriptures to the Church, and that in reading and making use of His Word, they must follow the Church as their guide and their teacher.'

---

[1] *P.D.*, xxiv.   [2] *Catholicism and Christianity*, 146.   [3] *P.D.*, xvii.

It is in opposition to this exaggerated obscurity that Calvin affirms, with perhaps bewildering emphasis, the perspicuity of the Bible. But certainly Calvin too can supply the correction to the other allegation that the Protestant consults no authority but his own heart for the interpretation of obscure passages. Despite this and all the other evidence showing the profound concern which reformed theology has shown and still shows for the historical interpretation of the Bible, R. A. Knox, not at his best when he attempts to present the reformed point of view, can contrast the Roman and the Protestant thus:[1] we Romans 'derive from our apprehension of the living Christ the apprehension of a living Church; it is from that living Church that we take our guidance'; Protestantism on the other hand 'claims to take its guidance immediately from the living Christ. But what is the guidance He gives us, and where are we to find it? That is a question over which Protestantism has always failed to answer the Catholic challenge'. If this really is the challenge which the Roman Church offers, an answer would be comparatively simple. The reformed Churches find their guidance in the Bible, and this not because it is a textbook of belief and conduct, but because this is where the living voice of Christ is heard in the witness of prophets and apostles to Him. The Roman on the other hand will have more than this. He looks for specific detailed articles of faith and precepts of conduct. The Roman Church supplies this out of itself, and claims that it has a divine character. The speaking Church takes the place of the living voice of God. ' "Let the Churches make up their own mind what they believe," says the ordinary Englishman, "then come and tell me," ' declares R. A. Knox.[2] How simple it sounds, and how false it is!

'Those who have no special intellectual interests—and the majority of the faithful belong to this class—find a Church where awkward problems are settled, or suppressed, by authority, more imposing than one which does not affect to possess any short cut to truth. The general anathema is a labour-saving device and it will always be popular.'[3]

Of course, the Protestant listens to what the Church—the whole Church and not only the ecclesiastical hierarchy—

[1] *The Belief of Catholics*, 109.   [2] *The Belief of Catholics*, 13.
[3] A. R. Vidler: *The Modernist Movement in the Roman Church*, 232.

has to say in interpreting Scripture. No doubt the Church speaks with a confusing diversity of voices. But for this the Roman Church, precipitating by its hostility to genuine reform the great schism of the sixteenth century, must bear primary responsibility. Yet the Christian can never rightly look to the Church for the kind of guidance which Rome professes to offer.

'We cannot offer [the enquirer] infallible instruction or guidance, but we can assure him that such a thing is not to be found in the Roman Church, and that to seek for such infallible guidance there is to deliver himself—now with his eyes open—into the hands of a hierarchy which, for all its vast pretensions, does not really know from where it derives its teaching and does not really care whether that teaching rests upon the revelation which God gave to the world in Jesus Christ or not.'[1]

It must now be asked how the hierarchical principle of interpreting the Bible really works. Here the recent publication of *The Catholic Commentary on Holy Scripture*[2] has placed us in an advantageous position. For we have in this book an up-to-date and (in its proper degree) authoritative document, expounding, for English readers at least, both in general articles and in detailed exegesis on each biblical book, the latest evidence concerning Roman theory and practice in the realm of scriptural interpretation. One or two preliminary remarks may be made. The book comprises an astonishing diversity of opinions. For one thing, a good deal of attention is paid to writers not belonging to the Roman Church, and their works are duly asterisked to make the position clear. Rightly or wrongly, one has the impression that in general more attention is here and elsewhere paid by the Roman Church to writers of other communions than by the latter to what Romans have to say. Further, differences of opinion between Roman exegetes and critics are frankly stated. We find no unequivocal statement of solutions· unanimously adopted and authoritatively declared for the chief problems of biblical study today. Whether the fact is found disappointing or reassuring, there is great diversity in the views expressed.

[1] R. Hanson and R. Fuller: *The Church of Rome—a Dissuasive*, 107.
[2] A large volume of something like a million and three-quarter words, published by Thomas Nelson & Sons in 1953.

This is due to the fact that interpretation is done by authorities which vary in the degree of authority which they exercise in a hierarchical scale. Sometimes the Church defines infallibly the correct interpretation of a text, or condemns a false interpretation. This high degree of authority belongs to the hermeneutical papal pronouncements. It appears that 'the number of texts infallibly interpreted by the Church is small. . . . It has been estimated indeed that the total of such texts is under twenty, though there are of course many others indirectly determined.'[1] Many people will be astonished to learn the smallness and indefiniteness of the number, and perhaps equally surprised that, even of these few, the infallible interpretation of a text 'does not necessarily exhaust its full meaning'. Lower in the scale of authoritative definition come the many other interpretations in the decrees of the Councils, Commissions, and congregations, which are said, though not infallible, to 'enjoy high authority'.[2] Moreover, there is the unanimous consent of the Fathers which has 'always' been regarded[3] as a norm of interpretation. In practice this standard is liberally understood: 'Moral unanimity is sufficient, i.e. if a good number of the Fathers in widely different parts of the Church, or of different ages, agree on a point, and no Father contradicts their teaching';[4] and in fact 'the number of texts determined by the consent of the Fathers is even smaller than that of the texts determined by the decrees of the Church'. Particular attention is paid to the so-called 'Replies of the Biblical Commission, designed to guide the Catholic along the lines of prudent exegesis'.[5] Submission to the decisions of the Com-

[1] *A Catholic Commentary on Holy Scripture* (subsequently referred to as *C.C.H.S.*), §42a.

[2] Op. cit., §42c.

[3] See Council of Trent, Session IV.

[4] *C.C.H.S.*, §42d.

[5] The Biblical Commission was set up by Leo XIII in 1902. It was, according to A. R. Vidler (*The Modernist Movement*, 96), 'at first regarded by the modernists as a promising development. The virtual removal of the decisions of biblical questions from the jurisdiction of the ordinary Roman congregations to this specially appointed commission, whose membership was at the outset comparatively liberal, seemed to imply that there would not now be any immediate and hasty condemnation of the whole critical movement'. It was thought that perhaps there had now begun the laborious process of explaining away *Providentissimus Deus*. The promise was not realized. In 1903, the membership of the Commission was enlarged to include a large number of new members. 'It was certain that henceforth it would be a bulwark of reaction, as has in fact proved to be the case' (op. cit., 128).

mission is enjoined as a duty, and 'this submission involves an internal assent'—an assent, however, which is not that of divine faith, for the pronouncements of the Commission are not infallible, but only 'based on the very high authority entrusted by the Vicar of Christ to the Commission'.[1] The contributors to the *Commentary* certainly exercise a great deal of freedom in giving and withholding assent, and often a disputed matter is simply left in suspense, or even apparently decided in favour of the commentator's own different view.

The Roman Church holds that Holy Scripture is infallible and inerrant. 'There is one great limitation to be set upon the operation of the divine condescension in its allowing the human author his head: it must be without formal error'.[2] Thus in *Divino Afflante Spiritu*, Pope Pius XII writes: 'Just as the substantial Word of God became like to men in all things, sin excepted, Heb. iv. 15, so the words of God, expressed in human language, became in all things like to human speech, error excepted'; and Pope Benedict XV in *Spiritus Paraclitus* declares that the Holy Spirit so operated on the writers of Scripture that 'they conceived correctly, and were minded to write faithfully, and expressed fittingly with unfailing truth, all those things and those only which He bade them write'. Yet behind this apparently imposing front, there exists an inner dubiety about the detailed interpretation of what Holy Scripture is thus infallibly and inerrantly saying which is at least disconcerting. In contrast to the alleged inerrancy of the Bible has to be placed the paucity of what this book can be understood as infallibly saying. When this is recognized, the real difference between what the Romans have to say in the interpretation of Holy Scripture and what is said by those who do not subscribe to their presuppositions or use their terminology is greatly diminished. The affirmation of biblical infallibility and inerrancy apparently secures for Rome no greater degree of unanimity when the meaning of the Bible is being interpreted.

This is by no means said in a spirit of veiled triumph, as though there was a kind of satisfaction in a *tu quoque* that

[1] 'The declarations of the Biblical Commission are not "definitions", but decisions, not either infallible or irreformable-legal pronouncements to which we must submit as representing the mind of the Church' (H. Pope: *The Catholic Church and the Bible*, 49).

[2] *C.C.H.S.*, §36j.

H

shows Rome to be in no stronger position in biblical interpretation than those who belong to another form of the Christian faith. On the contrary, the conclusion is to be regretted:
not in this way either is an easy solution to interpretative
problems obtained. It appears that the appeal to inerrancy
and infallibility does not exempt us from the labour of trying
to reach a common mind in matters of interpretation, or even
effectively guide us in them. But for those who claim for Holy
Scripture inerrancy and infallibility, the fact of ambiguity at the
level of interpretation clearly constitutes a grave embarrassment.

So far the striking thing is not so much the difference between
the Roman point of view and that of the reformed Churches
as the resemblance. But wide dissimilarity does in fact lie
behind the appearances. The interpretative function discharged by the Roman Church rests on three primary affirmations: first, that the Church is the owner of the Scriptures;
secondly, that Holy Scripture is the statement of the teaching
of the Church; and thirdly, that the Church is the living voice
of Christ and is therefore the legitimate and infallible interpreter
of Scripture. Each of these affirmations requires some notice.

The role of the Church in relation to the Bible is variously
characterized,[1] and with much of what is said there is no
cause for disagreement. All will be happy to agree that the
Church has always and rightly exercised solicitude and care
for the Scriptures and for the purity of the biblical text.
Further, 'because the Bible ranks among the most precious
jewels of her patrimony, the Church is the Bible's jealous
guardian and defender'. Nor is there need to quarrel with the
statement that the Church is the 'trustee' of Scripture. These
characteristics together declare that the Church both transmits the Scriptures and 'exercises a wise vigilance' over the
purity of what is transmitted. But quite another element is
introduced when it is stated that the Church is the 'owner'
of Scripture, and that the Bible is 'the Church's exclusive
possession' or 'property'.

'The Church holds [the books of the Bible] as sacred and
canonical . . . because, having been written under the
inspiration of the Holy Ghost they have God for their author
and *as such have been handed to the Church herself.* . . . The

[1] *C.C.H.S.*, §§7a-8a.

Church is, by God's donation, exclusive Owner and Trustee of the Scriptures.'

It is a pity that the two terms are thus linked together; there is an evident distinction of meaning between them. It is one of Tertullian's more unfortunate utterances, cutting at the root of the missionary power of the Scriptures, when he argues 'that heretics should not even be allowed to use the Christian Scriptures, because they no longer belong to the society which has the right of possessing these same Scriptures'. The same principle is assumed in *Providentissimus Deus* in the interests of maintaining correct interpretation. It is, however, not really difficult to permit the reading of Scripture to all without crediting authoritative interpretation to all. Nor would this impair trusteeship on the part of the Church.

The second affirmation concerns the nature or content of the Bible. The view is (quite rightly) dismissed that the Bible is 'the eclectic product of certain outstanding members of that divine society that has existed in the world ever since God called Abram out of Ur of the Chaldees'. The Bible is rather 'the divinely inspired crystallization of the spirit and teaching of that society at times and places specially chosen by the Spirit of God dwelling within it'.[1] Even if only a description rather than a definition, this is a remarkable enough statement. Outside the Roman Church the conviction has been steadily growing that, whatever other elements there are besides, the central message of the Bible is God—God's purpose, God's saving work, God's grace extended to mankind, God present in word and deed. The Bible certainly is the Church's book, if one cares to put the matter so; but to make of it a summary of the 'spirit and teaching of that society' is to exclude any reference beyond the Church. Here is disclosed the most significant and recurrent distinction between the Church reformed and the Church unreformed: both will quite happily affirm that the Bible is both the Church's book and God's book; but the Church reformed holds that the possessive case is used in different senses, the unreformed Church that it is used univocally. No wonder, then, that the Church is credited by Rome, not only with the trusteeship of Holy Scripture, but also with ownership.

[1] *C.C.H.S.*, §16.

The third affirmation immediately follows from what has been said. Holy Scripture is not a merely petrified record or 'dead letter'. There is 'a living teaching authority' which is 'prior to every single book of Divine Scripture'; and besides, the Scriptures still do become a 'living voice'.[1] One might so far be listening to the testimony of the Reformers—for example, the well-known passage in the *Institutes*[2] where Calvin speaks of God's Word orally transmitted by the patriarchs, and later committed to public records, to which should be added what is said in the following chapter, that in the Scriptures it is God who is 'the divine Speaker'. But where the Reformers and those that follow them hear in Scripture the voice of God, the Roman Church hears the voice of the Church. It is for it not God who takes the Scriptures and makes them the vehicle of His living Word; it is the Church's voice that is heard. The Church's ministry, which for both is the servant of the Word, is thus differently conceived. For the reformed Churches it is a ministry of God's Word; for the Roman Church it is fundamentally a ministry of the Church speaking.

'The fact is that, while the apostles looked upon themselves primarily as witnesses of Christ, the living organism "which is the pillar and the ground of truth", functioned as a *voice*, and its ministers were "servants of the word", the term "word" meaning the spoken word.'[3]

The Church 'possesses the living voice of Christ'.[4] The principle and its consequences are stated together: 'the Church is superior to the Bible in the sense that she is the Living Voice of Christ'.[5] We are faced again with the characteristic difference between the Churches of the Reformation and of the unreformed tradition: while both unhesitatingly declare the divine origin, nature and destiny of the Church, the first tradition affirms and the second denies that in speaking of deity one speaks of something beyond the Church. Putting it more bluntly, the second affirms, if not an identity between deity and Church, at least an assimilation between them. This the first cannot but deny, and for ground of its denial appeal to the reiterated evidence of Holy Scripture itself. If this is the core of the error, it matters very little whether what is

---

[1] *C.C.H.S.*, §1c.　　　[2] *Insts.*, 1. 6. 1, 2.　　　[3] *C.C.H.S.*, §1c.
[4] Op. cit., vii.　　　　　[5] Op. cit., §1e.

happening here is the elevation of the Church to the status of the divine, or the diminution of the divine to the level of the human. The Holy Scriptures will not retain their salvific power if, when we resort to them, we hear nothing but the Church speaking, or if we hear only the Church speaking of things which it has and knows from a source not outside or distinguishable from itself. If this is what the Roman Church is really saying, it represents a Titanism or a Prometheanism which must be rejected.

That what has been said occupies a position of central importance in the Roman faith, may be shown by the fact that, setting out from another point, it is to a similar conclusion that one is led. Romanism has never consistently surrendered the intellectualist bequest of Scholasticism that sees religion in terms of propositions and statements. Thus

'by religion we mean a system of beliefs concerning the divinity and of man's duties in regard thereto. If such a system, whether practical or theoretical, is based merely on what the human reason can discover by its own powers, it is called natural religion. If it is based on knowledge communicated by God to man in some way outside the working of ordinary providence, it is called revealed religion.'[1]

Here religion in general is intellectually conceived; natural religion is defined in terms which regard God as coming at the end of a process of reasoning as a deduction or conclusion reached by inferential thinking; revealed religion is defined as the transmission of information about deity.

This is a pity; for even among Roman writers there is apparent an attempt to open up a way behind the intellectualism of the official teaching and the scholastic terminology in which it is traditionally conveyed. *The Teaching of the Catholic Church*, for example,[2] makes a nice distinction between the necessary condition and the motive of the Christian's faith. 'The believer accepts a revealed truth not precisely *because he knows* that God has revealed it and *knows* that God is infallible. This knowledge is the necessary condition, but it is not the motive of his faith. He believes because *God* who is

---

[1] *C.C.H.S.*, §104b.
[2] Essay, 'Faith and Revealed Truth', by the editor of the volume, Canon G. D. Smith.

infallible has said it.' Here at least some attempt is made to add to the information conveyed in revelation the apprehended fact of the communicator of this information. So too and even more clearly, it is said earlier in the same essay: 'Religion is the act whereby God speaks to man, making a statement to the truth of which He testifies'; and 'religion implies a personal intercourse between God and man, wherein God truly speaks—i.e. makes an assertion, which man accepts on God's personal authority'. Even if the content of revelation is still regarded as truths, at least the religious man is regarded as apprehending behind the propositions conveyed the person of the communicator. Applying this to the Bible and what is communicated there, on the terms used above it is possible to think of God setting His own personal stamp upon the truths which the Bible is supposed to convey, and thus imparting to them such evidential power as to secure assent to them in the believer's heart. But where unmodified intellectualism operates, the only valid and real reason for distinguishing between revelation and doctrine, between the act of revealing and what the Church teaches, collapses. Ontologically they are indistinguishable. There is no longer a distinction to be drawn between the communication by God of Himself and the communication of truths concerning God; revelation and doctrine are no longer different things. The path is thus neatly prepared for the identification of God's revelation and the Church's teaching. 'There is, in a sense', affirms the Commentary, and with perfect right, 'but one source of revealed truth, viz. divine Tradition'. It is the further step that has to be resisted: the definition of this divine tradition as 'the body of revealed truth handed down from the apostles throughout the ages and *contained in the doctrine, teaching and practice of the Catholic Church*'.[1] In fact, once the Church's doctrine and the Holy Scriptures are put on an equality with one another, the normative superiority of the latter is lost, though here the utterances of the Commentary are inconclusive. Thus it is said that 'since that time [the death of the last of the apostles] there has been no new revelation to the Church, though, under the guidance of the Holy Ghost, knowledge and understanding of the original revelation has deepened and widened'. A mediating view finds expression when it is said that

[1] Italics not in the original.

'the question is sometimes asked whether all revealed truth
may not be found at least obscurely in Scripture. It is impossible, however, to make an absolute affirmation in terms
of the above question; but, relatively speaking, so much is
contained in the Bible, that it is difficult to assert that certain particular truths of Christian faith and conduct are
nowhere found in it'![1]

Again a statement a little bolder in tone appears,[2] when,
speaking of the dogma of the Assumption of the Blessed Virgin
Mary, the assertion is made: 'we may say with confidence
that [Holy Scripture] contains in germ most if not all of the
developed doctrine of the Church concerning her office'. The
hesitancy does the contributor credit, but it should blind no
one to the fact that the Roman Church claims and exercises
the right to add to the sum of saving revelation from outside
the Scriptures, that is out of itself.[3]

An easy solution is thus achieved to the tension between
revelation and doctrine, between the essence of the Gospel
and its expression in doctrinal terms. Revelation and doctrine
are one: 'For seeing that the same God is author of both the
Sacred Books and the doctrine committed to the Church, it is
clearly impossible that any teaching can by legitimate means
be extracted from the former which shall in any respects be
at variance with the latter.'[4] The application of this so-called
'analogy of faith' is of profound significance. The resolution
of the tension is virtual capitulation to one of the poles—namely,
the doctrine and teaching of the Church. There are practical
considerations which need not here be mentioned which will
always tend to give the dominant role to this side, rather than
to that of Holy Scripture.

Thus once again we are brought to the point where it

---

[1] *C.C.H.S.*, §1f.

[2] Op. cit., §86d.

[3] Jean Bainvel in *The Catholic Encyclopedia*, article 'Tradition', 12b, writes:
'Since the deposit of revelation has remained the same, the same also, in substance, has remained the taking possession of the deposit by the living faith',
and adds concerning the Immaculate Conception: 'the revealed truth was indeed
in the deposit of truth in the Church, but it was not formulated in explicit terms
nor even in clearly equivalent terms; it was enveloped in a more general truth
(that e.g. of the all-holiness of Mary), the formulation of which might be understood in a more or less absolute sense (exemption from all actual sin, exemption
even from original sin).'

[4] *C.C.H.S.*, §42e, qtg. *P.D.*

becomes obvious that the Church, given the kind of interpretative function assigned to it or arrogated for it by Rome, is superior to Scripture. It is indeed understandable and even acceptable (in some sense) that the Church be said to be the legitimate interpreter of Holy Writ. But the contention is unacceptable that such interpretation shall be such as does not conflict with the teaching of the same Church. In saying this, the Roman Church embraces a thesis which renders it irreformable in principle. Tertullian contends[1] that it is a virtue in the Church that it be *irreformabilis et immobilis*. In the sense of Eph. iv. 14 ('every wind of doctrine'), this is, of course, true. But in the stricter sense implied here the statement simply means that the Church no longer cares to listen to Holy Scripture and repudiates correction by it. The modern Roman Church too often simply equates reformer with innovator,[2] and so disposes of the matter by attaching a derogatory label. In fact, the very same issue raises its head here again, which in the early sixteenth century precipitated the disaster of schism, and turned the Reformation from being a movement for reformation of the Church into an occasion of the division of the Church. It is difficult to see how Churches, reformed in the days of Luther and Calvin and still capable of reform, can have very much to say to a Church which thus in principle shies away from the source of reforming power.

The familiar distinction between the literal and the spiritual meaning confirms the Church in its control of Scripture. In contrast to the fundamentalists, the Roman Church is wise enough to employ it to eke out the doctrine of infallibility and make its rigid system work. The *Commentary* refers to it thus:

'The literal sense of Scripture is that which arises directly from the text and is intended by the inspired writer. There is also frequently in Scripture another sense which we call the *spiritual sense*. This is a meaning authoritatively revealed by God to man. It is not, however, strictly speaking, the meaning of the words.'[3]

The *Commentary* is aware of the possibility of misuse of this distinction, and even criticizes Origen for abusing it. Here, between competing positions, the *Commentary* makes a right choice.

[1] *de virg. vel.*, 1.   [2] So *Pascendi*; see *The Doctrines of the Modernists*, 47f.
[3] *C.C.H.S.*, §39c.

Origen and Clement of Alexandria go so far as to deny the necessity of a literal sense, and the former seems at least sometimes to resort to a spiritual sense, because he cannot discover a literal sense.[1] Chrysostom, Jerome, and Augustine insist that the literal sense is basic and normative. St Thomas concurs, remarking that 'in the sacred page, we have not merely the literal sense which runs continuously, but also the mystical sense which need not be continuous'.[2] Through St Thomas's advocacy, this view becomes influential, and it is this that the *Commentary* is wise enough to adopt.

It continues: 'there is no sure road to the elucidation of the spiritual sense of Scripture save through the literal sense'. This is a salutary warning and sound good sense. The legitimacy of taking a spiritual sense out of words which for the writer bore no more than a literal sense is—perhaps a little naïvely—justified by the fact of the 'ambiguity of language'. Of the spiritual sense proper, it is said: 'Almighty God has thus willed that the persons, things and events described should often signify other persons, things and events.' St Thomas is quoted to justify this principle of type and antitype.[3]

This distinction between literal and spiritual senses helps to relate the Old Testament and the New. But it is never used to diminish or restrict the inerrancy of Scripture. 'Since [the writers] were God's instruments, their meaning was also God's meaning. They could not write down anything not intended by Him. "The things which He ordered, and those only, they . . . expressed in apt words and with infallible truth." '[4] The principle of infallibility extends to everything written in Scripture. Thus Scripture records Abraham's residence at Hebron. 'It is asserted in Scripture and is therefore infallibly true. The Church, as the champion of the Bible's inerrancy, has a right to condemn any denial of an authentic biblical statement.[5] At the same time, the Church regards such a fact mentioned in patriarchal history as secondary, 'which cannot

---

[1] Cf. F. W. Farrar: 'His system rose in reality not from reverence for the Scriptures, but from a dislike to their plain sense which had at all costs to be set aside' (*History of Interpretation*, 191, qtd. H. H. Rowley: *The Unity of the Bible*, 17, n. 3).

[2] *Expositio altera in Canticum Proemium*; see H. Pope's contribution to *St Thomas Aquinas*, 135 (Blackwell, 1925).

[3] *Quaes Quodlib*, 7. xiv.

[4] *C.C.H.S.*, §39c.

[5] Op. cit., §1f.

itself directly be matter for a positive infallible definition'. But the mind of the Roman Church seems to be uncertain about the question of the spiritual interpretation of Scripture. There is no doubt that the traditional acceptance of a four-fold sense served to put the understanding of the Scriptures farther than ever beyond the reach of the ordinary believer, and thus to deliver them more than ever into the hands of the officially recognized interpretative authority. 'The principle of authority of Holy Scripture', says St Thomas,[1] 'is the Holy Spirit, who in any one expression of Scripture meant far more than any expositor can expound or discover.' And, again, because two minds contribute to the composition of Holy Writ, 'there are two meanings: what God meant and what the human writer meant'.[2] Thus the Church is seen, for another reason, strong if not good, laying exclusive hands upon Scripture for purposes of interpretation. More recently, however, Rome seems to have become aware that the insistence upon spiritual interpretation can be turned against itself. It is still maintained that 'it is for the Living Voice of the Church to interpret what is obscure in the sources, and when she has spoken it is plainly perverse to use what is obscure to explain her clear decision'.[3] But the encyclical *Humani Generis* strikes a new note of caution, if not of alarm, when it decries 'false teachers' who maintain that 'the literal sense of Scripture . . . must make way for a new kind of exegesis, which they are fain to call "symbolic" or "spiritual" '. 'And thus, they tell us, all difficulties will disappear; difficulties which are felt to be so only by those who cling to a literal interpretation.' The encyclical judges that this ill accords with 'the principles and rules of interpretation which have been solemnly laid down by Our Predecessors, of happy memory; by Leo XIII in his encyclical *Providentissimus Deus*, by Benedict XV in *Spiritus Paraclitus*, and by Ourselves in *Divino Afflante Spiritu*'. There seems little doubt that the Church of Rome has been stirred to a renewed interest in the literal meaning of Scripture, and that

---

[1] *Quoadl.*, 7. 14 *ad fin.*

[2] *St Thomas Aquinas*, 134. So too *D.A.S.*, 31: 'For God alone was able to know the spiritual significance.' It is appropriate that the Church and the Church alone should be responsible for declaring this meaning. Here is the idea of a carefully hoarded mystery dispensed by the interpreting Church.

[3] Dom Ralph Russell in *The Downside Review*, 1951, article, ' "Humani Generis" and the "Spiritual" Sense of Scripture', 1.

this revival is the direct result[1] of the critical study of the Bible
to which reference is later to be made. Since, however, this
sensus litteralis is quite rightly understood, not as the meaning
of the English idiom, but as 'the sense intended by the author,
be it historic, poetic, metaphorical or that of some ancient
literary "genre" ', interpretation remains the exclusive pre-
rogative of the Church—that is, of the scholars with their
appropriate degrees of interpretative authority in the hierarchy. And further, since 'all interpretation is foolish and false
which either makes the sacred writers disagree with one another, or is opposed to the doctrine of the Church',[2] the
position which seemed to be threatened is recovered and re-
established in fatal security: Holy Scripture can say, and by
interpretation can be made to say, nothing that conflicts with
ecclesiastical doctrine. This is the assumption which Trent[3] first
makes, and which *Providentissimus Deus*, as already quoted,[4] with
its identification between Scripture and doctrine, only confirms.

Scriptural interpretation is thereby understood by the Roman
Church in a sense that subordinates Scripture to dogma. The
Church thus so controls and channels the Word of God in
Scripture that what finally survives its interpretation and reaches
utterance is only a reiteration or continuation of the monologue
which the Church independently carries on with itself.

b) *The relation of tradition and Scripture.* Another way in which
the unresolved differences between the Roman and the reformed Churches come to expression is the matter of tradition.
In what relation are we to think, firstly, that the Church stands
to Scripture, and secondly, that Scripture stands to tradition?

(i) *The Church and Scripture.* In *The Spirit of Catholicism*, a
beautiful and moving *apologia* for the Roman position, Karl
Adam raises the issue. To begin with, he finds the structure of
the Catholic faith capable of summary in a single sentence:
'I experience the living God through Christ realizing Himself
in His Church.' The 'certainty of Catholic faith rests on the
sacred triad: God, Christ, Church'.[5] It is not accidental that

---

[1] *Pace P.D.*, xiv; the Church 'has never required, nor does she now require,
any stimulus from without'.

[2] *P.D.*, xviif.

[3] *eum sensum quem tenet sancta mater ecclesia* (see Brunner: *Revelation and Reason*,
146, n. 25).

[4] *P.D.*, xvii.   [5] *Op. cit.*, 46.

Holy Scripture is not included among the basic factors. Adam holds that 'the Catholic does not come to Christ mediately and by literary channels, as by scriptural records, but immediately through personal contact with Christ living in His community'.[1] It is true that the Bible is 'a sacred book, written by the hand of God and therefore infallible in its definite doctrinal statements', and certainly the Catholic 'accepts with joy and gratitude the luminous portrait of Jesus that is drawn by the Gospels. . . . Yet the Catholic does not derive his faith in Jesus from the Scriptures.' The reason for this is that 'he had his faith already, before the first Epistle and before the first Gospel was written. His faith dates back to St Peter's confession at Caesarea-Philippi.'

Thus is introduced one of the cardinal arguments for subordinating Holy Scripture to the Church: the Church is prior to Scripture, and hence superior to Scripture. Once this is established, the implications are easily drawn, that the Church is the guardian of Scripture, the guarantor of Scripture, the possessor and owner of Scripture, and even its creator. This argument must be examined and assessed. (*a*) It can readily be allowed that the Church is the guardian of Holy Scripture, and even, in a carefully defined sense, its creator. That the Church is responsible for the canon of Holy Scripture is certainly true. It is fairly clear that one motive at work in the determination of the canon was to prevent the mutilation of the Scriptures in the interest of specific theological points of view, as by Marcion. The question of the criteria that operated is more complex. At least two are distinguishable, though they need not have been distinct—namely, apostolicity and general usage. Origen's testimony concerning the books later taken into the canon, that they were 'in general circulation', is important. Tradition no doubt rightly ascribed apostolic authorship to many of these books, which were accordingly honoured and revered. But just as certainly, the principle worked the other way round. Even Roman theology has come to realize the importance of the influence of the *communis sermo*, and the Semitic treatment with respect to pseudopigrapha has elsewhere been long recognized.[2] Books which were 'in general circulation' could readily be accorded an apostolic origin. At all events, the canon was defined by the Church, whether on

[1] Op. cit., 49.   [2] See *The Downside Review*, 1951, 422.

the ground of extensive Christian usage or by conciliar action, and in this sense Holy Scripture is quite dependent upon the Church. Further, it is entirely true that[1] the Church is 'the Bible's jealous guardian and defender', and 'exercises a wise vigilance' over the purity of the transmitted text. The argument, however, does not go a great distance. A constitutional monarchy is defined by the subjects over which it presides, and the person of the monarch is defended by a royal bodyguard. But these factors do not constitute the essence of monarchy. Similarly, we are at least entitled to look elsewhere for the essence of scriptural authority than to the Church by which it is defined and also defended.

(*b*) What is to be said about the relation of the Church to Scripture? What is the force of the statement that the Catholic 'has this faith already, before the first Epistle and before the first Gospel was written'?[2] The answer can be found by considering the relation of oral tradition to the written Scriptures. Adam's view has at least the merit of clarity. The oral tradition has for him, as for all Roman theology, a place of first-class importance—and quite rightly, if it be correctly understood. This oral tradition, Adam[3] designates 'the living word'. 'Jesus prepared His disciples for the miracle of Pentecost through His living word alone.' Further, the 'disciples too wished to be nought else but "eyewitnesses and first ministers of the word" (Luke i. 2)'. Finally, 'it was the living word which was to bring the new faith to mankind'. It is at this point, to which we might all cheerfully follow him, that the paths divide. Adam is only the mouthpiece for the Roman view when he comes to deal with the Scriptures and to relate them to the hitherto current oral tradition. Two points are made: the appearance of the Scriptures is late, and the oral

[1] As *C.C.H.S.*, §§7a-8a.

[2] It is the New Testament that is concerned here. The Old Testament was, of course, already in existence before the Christian Church was explicitly founded. Of this the Roman Church is aware. Thus Adam, with rather less charity and accuracy than usual, suggests that 'unlike all non-catholic communions, the [Roman] Church affirms, completely and entirely, the whole of Holy Scripture, both the Old Testament and the New' (op. cit., 147). M. J. Lagrange addresses the question specifically to the New Testament: 'Has the Church believed that, believing in Christ, it has sufficient authority to produce, not by a human principle, but by divine virtue, books which are the equal of the Old Testament?' (*The History of the Canon of the New Testament*, 6).

[3] Op. cit., 53.

tradition is continuous alongside the Scriptures. But the relative importance of the Scriptures is systematically depreciated. The recognition accorded to them is almost grudging.

'Certainly [he says][1] some [of the apostles] composed historical records of the life of Jesus, and of the acts of the chief apostles. And they wrote also letters to single persons and communities, wherein they set forth the Christian teaching and the Christian life according to the enquiries and the special circumstances of those to whom they wrote. Yet these written communications were only supplementary to their oral preaching, sometimes in confirmation of it or preparatory to it. Even the Epistles to the Romans, Ephesians and Hebrews, in spite of their more general range, are concerned particularly with the special needs of the people to whom they are addressed, and make no sort of claim to be an exhaustive exposition of the Christian faith. So little thought was given to any final literary expression of the Gospel, that some apostles left no writing whatever after them and that apostolical writings could even disappear (1 Cor. v. 9; Col. iv. 16).'

The conclusion follows: 'Therefore it was not literary records, incontestable documents, which were the primary means of bringing the message of Jesus to man.'[2] If Scripture is thus depreciated, some other channel or source for the perpetuation of the Christian message has to be devised. Adam is not at a loss, and he faithfully expresses again the Roman view when he finds this desideratum to consist in 'the broad stream of the uniform life of faith of the primitive Church, a life based on the preaching of the apostles and animated by the Holy Spirit'. The foundation of tradition according to the Roman view is thus securely laid. The argument is supplemented by a further consideration to which indeed all but those committed to a rigid scriptural literalism must be deeply sympathetic. At the heart of Christianity there must be a *living* authority; and He who is spirit and life cannot exercise mere rigorous compulsion over His followers. Where is this living quality in authority to be located, and how is it to be safeguarded? The Roman answer is given by Adam. Scripture will not serve:

[1] Op. cit., 54.   [2] Op. cit., 55.

'a living thing, in all its depth and all its extent, cannot be comprised within a few written sentences. Only that which is dead can be delineated in writing. . . . Therefore all literature, and even the Bible itself, is stamped with the character of its time, and bears a form which, however vital its content remains, yet all too easily seems stiff and strange to later generations.'

'The living thing is continually bursting the temporary form in which literature must perforce embody it. At the very moment that literature is endeavouring to arrest and fix it, the stream of life is escaping and moving swiftly on.' The real principle of life is to be found in the 'supernatural life of faith of the primitive Church'; and the New Testament 'is supported and dominated by this life. . . . Consequently the Bible possesses no independent authority apart from the faith of the Church.' Here then is the real seat of authority in the Christian religion according to Rome. It is 'the new life flowing out from the apostolic community', which 'spread ever wider and wider, and impregnated the world'. 'I learn the complete Christ, not from the Bible, but from the uniform life of faith of the whole Church, a life fertilized by the teaching of the apostles.'[1] 'I grasp the living Christ by means of the living Church';[2] *Ego vero evangelio non crederem, nisi me catholicae ecclesiae commoveret auctoritas.*[3]

It has been worth while to set out what Adam has to say at such length, not only because the terms in which he phrases it are persuasive and attractive, but because the position he occupies is typical of Roman theology. It need hardly be said that the matter is capable of an entirely different interpretation. It is not even so much the facts that are in dispute as the assessment made of these facts and their significance. The gospel was to begin with orally transmitted. This is the essential meaning of the term 'oral tradition', which Rome primes with a meaning which does not naturally belong to it.[4] The apostles preached to begin with, rather than wrote, and by their speech the Gospel was communicated to others—it was handed on orally. This is what Adam finely calls the 'living word' and which he rightly holds to precede all the written

[1] Op. cit., 56.　　　　　　　　　[2] Op. cit., 57.
[3] St Augustine: *Contra ep. Manich.*, 5.　　[4] See Hanson and Fuller, op. cit., 75.

record of the gospel. Further, this 'living word' incontestably continued alongside the written records. It is a fact witnessed to by the available evidence: 'these things I write', says St Paul (1 Tim. iii. 14), and to the same correspondent he gives the injunction, 'preach the Gospel' (2 Tim. iv. 2). Adam recognizes it when he says the 'written communication' and 'oral preaching' went on side by side. The really critical question on which the Roman and the reformed views differ fundamentally and irreconcilably is the meaning and value to be given to the written record which has meantime appeared. The question is critical in the sense that it divides not only the Roman view of Scripture from the reformed view, but also the Roman conception of the Church from that of reformed theology. On the Roman view, the written records—that is, the Scriptures of the New Testament—are incidental, almost accidental, the ancillary of or substitute for oral transmission. If this is so, it follows that provision must be made for the continuance of this oral transmission, and this provision is made by the supposition that the apostolic office is transmitted to successors. Those who succeed the apostles continue the apostolic function.[1] The Church equipped with apostolicity thus conceived, and credited with an internal but supernatural 'unitary life-stream' or 'vital movement',[2] is the real agent for transmitting the gospel, Christ and His benefits to men. On the view of reformed theology, the written records constitute the form in which the gospel is authoritatively transmitted by the Church—one of the forms in the early days while oral transmission persisted, the only form as this oral transmission ceased. That which begins orally is perpetuated scripturally. While those qualified to transmit orally live, the oral transmission of course continues alongside of the written transmission. With their disappearance from the scene and the end of the apostolic age, oral transmission ceases. There is no need for its continuance. That which has to be handed on is safely committed to writing. All that is necessary for salvation

[1] Op. cit., 56: 'The preaching authority was taken over from the dying apostles by disciples who had been commissioned by them and appointed as presidents and overseers of the Christian communities. This fact is plainly attested by history.' The latter sentence of the quotation is in general true, but in Adam's sense, of the taking over of an identical status and function, it is quite untrue. This may be worth discussing; but it is simply not a matter of historical certainty.

[2] Op. cit., 61.

is there. The apostles withdraw from the earthly sphere of
their labours. But the work of the Church of which they were
founder members continues. It is distinguishable from their
work, but of course not distinct. The Church has itself to live
by and at the same time to declare to others nothing but that
which is there in the Holy Scriptures on apostolic testimony.

The issue raised here is not only cardinal, but also delicate.
Neither rational nor even theological considerations alone will
ever be allowed to determine it. Loyalty to tradition is a strong
motive, and less respectable influences connected with *amour
propre* readily lend their support. But it seems worth while to
consider briefly the relative merits of the two views. Attention
should first be paid to the Roman suggestion that, in comparison with the stream of living tradition which pulsates
through the Church, the influence and authority of Scripture
is 'stiff' and 'dead', and can only 'arrest and fix' the stream
of life. This suggestion looks plausible enough. But Adam himself has sufficient Christian understanding to be aware of other
considerations which quite annul the advantage which it wins
for the Roman view. As already seen, he calls this continuing
tradition the 'living word'. It does not belong to this 'living
word' to achieve the initiation of faith. He assigns to it its
own part: it effects 'human faith, a purely human certitude'.
But real faith, 'supernatural, final, highest certitude', as he
calls it, comes 'from the working of the Spirit'. This so-called
'living word' is by itself inefficacious, and it becomes effective
only when the Holy Spirit makes it so. If this is so, then the
appearance of life which the 'stream of living tradition' presents is spurious. It may attract, but it cannot by itself repro-
duce itself or evoke new life without the aid of the Holy Spirit's
operation. On this count therefore no real advantage accrues
to the Roman view. For precisely this claim is made by reformed theology for Holy Scripture. By itself, it is impotent
and inefficacious, and it only operates to the creation of faith
when it is supplemented or informed by the activity of the
Holy Spirit. It is quite true that those who maintain a rigid
scriptural literalism give to Scripture the appearance of a fixed
and frozen thing. Against them the considerations urged by
Karl Adam may have some relevance. But even they do not
exclude the operation of the Holy Spirit. Their fault, as has
been seen, is not that they disregard the Holy Spirit, but rather

I

that they lock up the Holy Spirit within Scripture, and thus deny, not His existence, but His independent sovereign action. For other reformed theology, Scripture is held to *become* the living Word by the power of the Holy Spirit. Where instruments or agents are thus under consideration, of which the Holy Spirit makes use, there is little to choose between a 'stream of living tradition' and a written record. Karl Barth appreciates this hypothetical equality clearly when[1] he insists that there is no assignable reason why the perpetuation and transmission of the gospel should not have been contrived by way of a 'stream of living tradition'. But if there is a real equality here, no advantage can be claimed for the Roman view. In the disposal of the Holy Spirit, a written record and a continuing and present Church can equally be utilized as tool and instrument. The question cannot be decided *a priori* in these terms; nor has it so far been resolved *a posteriori*. But this is what must now be considered.

If the living quality of a present-day Church secures no clear advantage for the Roman view, neither does the strongly contingent character of the written record constitute a disadvantage for the reformed view. As already seen, Adam notes the adventitious character of the apostolic writings. They were, he says, prompted by specific situations and addressed to individual needs. Moreover, to the adventitious character of their origin and intention there must be added the contingency of the form which all literature, the Bible not excepted, bears. Here is the problem to which Bultmann has addressed himself and in which he has aroused so much interest. At this point, Bultmann, moved as he is by the best evangelical motives,[2] joins hands with the persuasive apologist for Rome. Both regard it as a disadvantage that the Bible is so tied up with and impregnated by temporal forms; both might agree that these render the Bible 'stiff and strange to later generations'. While, however, the Roman apologist regards this as disabling the claim of Scripture to be finally authoritative, Bultmann embarks on the hazardous task of divesting the gospel of these forms. The assumption common to both is that these temporal forms are an essential disadvantage and handicap.

---

[1] *Kirchliche Dogmatik*, I/1, 117.
[2] See 'Neues Testament und Mythologie' in *Kerygma und Mythos* (ed. H. W. Bartsch) 16.

Is this assumption justified? It is neither possible nor necessary to deny the contingency with which the gospel in the written record is presented. The facts are there, though (as will be seen shortly) Adam is inclined to exaggerate them, and it is open to anyone to ask with dismay why the Gospels should not have been more circumstantial and accurate, why the Epistles should not have been more systematic and theologically exhaustive, and why the prospects held out to mankind by Christianity should have been communicated in so forbidding a Semitic apocalyptic form. It is further legitimate and indeed our duty to reckon apologetically with the embarrassment these facts occasion. What is illegitimate is theologically to demand, either explicitly (as do critics of the Christian faith—for example, the *Deutsche Christen* of recent years in Nationalist-Socialist Germany), or implicitly (as does Bultmann) that they be altered or removed. There is an exact parallel between this demand and the querulous complaint that the Saviour of mankind was not born an Englishman or that the scene of the event of all history should have been located in a semi-civilized country under pagan hegemony. There is no final answer to either set of questions. Karl 'arth is right in affirming that we cannot know *why* it should be so, but only *that* it is so, and that this is inherent in the essential historicity of the divine scheme of salvation. It is the odd kind of price that has to be paid (if we may put it so) for a religion in which a real incarnation takes place. For this means that one time is taken and not another, one place chosen and not everywhere, and one single human body assumed. That the Bible has an essentially incidental character no more unfits it to play its part as the 'living word' (and this in a much more real sense than Adam can allow the term) than the fact that Jesus was born of Mary in the reign of Tiberius disqualifies Him from playing the role of Saviour of the world.

Further, it suits modern Roman apologetic, in its disparagement of Scripture in the interests of tradition, to magnify the incidental character of the Scriptures into a positive defect and imperfection. In the days of the Reformation, this tendency on the part of the Roman Church was already noticeable. The Reformers insisted upon the presence of a *mandatum scribendi*, whereas the Romans denied it. If Scripture is substantiated by a divine *mandatum*, it cannot be held to be defective or insufficient. The absence of a *mandatum* leaves Scripture open to adventitious influences, which the Roman Church exploits in the interests of its own theory of Scripture. The specific interest which is thereby conserved is to establish alongside Scripture, and continuing after the apostolic age has closed, the existence of an unwritten tradition claiming to be dominical and *a priori*. This conception will fall to be considered in greater detail later. In the meantime, there is no reason to suppose, and certainly no evidence to indicate, that there was intentionally or unintentionally omitted from the written records any cardinal and indispensable item or portion of the Christian faith. The fact that the Scriptures have an incidental character really excludes the preposterous suggestion that there was deliberate omission from them of certain things, doctrines or truths, requisite for the Christian life and faith.

> 'It is indeed a stupid insult to the memory of the four evangelists and of St Paul and the other apostolic writers, to suggest that they failed in the first aim of their writings, which was to convey the meaning of the Christian gospel to their hearers. . . . The Bible, in short, contains the whole of the only tradition of doctrine which the primitive Church required its members to believe as necessary to salvation.'[1]

The Roman supposition, then, that the written tradition is defective is quite improbable. But this is not all. Even before the harsh doctrine of infallibility was formulated, the Scripture enjoyed an authority and prestige which was paramount. It is unintelligible that this should have been the case if at the same time it was realized that it was defective and required to be supplemented from quite another source. When the authority of Scripture is interpreted in terms of infallibility, the discrepancy becomes even more apparent. How could infallibility be accorded to something which is known to be, not merely defective and curiously incidental, but actually incomplete? Modern Romanism can hardly reconcile these facts. On the other hand, the facts can quite simply be explained on the supposition that no such defect as is alleged was earlier attributed to the written tradition. Without such known defect, they move up at once into a place of supreme authority.

[1] Hanson and Fuller: *The Church of Rome*, 95.

That this is formulated later as infallibility is understandable if also unfortunate. When it is regarded as necessary to maintain the existence of an independent oral tradition to be placed alongside of Scriptures, in order to make room for it the Scriptures are supposed to be defective. The supposition is introduced to accommodate and guarantee quite another interest, namely the existence of the independent unwritten tradition. The early affirmation of the authority of Holy Scripture has been overtaken by the supposition of an independent oral tradition exalted to equal rank alongside of Scripture, and the sufficiency of Scripture is impaired in order to make room for this perverse supposition. This at least makes sense of the facts that are known to us, while the Roman account falls into contradiction with itself. To put the matter in other words, there is in fact no room in Christianity for both an infallible Church and an infallible (or even a really authoritative) Bible. C. J. Cadoux is justified when he says:[1] 'without the infallibility of the Church, tradition would be utterly worthless. On the other hand, given the infallible Church, tradition is as much a superfluity as Scripture is.' Scripture forms 'an erratic boulder in the Catholic system'.

(c) Further, it should be noted how near the truth the Roman doctrine as expressed by Karl Adam comes when it speaks of a 'living word', and how far away it inevitably remains in virtue of the false construction it places on this phrase. Roman doctrine is quite right in placing authority in a living word. So firmly does it maintain this insight that, deprived by its own action of Holy Scriptures as a living word, it finds it necessary to fabricate something else to replace it. Rome puts up a living tradition in place of the Bible which it has deprived of life. Over against the wing of reformed theology which holds a fundamentalist doctrine, Roman theology at this point holds a distinct advantage. It has frequently been observed that there is little to choose between fundamentalism and Romanism here. C. J. Cadoux speaks[2] of the 'sameness in essential principle' between the infallible Church and the infallible Bible; and he quotes John Oman[3] as asserting that fundamentalism is a purely Roman Catholic position. But the identity is in fact only partial: it extends only to the fact 'that

[1] *Catholicism and Christianity*, 297.   [2] Op. cit., 115.
[3] In *Daily News*, 24th March 1926; *Christian World*, 1st April 1926, 7.

both locate the final authority in an *external* thing believed to be infallible'.[1] Putting it bluntly, both deprive the Bible of life. But there is also difference. For while fundamentalism is burdened with a dead principle of authority, Rome at least recognizes the importance of some living principle and locates it in the 'broad stream of life' in the continuing Church. Here is a living word by which Christian life and faith is nourished and ruled. Adam's book is a telling exposition of how the Church can be represented as playing this part. But, however telling the exposition, it is based upon a false assumption. The living word is otherwise to be defined and elsewhere to be located. Already in the Old Testament the living voice is to be found, calling Abraham, sustaining Israel, inspiring the prophets, and all the time inviting the men of the Old Testament to know and to acknowledge the God who works savingly. It is in the Old Testament indeed a muffled voice, and the men who listen fail in their understanding, their reporting and their consequent action. When the Word becomes incarnate, while for many the voice is still indistinct and even inaudible, it begins to be heard at least by some in its fulness. These then begin to preach. In the oral tradition the living voice is heard, not indeed in the oral tradition in its own right, but in and through it as made alive by the Holy Spirit. This oral tradition then undergoes the momentous transition of becoming a written tradition. The Scriptures of the New Testament are given to mankind. The living word 'crystallizes'[2] into the Scriptures—but if crystallization implies rigidity and death, it is the wrong term to use. As oral tradition by itself must await employment by the Holy Spirit in order to become the living word, just so, no more, but certainly no less, the Scriptures in the employment of the Holy Spirit become the living word which Christian faith and life require for rule and for nourishment. Here is the primary testimony. Strictly speaking, it is the primary testimony to fulfilment, just as the Old Testament is the primary testimony to the promise. With a sure instinct, the Church placed these new Scriptures, which it had only just contrived to perpetuate the oral tradition, alongside the Old which it had received. The theme of their message is identical, though the angle from which the theme is

---

[1] C. J. Cadoux: op. cit., 115, n. 1.
[2] Hanson and Fuller: *The Church of Rome*, 70; cf. *C.C.H.S.*, §1b.

spoken of differs, as prospect differs from retrospect. But the two form one whole. Holy Scripture forms a unity not excluding diversity. It is the primary antecedent and consequent testimony. It is sufficient, for it witnesses to Christ in the fulness of His redemptive life and work. It is complete, and 'the Church in no sense completes the Bible'.[1] It is living, because the Holy Spirit takes of the things of which it speaks and shows them to men.

These are truths which the Roman Church is unable and perhaps unwilling to recognize, for recognition would alienate from the Church the authority which it has wrongly attracted to itself and which rightly pertains to Holy Scripture. Yet Adam retains a genuinely reformed insight, when he allows that in his terminology, the 'living word' must, to be effective, have 'added' to it the Spirit. This opens the door to an occasional note of striking humility when speaking about the Church: 'we need a poor mother, for we ourselves are poor', though indeed this 'redemptress mother' is 'celestial in the deepest recesses of her being'.[2] Moreover there is a real approach to reformed theology when he affirms that the Church, by its preaching and its attestation, 'can make credible to me the supernatural mystery of Jesus. Its preaching prepares the way for my faith in Jesus. Her testimony becomes in that measure a motive of credibility, as the Schools express it.'[3] Calvin himself does not better say what is needful, when he is interpreting the Augustinian *crux interpretum*.[4]

(ii) *Scripture and tradition.* There remains a narrower and more restricted issue. The Roman Church is wrong in attributing priority to the Church over Scripture. In any realistic appraisal of what the Bible means, it is farther from the truth to say that the Church makes the Bible than to say that the Bible makes the Church; for the Bible is the testimony of those who lived before and after the incarnation, and this testimony becomes the living Word by operation of the Holy Spirit, and on the living Word, whether written or unwritten, the Church depends and rests. The narrower question concerns the nature and significance of tradition. What is the character of this continuing 'living stream' of Church life and worship in which

---

[1] Hanson and Fuller: *The Church of Rome*, 95.
[2] K. Adam: *The Spirit of Catholicism*, 228.
[3] Op. cit., 57f.   [4] *Contra ep. Manich.*, 5.

the gospel message has been carried down from the days of our Lord Himself to the present day? The Roman Church calls it tradition, and it holds it to be the gospel. The stream of Church life is identical with the gospel because the Church is 'celestial in the deepest recesses of her being'. It is there that men meet with Christ. This, moreover, is said not merely in the sense that the Church is the occasion of their meeting with Christ. It is not even just the Body of Christ with which they are in touch, but Christ Himself. In this way there is repeated in a different form the doctrine of transubstantiation. The Church *is* 'celestial' in substance, whatever appearance its accidents may present. The sacramental relationship is jettisoned in favour of a transubstantial identity between Christ and the Church. Instead of a relationship in which the tie consists of the promise and gracious activity of God and which has thus a theologically secure basis, the Roman Church substitutes a substantial identity masked by accidents. Roman theology often protests against the criticism that it interpolates the Church between Christ and the individual believer. There is some truth in the charge, though Karl Adam has enough evangelical understanding to escape its application, and R. A. Knox[1] and others evade its full weight by restricting the intermediacy of the Church to its interpretative function. But the full charge against the Roman Church in general is in fact more serious. It is not that it interpolates the Church between Christ and mankind, but that it substitutes the Church for Christ. This finds illustration when the relation of tradition to Scripture is examined.

There are at least two conceivable relations between tradition and Scripture. The first is that tradition arises out of and is ultimately dependent upon Scripture; the other is that tradition exists as an independent factor alongside of Scripture. Between these two views, out of the Bible or alongside the Bible, the Roman Church has never quite decided. On the one hand, J. H. Newman writes[2] in a frequently quoted passage:

'Nor am I aware that later post-Tridentine writers deny that the whole Catholic faith may be proved from

---

[1] *The Belief of Catholics*, 109.
[2] *The Development of Christian Doctrine*, Chap. 7, 342.

Scripture, though they would certainly maintain that it is not to be found on the surface of it, nor in such sense that it may be gained from Scripture without the aid of tradition.'

The ominous ambiguity of the last phrase is notable. How far is it legitimate to make use of the 'aid of tradition', and where is the line to be drawn which separates tradition as the interpreter and expounder of what is in Scripture and as the supplier of what makes no pretence to be included in Scripture? C. J. Cadoux[1] considers that this ambiguity justifies the classification of even Newman with the 'traditionalists'.

The *Catholic Encyclopedia*, when it deals with 'Tradition', quotes Newman and emphasizes the independence of tradition. The Council of Trent clearly held that there are 'divine traditions not contained in Holy Scripture, revelations made to the Apostles either orally by Jesus Christ, or by inspiration of the Holy Ghost and transmitted by the apostles to the Church'.[2] Karl Adam declares[3] that 'by the side of the Scripture stands extra-scriptural tradition'; and Knox:[4] 'you cannot expect every single element of that tradition to appear in written form among the scarce literary relics that have come down to us from the first two centuries'. Two pages later he affirms that 'the Catholic Church is not inspired. She has no mandate to improve upon the deposit of tradition which was entrusted to her at the first.' But an independent stream of ecclesiastical tradition has already been included in the term 'tradition', by which the Church has really 'improved' the Bible. With this modern exponent may usefully be compared the contention of an earlier champion of the same view, Manning, who declares 'that all appeals "*from* the living voice of the Church" to Scripture and antiquity are "treason" to the Church, because that living voice is supreme'. A further illustration of the failure of the Roman Church to make up its mind is found in the story of the promulgation of the doctrine of the Assumption of the Blessed Virgin Mary and its declaration as a dogma *de fide* in *Munificentissimus Deus* of 1950, and the spirited defence which was offered for English readers

---

[1] *Catholicism and Christianity*, 257.
[2] H. Bainvel: op. cit., §111.
[3] *The Spirit of Catholicism*, 147.
[4] *The Belief of Catholics*, 138.

in the *Tablet*.[1] All the four usual principles are employed to account for the declaration of the dogma: *ex scriptura, ex unanimi consensu patrum, ex consensu fidelium,* and *ex sese* or *ex cathedra.* Its grounds and reasons, that is to say, were to be found in the Bible, in the Church Fathers, in the mind of the present-day Church, and in the decision of the Holy Father. There is no necessity to determine here whether the argument carries conviction; nor need we stop to try to assess the relative importance of the suggested sources. It is enough to observe that both scriptural and non-scriptural grounds are advanced for the explanation and justification of the doctrine, and that the impression left on the candid reader is that of failure, or rather refusal, to choose between them.

At the same time, while individual advocates can be found to champion both sides, and while one may perhaps without injustice suppose that the Roman Church is willing to employ pragmatically each principle in turn for the defence of especially its more recently declared dogmas, there can be little doubt that the principle which really controls the thought and action of Rome is that which reckons tradition as a stream of development independent of and hence uncontrolled by Scripture, and officially placed on an equality with Scripture. This equality can at best be only theoretical. The proximity and accumulating weight of tradition so conceived will inevitably eclipse its partner and exercise the dominant influence. A corollary of this has already been noticed in the disparagement which Scripture suffers at the hands of even those

---

[1] Patrick Bushell in the issue of 19th August 1950 on the impending definition of the dogma. The writer says: 'Petitions have poured into Rome asking for a formal definition of the traditional belief of Catholics that Our Lady was taken to Heaven body and soul.' 'Christians who accept the Resurrection and Ascension, as Protestants no less than Catholics do, can have no additional intellectual or imaginative difficulty about the Assumption of Our Lady. Nobody can recite the Apostles' Creed with conviction and go on to say that they have rational objections to the doctrine of the Assumption, . . . nor is there any difficulty to the Christian mind in believing that what God wills He can do.' G. D. Smith, in a subsequent issue (28th October 1950), says: 'Scripture yields nothing that is directly relevant to our inquiry. . . . In the absence of clear scriptural evidence, it is to the second source of revealed truth, divine tradition, that theologians turn to discover our doctrine. . . . With this infallible definition, there is an end to any doubt the faithful may have had whether the Assumption is divinely revealed. . . . It is not for the individual Christian to declare what the *depositum fidei* contains, but only for the Church's Living Voice.'

Roman expositors who desire to emphasize its importance.[1]

This inherent likelihood is borne out in the official documents of the Roman Church. As early as the Seventh General Council of Nicaea in 787, those were anathematized who should decline to receive doctrines on the authority of Fathers and Councils or the tradition of the Church, unless they could be shown to be plainly taught in the Old and New Testaments.[2] Trent[3] speaks of 'the truth contained *in libris scriptis et sine scripto traditionibus,* accepted by disciples from the mouth of Christ, or coming to us from the apostles themselves, the Holy Spirit dictating (*spiritu sancto dictante*), as transmitted by their hands'.[4] It proceeds to make a distinction between the written and the unwritten, and its insistence on equal reverence only emphasizes the relation of independence in which the two stand. Thus there are 'all the books of the Old Testament and the New Testament of both of which the One God is author'; and there are 'along with them [*nec non*] the traditions themselves so far as either spoken by Christ or dictated by the Holy Spirit and conserved by continuous succession in the Catholic Church'. Both these are to be accepted and honoured *pari pietatis affectu ac reverentia.* From the time of its formulation at Trent, this has remained the standard official doctrine.

What then is the nature of this *traditio sine scripto?* There are three possible answers to the question.[5] The tradition which is spoken of here may be thought of as apostolic tradition and distinguished clearly from ecclesiastical tradition. Authority will then be accorded and reverence offered to the first primarily and not in the same measure to the second. But the Tridentine statements make it clear that, whatever the tradition is of which they speak, it has been 'conserved by continuous succession in the Catholic Church'. No attempt is made at this crucial point to make a distinction. If it is thought that there ever was a distinct apostolic tradition, it has been

[1] Cf. Karl Adam: *The Spirit of Catholicism,* 54, 147; R. A. Knox: *The Belief of Catholics,* 138, 'scarce literary relics'.

[2] C. J. Cadoux: *Catholicism and Christianity,* 256, who cites Neander: *Church History,* v, 320, and Salmon: *Infallibility,* 320.

[3] Sess IV: Decretum de canonicis scripturis.

[4] The same statement in almost identical terms is repeated in Concil. Vat. Sess. II. ii de revelatione, and also in *P.D.,* opening paragraph.

[5] See C. J. Cadoux, op. cit., 294, who makes short work of the two which mitigate the importance of tradition.

drawn into the veins of the Church in which runs the ecclesiastical tradition, and there merged indistinguishably with it, not, however, without imparting to this ecclesiastical tradition the prestige and authority which once belonged to it alone. Secondly, the tradition thought of here may be construed as the Church's own commentary upon Holy Scripture. As interpretation and exposition of the Scriptures, tradition might plausibly be held to participate in the authority which Scripture enjoys. It could be rightly placed alongside Holy Scripture, not indeed as an independent source of authority, but as an ally and ancillary of Holy Scripture, the two being necessarily held together to be practically effective, but the authority of the second being wholly derivative from and its usefulness wholly subservient to the first. There was a time when this clearly was the meaning assigned to the term 'tradition'. In the patristic writings, there is frequent reference and appeal to the 'tradition of the Church', the 'Church's rule of faith', and the like. What is meant is the Scriptures as interpreted by the Church, because 'to the Fathers, the Scriptures *are* the Church's tradition'.[1] Whatever distinction existed between tradition and Scripture was accordingly a fine one, and the order of pre-eminence is plain. If the Church contributed anything to what was contained in Holy Scripture, it was a tradition of scriptural interpretation and exposition. By the time of the Council of Trent, however, this simple and reasonable meaning of the term tradition is no longer in use. This becomes clear in the controversies in which the reluctance of the Roman Church to reform involved the Reformers. As C. J. Cadoux points out,[2] it was the thesis of Luther, Calvin, and the other reformers that Scripture was authoritative and alone authoritative for Christian life and faith. The retort offered by the unreformed Church was not to meet the Reformers on their own ground and by reference to Scripture only to justify the Roman system. Instead, they elected to defend it by appeal to a source of authority other than Scripture—namely, tradition. By this time, then, the term tradition had acquired in the unreformed Church a different meaning from that which it had possessed when the Fathers used it. Its connotation was disconnected from its relation to Scripture, and therefore

---

[1] Hanson and Fuller: *The Church of Rome*, 71.
[2] C. J. Cadoux: *Catholicism and Christianity*, 294.

from its dependence upon Scripture. Tradition stands now alongside Scripture as an independent source and authority. The Roman Church, in other words, imposes on the term a third meaning, and it is this third meaning which calls for examination.

What, we may ask, is the nature and content of this extra-scriptural tradition? There is every reason to think that all that was cardinal in the original oral tradition by which Christianity was proclaimed reached written expression in the Scriptures of the New Testament, despite their incidental character, and that nothing is there lacking for the nourishment and rule of Christian life and faith. The real reason for their sufficiency is not that every tenet of the faith and every ethical precept of the Christian life, or even that the seed and germ of every such tenet and precept, is necessarily included in the New Testament Scriptures. To think that this is a necessity is to misunderstand the nature and the purpose of both oral tradition and written Scripture. And it is this misunderstanding of Scripture which is characteristic of Roman theology. Rome, as has been said, has never discarded the intellectualist view of faith and of the Scriptures on which the faith is based; and here once again we come across the fruits of this pervasive misunderstanding. Neither in Scripture or anywhere else does the Christian faith possess a *system*, whether of doctrine or of conduct, to which it may point and declare: Accept and obey this in order to be saved. The real ground of the sufficiency of the Scriptures is that they testify to Him in whom in order to be saved men must believe; and the doctrine and the conduct, the faith and the life, have their origins there. In this sense, much less than what we have in the New Testament, always provided that it had the authentic character of witness and testimony, would suffice; and on the other hand there is no reason why we should not have had much more. The fact is that, in the providence of God, through the careful guardianship of the early believers, there has been handed down to us this actual quantity of authentic primary witness. Of this the Holy Spirit makes use, 'from time to time', as Karl Barth would say, to bring men into the presence of Him who is *dominus et rex scripturae.*

It is because the Roman Church does not believe this that it is driven to impose another meaning upon the term 'tradition'. It constructs the hypothesis of a strand or seam of tradition which never reached written form, delivered by our Lord or by the Holy Ghost,[1] to the apostles, and by them orally transmitted to those who by the further hypothesis of apostolic succession, narrowly conceived, are regarded as not only their successors, but their equals in status and function. Once this desperate plunge is taken, the hypothesis can become the convenient bearer of anything that by one means or another the Church has come to believe or do. We contend, says R. A. Knox,[2] 'that a doctrine which is "late" in the sense that (say) St John Damascene was the first author who put it on paper in distinct form, may yet be part of the primitive tradition'. The theory has some kind of frail support in the writings of Origen, who holds that our Lord communicated certain secret teachings to His disciples, and that they in turn transmitted them to disciples of their own.[3] But had Origen known of any continuous secret tradition, scrupulously guarded and carefully and discreetly transmitted, we must expect him to have registered the fact, for nothing would have been more convenient for him in support of several speculative theological tenets which he was concerned to propound. In Clement of Alexandria too there is some kind of evidence for secret dominical teaching.

'But when we come to inspect specimens of the secret teaching of these two writers, it is quite impossible to see in them resemblance either to the original teaching of Christ and His apostles or to the sort of doctrines claimed by the Roman Church today to derive from the traditions of the Church independent of the Bible. It is obvious that Origen in his assertion that his secret teaching was identical with Christ's was simply guessing, and the conclusion is irresistible that Clement was doing so also.'[4]

A modern expositor of the Roman position, R. A. Knox,[5] feels himself driven to an expedient of which others have made use in the defence of this far-fetched hypothesis. 'We know', he says, 'that there was in the early Church a *disciplina arcani*,

---

[1] See Trent, Sess IV. [2] *The Faith of Catholics*, 138.

[3] *Con. Cel.*, I. 31, II. 2, III. 37, 58, VI. 6; *Comm. ad Mt.*, XII. 17, XIV. 12; *de Prec.*, II. 5; *Hom. ad Josh.*, XXIII. 4; see Hanson and Fuller: *The Church of Rome*, 71.

[4] Hanson and Fuller: *The Church of Rome*, 78, n.1.

[5] *The Belief of Catholics*, 138.

a system by which sacramental doctrine was expounded, not
to all comers, but only to those who were actually under instruction.' Of course, other Churches than Rome know this.
It is the ground for the traditional distinction between the
Liturgy of the Catechumens and the Liturgy of the Upper
Room, for the Scottish tradition of 'fencing the tables' and of
Communion tokens and cards, and for the obligatory confirmation class for catechumens. But there is not the remotest connexion between this and the impartation of some secret and
esoteric non-scriptural information, which savours more of the
mystery religions than of Christianity. The hypothesis is quite
improbable. Nor is it ancient, and if the Tridentine resolu-
tions imply that it is, we must decline the invitation of *Providentissimus Deus*[1] to find in this Council a 'return' of 'the great
age of the Fathers'. C. J. Cadoux[2] delivers a more pungent
judgment: 'the Tridentine doctrine is simply an extremely
clever device for vindicating Roman ordinances against the
charge of novelty.'

The fact is that there is no evidence for the survival of an
independent oral unwritten doctrinal tradition after the Scriptures have appeared and begun to circulate. While the apostles
live, oral and written tradition operate side by side. Once the
apostles have disappeared from the scene, the sole normative
and authoritative tradition is Scripture. Of course, after this
time ecclesiastical tradition continued and grew. But there are
two meanings of tradition which may not be confused. 'There
is the doctrinal tradition of the Church, that gospel which
God has given it to proclaim, to witness to. And there is the
traditional manner in which the Church proclaims it or witnesses to it; there is the tradition which the Church inevitably
creates as it proclaims its tradition.'[3] The writers of this statement contend that the Roman Church may have confused
these two meanings. It would, however, argue: the way in
which we do things is on an equality with the gospel tradition
itself, because the Church too has Christ and the Church is
divine. At this point, it is to be feared, all conversation between
the unreformed and the reformed Churches comes to an abrupt
end. So long as the Roman Church shelters from the Bible
behind its own developing tradition, it is unable to listen to

[1] P.D., xiv.
[2] *Catholicism and Christianity*, 297.
[3] Hanson and Fuller: *The Church of Rome*, 76.

the living voice that comes through Scripture. It can no doubt
have long and even edifying monologues with itself, but in the
last resort it rests in a refusal to 'let itself be told something'
from outside itself.[1] Until the Roman Church resile from the
position which it thus occupies, nothing very fruitful can be
said or done.

One could think and wish that the idea of development, to
which the Roman Church is not unsympathetic, might afford
the prospect of a *détente*. Newman wrote[2]

> 'that the increase and expansion of the Christian Creed and
> Ritual, and the variations which have attended the process
> in the case of individual writers and Churches, are the
> necessary attendants on any philosophy or polity which
> takes possession of the intellect and heart and has had any
> wide or extended dominion; that, from the nature of the
> human mind, time is necessary for the full comprehension
> and perfection of great ideas; and that the highest and most
> wonderful truths, though communicated to the world once
> for all by inspired teachers, could not be comprehended all
> at once by the recipients, but, as received and transmitted
> by minds not inspired and through media which were
> human, have required only the longer time and deeper
> thought for their full elucidation.'

The denial that the subsequent recipient minds are inspired
may be at once rejected. But the substance of what is said is
otherwise true. Yet development so conceived clearly belongs
to tradition defined as the way in which the Church does
things and dogmatically formulates the original Gospel. At
times even Roman theologians register agreement here. Thus
R. A. Knox[3] declares that 'the only "development" to which
[the Church] will plead guilty is a growing rigidity of doctrinal definition'; and he uses the illuminating analogy of the
way in which the soles of the feet in the course of usage develop
a defence of toughness. It can, however, only be surmised how

---

[1] *Kirchliche Dogmatik*, I/1, Eng. trnsln., 167: 'letting ourselves be told something'.
H. Pope: *The Catholic Church and the Bible*, 49, writes: 'Who produced [the Bible]?
The Catholic Church. Who preserved it? Again the Catholic Church. And still
men maintain that the Church is afraid of the Bible!' And certainly with right.
It is just as effective to smother what you are secretly afraid of as explicitly to
deny or discard it.

[2] *Development*, 27, qtd. A. R. Vidler: *The Modernist Movement*, 56.

[3] *The Belief of Catholics*, 140.

such dogmas as those of the Immaculate Conception, Papal Infallibility, and the Assumption of the Blessed Virgin Mary can possibly be brought under this excellent rubric. The development here supposed to take place is quite different, and is based on the supposed ability of the Church, unrestricted by the only real and original tradition, to initiate development out of itself. We are back again with the erroneous idea of 'the living idea of Christianity in the mind of the Church',[1] and the 'broad stream of the uniform life of faith'[2] as independent uncontrolled sources of tradition. Karl Adam does nothing for this conception of development by applying to it the biological analogy of growth. 'The life of Catholicism grows', he says;[3] and again: 'Christianity is an intimate organic unity, a vital unity, which unfolds itself indeed to its fullness progressively . . . development has been effected . . . by the one spirit of the Whole Christian community.'[4] And again:[5]

'The Gospel of Christ would have been no living gospel, and the seed which He scattered no living seed, if it had remained ever the tiny seed of A.D. 33, and had not struck root, and had not assimilated foreign matter, and had not by the help of this foreign matter grown up into a tree, so that the birds of the air dwell in its branches.'

Adam forgets that the seed must die and come to life again before growth is possible: the Word is committed to writing, but brought to life by the Spirit of the living God. The trouble is that the argument glosses over the very point at issue, whether the Church can be thus naturalistically conceived as an independent and self-developing entity, with powers of growth resident in itself. On the other hand, the statement that the dogmas and usages of Rome are all implicit in the original gift of Christ and tradition is simply their right explication and development to discernible fruit, seems not only to be incapable of proof, but to have the relevant evidence against it.[6] *Providentissimus Deus* cites[7] Augustine,[8] who confesses that there was more that he did not know in Scripture than what he knew. This is a weapon that can be turned against the Roman doctrine. The locus of development lies

---

[1] Bainvel, in *The Catholic Encyclopedia*, article 'Tradition'.
[2] *The Spirit of Catholicism.*   [3] Op. cit., 150.   [4] Op. cit., 60.
[5] Op. cit., 3.   [6] C. J. Cadoux: *Catholicism and Christianity*, 298.
[7] *P.D.*, Summary xxxv.   [8] *Ep ad Januar*, iv. 6.

not in ecclesiastical tradition, but in men's understanding of the apostolic and original tradition. In other words, the only legitimate development is and remains in the sphere in which the Church comments upon and reformulates what it has received, knowing all the time that it is also being judged by it. It is this subordination of the Church to Holy Scripture, and the consequent subordination of ecclesiastical to original tradition, that the Church of Rome refuses to allow. Until some change takes place here, the sad conclusion must be drawn that every step it takes at the prompting of this erroneous conception of development must increase the distance that divides it from the reformed Churches. If today the Roman Church is farther from the reformed Churches, as R. A. Knox suggests, the reason lies here.

c) *Higher criticism.* The remaining issue illustrative of the Roman attitude to Scripture concerns critical biblical study. The Roman Church has in the past regarded the new learning hesitantly. This is admitted by the *Catholic Commentary*. This work is compiled in the belief that 'biblical learning must be integrated with traditional Christianity if it is to bear any spiritual message or fruit for modern society'. It is candidly acknowledged that the Roman Church was late in entering the field of criticism. This had, the *Commentary* says, disadvantageous results: 'the critical analysis of the Bible, when it came, was entirely non-Catholic—indeed, anti-Catholic—and vastly more irresponsible and destructive than it need have been'. Not till the end of the nineteenth century did Catholic exegetes take the new study seriously, and 'catholic scholarship in this matter has not yet made up for its late start'. This is one way of putting the matter. In fact, the warfare which Loisy, Tyrrell, and Miss Petre were bold enough to wage on behalf of criticism was rendered personally inconclusive by various equivocal submissions to authority. It was also rendered ecclesiastically ineffective. Tyrrell wrote: 'I feel my work is to hammer away at the great unwieldy carcass of the Roman Communion and wake it up from its medieval dreams. Not that I shall succeed, but that my failure and many another may pave the way for eventual success.'[1] Has the time to which Tyrrell looked forward now come?

[1] *Life*, II, 273, qtd. A. R. Vidler: *The Modernist Movement*, 172, n.1.

Two questions arise here. The first is: Has the official attitude to higher criticism substantially changed? And the second: With what success can the practice of criticism be carried on under the restrictions that remain?

(i) First, then, may we see in *Providentissimus Deus* and *Lamentabilis* of ten years later the high tide of intransigent and not very well-informed opposition to criticism, and has there been a recession since? *The Contemporary Review*[1] expressed the hope that *Providentissimus Deus* might 'prove a tremendous bridge spanning the broad abyss that now divides alleged orthodoxy from established science'.[2] More recently, H. J. T. Johnson says that it 'marked the starting-point of a revival of biblical studies in the Church which in spite of setbacks has continued since'.[3] It is debatable whether the encyclical has had such an effect. Gore said of it[4] that 'it might have been written by a being in another world, so remote did it seem from the problems which were agitating the minds of scholars'. The appointment of the Biblical Commission raised hopes that a genuine understanding of the nature, aims and results of criticism might now be expected. One of the objects for which it was constituted was the promotion of up-to-date and enlightened critical study. But it was at the same time charged with the duty of seeing that the encyclical of 1893 was duly obeyed. This duty was said to be 'to recall interpreters of the Sacred Books to the sound rules of Catholic exegesis which the holy Fathers, the Doctors of the Church, and the Popes have delivered to us'.[5] It appears that this object has proved the dominant concern. The judgment of C. J. Cadoux is[6] that 'the decisions already given by the Commission are . . . almost all hostile even to the most widely accepted critical conclusions'. A study of the *Catholic Commentary* bears this judgment out only too clearly. *The Catholic Encyclopedia* of 1908 has an article on 'Higher Criticism' which is still frankly hostile. 'Its undeniable effect', says the writer,[7] 'is to depreciate tradition in a great measure.' Even the moderate criticism of British Protestants is incompatible with Catholic orthodoxy.[8] The reason

[1] April 1894, 576.

[2] Qtd. A. D. White: *The History of the Warfare of Science with Theology in Christendom*, II, 364.

[3] In *The Downside Review*, 1951, 414.   [4] Qtd. ibid.

[5] Leo XIII, *Acta*, XXII, 232.   [6] *Catholicism and Christianity*, 288.

[7] G. J. Reid.   [8] C. J. Cadoux: op. cit., 289.

for this judgment is not difficult to discover. The doctrine of inerrancy is unsympathetic to criticism, and to this doctrine in its strictest form the Roman Church is inalienably pledged. *Spiritus Paraclitus* of 1920 issued by Benedict XV does not seem to mark any very significant advance. It expressly adopts the attitude of *Providentissimus Deus*. The doctrine of inerrancy is proclaimed as implacably as ever, and this alone suffices to dash hopes that a more accommodating attitude to criticism will be expressed. In the latter part of the encyclical, attention is given to the matter of reading the Scriptures, and the practice is for the first time clearly commended for laity as well as clergy. Leo XIII[1] had already expressed his

> 'earnest desire that greater numbers should daily adopt and perseveringly maintain the cause of the Sacred Scriptures, and that those especially who have been called by divine grace to sacred orders should devote more and more diligence and industry to their duty of reading them, meditating upon them, and explaining them'.[2]

Pius X commended the Society of St Jerome, 'whose object is to encourage the faithful in the laudable practice of reading and meditating upon the Holy Gospel, and to facilitate it for them in every possible way', with the object of disposing of 'the suggestion that the Church has any objection to the reading of the Sacred Scriptures in the vernacular or places any obstacle in the way of the practice'.[3] *Spiritus Paraclitus* was more explicit, exhorting 'all the children of the Church, and especially clerics, to venerate the Sacred Scriptures, to read them devoutly and meditate on them with perseverance'; but 'the chief use of the Sacred Scriptures lies in their being employed for the holy and fruitful ministry of the divine Word'. This encyclical commemorates the fifteenth centenary of the death of Jerome, and his rubric, which is quoted, *ignoratio scriptuarum est ignoratio Christi*,[4] acquires a wider application than hitherto Rome has normally allowed it. Yet when the encyclical comments upon the critical study of Scripture, its commendation is, just as in the case of *Providentissimus Deus*, robbed of all real force. Such study is to be 'progressive' only in accordance with 'sound principles'. The restriction is

[1] *Acta*, XIII, 328.   [2] See *D.A.S.*, §6.
[3] Op. cit., §12.   [4] *In Isaiam Prol.*, *P.L.*, XXIV, 17.

reasonable enough, if only the meaning read into it werç not the same as always: nothing may conflict with the already formulated doctrine of the Church.

It is safe to say that the first official pronouncement from which it can be gathered that the Roman Church is aware of what was taking place in the sphere of the critical study of the Bible is the encyclical, *Divino Afflante Spiritu*, by Pius XII of 1943, even if this document too purports to build upon earlier pronouncements. It lists several actions by previous occupants of the Roman see since 1903 which have contributed to the promotion of interest in the Bible and of its critical study. Most significant of these was the foundation by Leo XIII of the Pontifical Biblical Institute 'to promote biblical learning and subsidiary sciences as effectively as possible *and in accordance with the spirit of the Catholic Church*'.[1] The encyclical observes that 'the conditions of biblical science and of subsidiary studies have changed considerably in the course of the last fifty years',[2] and, notes as contributory factors to this change, exploration and the study of recently discovered and ancient manuscripts. It approves the revived interest in the ancient languages of the Bible,[3] and with reference to textual criticism declares that after an initial arbitrary and tendencious employment, the art 'has achieved such stability and sureness of principle, that it has become an excellent instrument for producing a purer and more accurate edition of the word of God; and any abuse of the art can now easily be detected'.[4] The Tridentine primacy of the Vulgate is diminished by interpreting it purely as primacy among Latin texts then current, and its authority is now held to be in no way incompatible with concern for the originals of which it is a translation. A further indication that it is really the intention of Rome to diminish the Tridentine estimate of the Vulgate can be recorded from an article in *Vers Verité Chrétienne*, issued by the Istima Study Centre, Paris, in May 1954: 'Has not the severity which marked the period after the Council of Trent been mitigated, since Pius XII—

---

[1] *D.A.S.*, §9, italics not in original. This Institute enjoys growing prestige; it confers degrees of equal status with those already obtainable in Sacred Theology and Canon Law (op. cit., §10); and increasing care is being taken that professors of Roman theology be trained in biblical science by it. It may be surmised that the activities encouraged by it resemble the kind of critical study long pursued by the reformed Churches.

[2] *D.A.S.*, §16.   [3] Op. cit., §19.   [4] Op. cit., §23.

by publishing a new Latin Psalter—inflicted a rude blow on the sacred unimpeachable totality [*bloc*] of the Vulgate which had been canonized by the holy Council?' As will later appear, this movement away from the Vulgate is a matter of importance, and heralds the explicit transference of inerrancy to a hypothetical pure and original text.[1] Interpreters are enjoined 'to discern and determine what is known as the *literal* sense of the words of the Bible',[2] though 'commentators have as their chief object to show what is the theological doctrine touching faith and morals of each book and text',[3] and this involves the 'spiritual significance' which 'God was able to know . . . and reveal to us'.[4] But here a severe restriction is imposed: this spiritual sense is already 'shown in the perpetual and traditional teaching of the Church', and it is 'only profitable if kept within reasonable bounds for illustrating doctrines of faith and commending moral truths'.[5] At the same time, it is realized that 'there are many matters, especially historical, which were insufficiently or hardly at all developed by the commentators of past centuries, because they lacked nearly all the information needful for elucidating them'. Thus there remain (or rather have been recently raised) many questions for study by those who do not 'fail to appreciate the conditions of biblical study'.[6]

Interpreters are urged to 'take advantage of every indication provided by the most recent research in an endeavour to discover the distinctive genius of the sacred writer, his condition in life, the age in which he lived, the written or oral sources he may have used, and the literary forms he employed'.[7] He has

'to go back in spirit to those remote centuries of the East, and make proper use of the literary forms the writers of that early age intended to use, and did in fact employ. For to express what they had in mind, the ancients of the East did not always use the same forms and expressions as we use today; they used those which were current among people of their own time and place; and what these were

[1] Op. cit., §26f.   [2] Op. cit., §28.   [3] Op. cit., §29.   [4] Op. cit., §31.
[5] Op. cit., §32.
[6] Op. cit., §36. Contrast the defence of the Fathers against the charge of ignorance undertaken in *Pascendi*, 55.
[7] Op. cit., §38.

the exegete cannot determine *a priori*, but only from a careful study of ancient Oriental literature.'[1]

Yet these 'approximations' in no sense impair the inerrancy of Scripture; 'for just as the substantial Word of God became like to all men in all things "without sin", so the words of God, expressed in human language, became in all things like to human speech, except error'.[2] It is alleged that

'even among non-Catholic writers there are some who have been led by a serious and impartial examination to abandon the views of the moderns and to return, in some cases at least, to the older opinions. The change is due in great part to the untiring labour of Catholic scriptural exegetes who, undeterred by difficulties and obstacles of every sort, have devoted all their efforts to making a proper use of the contributions made by the research of modern scholars, whether in archaeology, history, or philology, towards the solution of new problems.'[3]

It is more than difficult to accept this as an accurate statement of the case.

Yet the notable change which all this reflects in the official attitude to biblical criticism must be gratefully acknowledged. It might seem that the Roman Church were really prepared, in Tyrrell's phrase, to wake up from its medieval dreams. But the importance and reality of the change must not be exaggerated. The severe restriction upon the exercise of the new critical disciplines is repeated before the encyclical ends in even more forbidding terms.

'Prompted by a practical and ardent love of his science, and sincerely devoted to Holy Mother Church, [the Catholic interpreter] must grapple perseveringly with the problems so far unsolved, not only to repel the attacks of opponents, but also in the effort to find an explanation which will be faithfully consonant with the teaching of the Church, particularly with the traditional doctrine of the inerrancy of Scripture, while being at the same time in due conformity with the certain conclusions of profane sciences.'[4]

That profane sciences should be allowed certain conclusions

[1] Op. cit., §39.   [2] Op. cit., §41.   [3] Op. cit., §45.   [4] Op cit., §48.

in this connexion is probably here for the first time officially conceded. That these certain conclusions will be found to be faithfully consonant either with the teaching of the Church or with the doctrine of inerrancy is a speculation, which only shows that the Roman Church still holds critical study at arm's length. This is only to be expected. If it does not recognize the supremacy of the Word of God spoken in Holy Scripture, it is not likely to be more impressed by the Word of God spoken from a Holy Scripture illuminated by critical study.

(ii) The second question proposed concerns the degree of success possible for those who must pursue critical studies within the limitations officially prescribed. Some individuals seem to be discontent with the situation and prepared to call in question or deny the validity of the limitations. H. de Lubac[1] writes as follows:

'Spiritual interpretation, though it be interpretation of history in an eminent sense, must not interfere indiscreetly or prematurely with historical work. Still less should it be taken for history, even religious history, or substitute itself for history. . . . There is ground for reaction against a practice of spiritual interpretation, which encroaches too much or too immediately upon the historic situations of the Old Testament, in the name of the religious value of the Old Testament considered in its literal sense.'

If words mean anything, this is an invitation to disregard the limitations which are in fact officially imposed. Even more explicit is such a statement as that of H. J. T. Johnson.[2] Asking, 'Does Scripture contain error?', he replies:

'Probably the majority of highly educated Catholics hold that it does; most semi-educated and uneducated ones that it does not. The former opinion is based on admittedly apparent discrepancies between the sacred text and what are generally taken to be ascertained facts, the latter in part on ignorance of the progress of knowledge or of the Bible itself.'

It is a good thing that such things should be said, and they must be welcomed, and writers who dare[3] to this extent must

---

[1] *L'Histoire et Esprit*: 'L'Intelligence de L'Écriture d'après Origen', 398.

[2] In *The Downside Review*, 1951, 427.

[3] J. Coppens: *L'Histoire critique de l'Ancien Testament*, 195, writes: '*les exégètes ont relativement peu à dire dans l'Église, mais ce peu, ils se doivent de le dire avec courage*'.

be wished all success. In the meantime, while it is still far from clear that they will be able to make a real impact or effect any change, how does the work of criticism proceed in the Roman Church?

At all costs the inerrancy of the Scriptures must be maintained; but on the other hand the validity of much of the work of the critic is not denied. So far as can be ascertained, two measures are adopted to bring these two assumptions into something like compatibility. The first consists in the adoption of certain critical methods by which the *sensus litteralis* of Scripture is extracted, that is the meaning the writer intended, in order that another sense may be imposed upon it, presumably something like the spiritual sense, which God intends and which the Church alone declares. Official sanction for this may be found in the reference of *Divino Afflante Spiritu* to the 'theological doctrine' or 'meaning'.[1] Thus the apparatus of criticism becomes available and necessary to the interpreter of Scripture. This practice is not essentially different from that of other biblical scholars in the reformed Churches, but Rome, of course, is applying it to a book whose inerrancy is not in doubt.

The *Commentary* regards literary forms as important. The plea is (quite rightly) made that for example history, in the scientific sense in which the term is now used, was a mode of writing unknown to the original writers. Of the first chapters of Genesis it is said that 'one can neither affirm nor deny that they are history without applying to them the standards of a literary genre which does not fit them'. And again: 'It is impossible to deny or to affirm their historicity as a whole without unduly applying to them norms of a literary type under which they cannot be classed.' It is therefore not surprising that the *Commentary* shows a profound interest in the investigations of the *Formgeschichte* school. 'These [biblical] forms do not correspond to any of our classical categories and cannot be judged in the light of the Graeco-Latin or modern literary types.' Hence 'to declare *a priori* that these narratives do not contain history in the modern sense of the word might easily be understood that they do not contain history in any sense', and this again is not rightly affirmed. 'In the meantime, it is necessary to practise patience which is a part of prudence and the wisdom of life.'[2] Once more the issue is left

[1] Op. cit., §29.   [2] *C.C.H.S.*, §53m.

in suspense, pending further work along these lines. 'Thus a knowledge and careful appreciation of ancient modes of expression and literary forms and styles will provide a solution to many of the objections made against the truth and historical accuracy of Holy Writ.'[1] A similar hope is entertained by those belonging to the reformed Churches; but it is not an identical hope. The commentators look to the study of literary forms to justify their adherence to scriptural inerrancy; others look to it with the desire that they may more adequately interpret the meaning of the Bible.

There is also need for the study of the whole background of the Bible. 'It is absolutely necessary for the interpreter to go back in spirit to those remote centuries of the East, and to make proper use of the aids afforded by history, archaeology, ethnology and other sciences.'[2] But critical methods may not operate freely. The standpoint of the *Commentary* is typical of Roman theology: to venerate as virtually unassailable the verdicts of the Fathers and the decrees of the Councils. The onus of their disproof is laid upon the critic. Thus in the section entitled 'The Gospels and Non-Catholic Higher Criticism',[3] the distinction is clearly drawn, not between right and wrong criticism, but between critics favourable and critics 'hostile to the views of tradition'.

> 'On the whole it must be said that both in its origins and in its later development higher criticism has signally failed in respect for external historical evidence about the composition of the Gospels. Right from the beginning, it put its trust in its power of literary analysis rather than the broader approach which includes analysis and historical tradition alike.'[4]

The familiar allegation is repeated here that criticism 'owes its beginnings and rise' partly to the desire to deny the possibility of miracles.

Thus even where criticism is accepted and used there is failure to do full justice to its significance. It is not realized, despite the partial admission of *Divino Afflante Spiritu*,[5] that criticism provides a really new approach to the Scriptures. Evidence of this failure is abundant. Lagrange writes typically:[6]

[1] Op. cit., §38a.   [2] *D.A.S.*, §39.   [3] *C.C.H.S.*, §604a.
[4] *C.C.H.S.*, §604e.   [5] Op. cit., §36.
[6] *Évangile selon saint Jean*, qtd. A. R. Vidler: *The Modernist Movement*, 224.

'L'Église catholique a rangé parmi les livres canoniques les évangiles selon Matthieu, Marc, Luc et Jean. Le quatrième évangile a donc été écrit sous l'inspiration de l'Esprit-Saint. Pour nous c'est un dogme, ce n'est pas une question. Ce n'est pas non plus une question de savoir s'il a eu pour auteur le disciple bien-aimé, Jean, fils de Zébédée. Ce point est fixé par la tradition ecclésiastique.'

With this should be compared the story of the opposition offered by the hierarchy to Loisy, as told by A. R. Vidler.[1] Loisy's sad concluding judgment is worth recalling: 'Je veux rester prêtre et savant, *res dissociabiles*.' It is because the approach of criticism is novel that the findings of the Fathers have come under fire. There are two possibilities here: either criticism is allowed to do its work unrestricted by extraneous considerations, in the full confidence that finally nothing but a fuller and better understanding of the Bible will result, though some of the opinions the Fathers expressed will no longer be tenable; or the opinions of tradition are surrounded with a sacrosanctity similar to that of the Bible itself, which enables them to be preserved practically inviolate. It is the latter alternative that the Roman Church is bound to adopt. Tradition is of two parts, Holy Writ and the teaching of the Church; and of these, the more practically important is the latter. Hence *ab initio* the Roman Church can only operate criticism under the severest of restrictions.

Other devices are borrowed from criticism to prevent the collapse of verbal inerrancy.[2] A *communis sermo* is detected and distinguished. This is a kind of extension of the doctrine concerning the position in Holy Scripture of what Newman called *obiter dicta*, a theory he propounded in the teeth of the opposition of Cardinal McCabe, who pronounced the conception to be inadmissible. By the application of the idea of *communis sermo*, we read, such perpetual embarrassments as the 'lying spirit' sent to the false prophets,[3] and the divine command to number the people which is followed by punishment of the action,[4] are relieved. The Semitic habit of ignoring secondary causes and attributing morally questionable actions directly to God may be similarly explained, and also the custom

[1] Op. cit., chaps. IX-XVI.
[2] H. J. T. Johnson in *The Downside Review*, 1951, 422ff.
[3] 1 Chron. xxii. 23.　　　　[4] 2 Sam. xxiv.

of attributing pseudepigrapha to familiar and authoritative
writers.

Again the doctrine of 'implicit citations' is invoked. By this
means, it can be held that the Bible contains statements which
carry no guarantee of accuracy. This device has, however,
had a chequered career. It was sanctioned by the Biblical
Commission in 1905 with reservations, despite its condemnation by *Pascendi*[1] under the name of 'tacit citations'. *Spiritus
Paraclitus* is careful to reprove those who disregard the judgment of the Church *nimis facile ad citationes quas vocant im-
plicitas . . . confugiant.* This device is said to displace the
time-honoured attribution of error on the part of transcribers,
which has been found to be unsatisfactory.

Another device consists in distinguishing 'statements which
the Bible makes its own and those which it does not'. Error,
it is stated, is not included in the former, *omne id, quod hagio-
graphus asserit, enuntiat, insinuat, ratineri debet assertum, enunciatum,
insinuatum a Spiritu Sancto.*[2] For example, Lev. xi. 6 and Deut.
xiv. 7 declare the hare to be a ruminant. This zoological mis-
statement is set down as a piece of Semitic lore incorporated
in Scripture, and thus carries no scriptural guarantee.

The second measure for maintaining biblical inerrancy in
face of criticism is perhaps even more significant. Textual
criticism involves difficulties for us all, but they are of course
most acute for those who maintain a doctrine of inerrancy.
For Rome therefore it is a matter of life or death that some
relief should be found; for others not committed to inerrancy,
it is a matter only of great practical importance. How does
Rome then face the difficulty occasioned by textual criticism?
The answer is: by a wide application of the principle quoted
already, to which St Augustine gives expression:

> 'If I come upon anything in Scripture which seems con-
> trary to the truth, I shall not hesitate to consider that it is
> no more than a faulty reading of the manuscript, or a
> failure of the translator to hit off what his text declared, or
> that I have not succeeded in understanding the passage.'[3]

In other words, it is to the original documents and texts that
inerrancy belongs; any apparent error must then be due

[1] Op. cit., 29.   [2] The Biblical Commission, 1915, on the Parousia.
[3] *Ep.*, 82. 1, qtd. *D.A.S.*

to adventitious causes only. An official suggestion of this doctrine has already been detected in *Divino Afflante Spiritu*:[1] 'Criticism has achieved such stability of principles that it has become an excellent instrument for producing a purer and more accurate edition of the Word of God'; which is only a step towards the 'original texts' mentioned a little later.[2] It is this hypothetical original text that is inerrant—'an infallible Bible-X', as Brunner calls it.[3] *Ex hypothesi* this text is immune from criticism; the aim of criticism is to establish it, and with its establishment the task of criticism ends. Thus the Roman Church has an essential interest in the work of textual criticism; but the interest is controlled by the specific object of recovering an original text known *a priori* to be inerrant. Whether criticism is best conducted under the pressure of such a requirement is more than doubtful. The *Catholic Commentary*, for example, is hopeful, but it is content to leave the outcome in suspense. In any case, there is a noteworthy parallelism between this unverifiable hypothesis of an original sacred text that is inerrant and that other equally unverifiable and unlikely hypothesis of an extra-scriptural oral tradition.[4]

It is clear on this evidence that Roman theology has, in a genuine if also limited way, taken the powerful solvent of biblical criticism into its system. For the moment the distinction between literal and spiritual meaning suffices to camouflage what is going on, and the hypothesis of an inerrant original text gives a breathing-space for those who still cling to the infallibility of the Bible. But this uneasy position may not last. If it does not, Rome will have to choose between a recession of sympathy towards criticism and a diminution of the principle of biblical inerrancy.

[1] *D.A.S.*, §23.   [2] Op. cit., §§26f.   [3] *Revelation and Reason*, 274.
[4] A less agreeable parallel may be suggested. As we know, 'Mohammedan theologians consider the Quran an earthly copy of the heavenly book' (Eduard Nielsen: *Oral Tradition*, 62, n.1); and Rome thinks in similar terms at this point.

V

The Inspiration of the Bible

———

In this and the following chapter, we are to deal with two views of the authority of Holy Scripture which do not so clearly or specifically reach expression in theological works, but which exercise a very powerful and widespread influence upon the thinking of ordinary Christians.

'All scripture is given by inspiration of God', says St Paul in 2 Tim. iii. 16. If a reason for reading Scripture and a defence of it against neglect is needful today, they would be supplied by showing that it is inspired. The believer would then wish to put himself where such inspiration is present or conveyed. The unbeliever will feel encouraged to search the Scriptures, if only to see whether the claim is valid.

Adherents of the Christian faith commonly believe that Scripture is inspired. But it is necessary to define what is meant when this is said. What has inspiration can rightly claim some kind of authority. It will have the right to speak, and we shall have the obligation to attend. But where is inspiration to be found in the Bible, and in what does it consist? These are not mere academic questions but vital concerns. For the nature of the authority will be determined by the locus and nature of the inspiration. Sanday[1] equates authority and inspiration: 'That which gives to the Scriptures this authority and sacred character is more particularly the fact that they are inspired by the Holy Spirit.' But this requires further examination.

To the question: What is meant by the Scriptures being 'inspired by the Holy Spirit'?, many answers can be given; but in the main they fall into two classes. It is either the *words* or the *writers* that are inspired. The simple scriptural state-

[1] W. Sanday: *Inspiration*, 31.

ment in 2 Tim. iii. 16 seems to attach inspiration to the words, and the term used is *theopneustos*. But when inspiration becomes an object of reflection by theologians of the early Church, it is rather *pneumatophoros* that is thought of and inspiration is applied to the writers.[1] In fact, there is a connexion between the two types of view. If the words of Scripture are inspired, since they are admittedly written if not composed by human agents, these human agents must have been moved to their writing in some unusual way, and this can mean only inspiration. On the other hand, the view that the writers are inspired need not involve the inspiration of the words. Hence inspiration of the words seems to be inclusive of but not coincident with that of the writer's inspiration.

Each view must occupy attention. That which maintains the object of inspiration to be primarily what is written is the later of the two, and represents a hardening of the conception of inspiration. But for purposes of exposition, especially in view of the situation to which the Bible has to commend itself today, it will be better to follow the other order and think first of inspiration as attaching to the contents of Holy Scripture.

a) *Inspiration of the words.* Sanday's great work, even if some of the conclusions cannot be accepted, is a mine of information on the subject of inspiration and the place it has occupied in the understanding of the Scriptures. Here something must be said about the view of the Bible which, holding what is there written as the direct communication of God, usually goes by the name of verbal inspiration. In the previous three chapters, the view has already made its appearance. It was there asked whether Calvin held such a view, how it came about that Protestant scholasticism adopted it, and how the Roman Church tries to find relief from some of the embarrassments which it occasions. Now the attempt must be briefly made to assess this recurrent conception.

Even if it arises later than the view which thinks of the writers as properly the objects of inspiration, it is still a very early Christian view. This is not surprising, for the Jews held their Scriptures to be verbally inspired, and it was natural

[1] See Sanday, loc. cit. His first authority from early days is Theophilus of Antioch, who uses the term *pneumatophoros* twice. There follow citations which show preoccupation on the part of the writers with the biblical authors rather than the content of Scripture as object of inspiration.

that, as the Christian documents were accorded a rank equal to that which the books of the Old Testament enjoyed and a place alongside of these books, they should also share this characteristic with them. Irenaeus and Tertullian 'regard inspiration as determining the choice of particular words and phrases'.[1] The doctrine sometimes passes over into the assertion of the absolute perfection and infallibility of the Scriptures. Irenaeus affirms that the Scriptures must be 'perfect, as having been spoken by the Word of God and His Spirit';[2] while Novatian 'says roundly that the Scriptures are infallible (*nunquam fallunt*)'.[3]

Those who today hold that the Bible is verbally infallible and inerrant do not necessarily hold the very same doctrine as Irenaeus and Tertullian, however similar their expressions and assertions may be. As said already, A. G. Hebert[4] points out that inerrancy of the Bible as held today is a new doctrine, 'and the modern fundamentalist is asserting something that no previous age has understood in anything like the modern sense'. The terms used are the same; what is meant by the terms is different. The ground of the difference lies in the emergence of what may be called 'exact science'. A writing that touches upon the making or constitution of the world in which we live is immediately thought to be pronouncing a judgment of a physical or biological or astronomical kind. A record that relates an event of the past is classed with the writings that narrate exact history, and it is by the standard of exact history that it is liable to be judged. Thus[5]

'the truth of the Bible is judged by its reliability in matters of historical and physical fact. The ordinary modern reader of a biblical narrative wants chiefly to know what exactly it was that happened, or what a trained observer would have seen if he had been there; and he thinks that this is the real truth of the matter'.

Nothing would in fact have given greater surprise to the writers of the Bible than to find their work judged by any such standards. Not only have such scientifically exact standards not yet been conceived; even if they had been, the writers

---

[1] So W. Sanday: *Inspiration*, 34.
[2] *Adv. Haer.*, 2. 28. 2, qtd. Sanday, op. cit. 36f.
[3] *de Trin.*, 30, qtd. Sanday, op. cit., 38.   [4] *The Authority of the Old Testament*, 98.
[5] A. G. Hebert: *The Authority of the Old Testament*, 98.

would still have composed a kind of writing to which they were inapplicable. The writer of Genesis would have repudiated the idea that what he wrote could really compete on common ground with the modern geologist or geographer. Similarly, in the case of the Gospels: it has become more and more clear that even Mark, the most 'historical' of the four Gospels, has neither the desire nor the intention to give his readers a photographic picture of Jesus Christ. The writers of Genesis and the second Gospel use material that can also be used by the modern scientist and the modern historian; but they write with a difference of intention.

Not only is the sense in which these writings are often today understood quite alien to the writers themselves; it is also alien to the way in which for most of the Christian era these writings have in fact been understood. The 'infallibility' early affirmed of the scriptural writings both of the New Testament and of the Old is usually helped out by various methods of *interpretation*. Indirect evidence of this is supplied by Sanday: no sooner has he traced the doctrine of infallibility to an early stage of Christian thought, than he finds it necessary to pass to consider the 'stress which is laid upon their interpretation',[1] though this fact is adduced for the different purpose of demonstrating the sacredness with which Scripture was invested. By A.D. 170, it is asserted, 'the allegorical method is already fullblown'. It is easy to ridicule and deprecate the methods which enabled Origen and Clement of Alexandria to prove almost anything they pleased. The really important point is different. Though the temptation of extravagant interpretation often proved irresistible, yet *abusus non tollit usum*, and the methods of interpretation used throughout the history of the Church are in fact much closer in spirit and atmosphere to the writings as originally composed than the attempt to read the Scriptures as though they contained the conclusions of 'exact science'. St Bernard declares that the literal interpretation of Scripture, having no spiritual nourishment in itself, is like the outside crust of bread, indigestible and dry, and he accordingly employs the allegorical method of interpretation. Stephen Langton exemplifies the fourfold allegorical scheme[2] by

---

[1] *Inspiration*, 39.
[2] Thus: Litera gesta docet; quid credes, Allegoria;
Moralis, quid ages; quo tendas, Anagogia.

reference to Jerusalem, which literally is the city on Mount Zion, allegorically is the Church Militant, anagogically or mystically is the Church Triumphant, and tropologically or morally is the faithful soul. Mr Raymond Abba[1] quotes Master Rypon of Durham as saying that 'the Books of Moses are rude when considered historically, nevertheless within they are full of moral senses and doctrines, useful alike to the preacher and to his audience'. We may not indeed agree with all the ways in which the method was employed or endorse all the conclusions reached. But at least the method really 'made the Bible work'. Those who used it share with the biblical writers themselves an interest in the spiritual and moral significance of what is written, and this is lacking in those who read it in the light of 'exact science'. If the choice lies between an allegorization of the Scriptures and a rationalization, it is the former that better recaptures and transmits the spirit of their writers. When allegorization is simply dismissed as a whole, without any attempt to distinguish between a right and proper allegorism and an unreliable and false allegorization, a bare literalism alone remains. When this bare literalism is in turn allied to the expectation of finding in Scripture the same kind of thing that is so successfully supplied by science, as happens in modern fundamentalism, then there emerges the 'new doctrine' of infallibility of modern times which has no real precedent in previous ages. It is out of this unhappy alliance that there develops the acute and distressing tension and conflict between science and religion. Moreover, the term 'alliance' disguises what is going on here. It is not that an 'ancient literalism'[2] is simply supplemented by an aspect observable from another standpoint. In fact, the 'ancient literalism' is not retained in and by itself; it is rather subjected to another kind of interpretation—and one which can at least as effectively as the traditional allegorism prevent the real meaning of the Bible from being apprehended.

The traditional view of inspiration did in practice contrive to retain a certain measure of flexibility.

'The Bible as a whole and in all its parts was the Word of God, and as such it was endowed with all the perfections of that Word. Not only did it disclose truths about the

[1] In *The Scottish Journal of Theology*, Vol. 4, 227.
[2] The phrase is Charles Gore's, and has already been quoted in Chapter I.

Divine nature and operation which were otherwise unattainable, but all parts of it were equally authoritative, and in history as well as in doctrine it was exempt from error. It was not quite a hard and fast view. Some kinds of error might be admitted, and there might be no clear dividing line where these possibilities of error were to stop, but it would be agreed that they could not extend to anything of importance. They would belong chiefly to the sphere of the text: it might be allowed that the true text could not always be discovered; but when once it had been discovered it could not be otherwise than infallible.'[1]

This flexibility, however, is an advantage of which the modern view of infallibility cannot so readily avail itself. Once the principle of 'exact science' is invoked and its categories applied, rigidity settles down upon biblical interpretation, and we have on our hands immediately the grave embarrassment of trying to reconcile what is said in the Bible with contradictory conclusions which seem to be on other grounds inescapable. In this situation the appeal to scriptural authority does not solve the problem; it only precipitates intellectual chaos.

One attempted evasion of the dilemma may be briefly mentioned. It is the notion of 'degrees of inspiration'. Some words of the Bible will be credited with a greater 'degree of inspiration' than others. But this proposal raises as great difficulty as that which it tries to solve. There must be on this view some standard by which the degrees are judged and assessed. What this standard is it is impossible to say; or rather, so many possibilities at once offer themselves as standard, that it is impossible to choose between them. But in fact 'the "conservative" view, both in its Catholic and its Protestant forms, always refuses . . . to accept the notion of "degrees of inspiration" '.[2] Yet it is obvious, as Hebert goes on to say, that 'there are degrees of *something*'. God cannot rightly be thought of as granting greater and smaller quantities of inspiration, if they are inspired words that we have in the Bible. If there are degrees to be found, then they must be rather upon the human side—in the recording by men of what God gives. But this is to apply inspiration not to the contents of Scripture as such, but to its writers.

[1] Sanday: *Inspiration*, 392f.
[2] A. G. Hebert: *The Authority of the Old Testament*, 101.

The view that it is the words of the Bible that are inspired and the consequent controversy about 'verbal inspiration' has done much to sidetrack attention from what is the important thing at stake. The really crucial question concerns not the words, letters and vowel points and their origin, but the method of God's operation with men. One view of His chosen method is that He intervenes in the course of the ordinary natural and psychological processes to insert something that is directly and exclusively His own. This apparently is what is usually meant by the term 'plenary inspiration': it is the injection, if we may put it so, of foreign bodies into the blood stream. This is expressed by what B. B. Warfield says of Calvin.[1]

'It is not unfair to urge that this language [about "dictation"] is figurative and that what Calvin has in mind is, not to insist that the mode of inspiration was dictation, but that the result of inspiration is as it were by dictation, viz. the production of a pure word of God free from all human admixtures.'

Thus 'dictation' describes 'the effects rather than the mode of inspiration'. 'The important thing to realize is that . . . the Scriptures were so given that—whether by "literal" or "figurative" dictation—the result was a series of documents errorless in their original form.'[2]

If this is the way in which God works, it matters very little in what exactly the insertion is held to consist. Plenary inspiration may be held to apply only to the thoughts or ideas of Holy Scripture, or only to certain of them. As already seen, this is a familiar way in which the attempt is made to rescue Luther and Calvin from the charge of literalism. It may indeed do something to loosen the tension apparent in their writings. But it will not in the last resort save them from the charge of believing that in Scripture we have an abrupt and pure divine interpolation. In fact, if God thus works by the insemination of something purely His own, there is no reason why He should be restricted to 'ideas' only. Words, letters and vowel points might just as well be interjected or imposed by this means.

The Bible is on this view credited with an impressive if also inflexible authority. There is no *a priori* reason why the Bible

---

[1] *Calvin and Calvinism*, 63f.
[2] E. A. Dowey: *The Knowledge of God in Calvin's Theology*, 101f.

should not have this origin and character and the authority that goes along with it. If it did, it would suit admirably the longing in men to take refuge in an authority against which there can be no appeal, and this longing might have been gratified. Whether, however, it has in fact been gratified is quite another question. It is often argued that there are 'unworthy conceptions' of God contained in the Bible, and 'immoral actions' in which God is reported to be implicated; and such things are sometimes adduced as evidence that finally disposes of the idea that the Bible comes directly from God by verbal inspiration. But the evidence does not suffice to support this conclusion, since it is evidence that involves resort to other standards of judgment, which are ruled out of order, if the Bible is simply and directly God's handiwork, interpolated like a bolt from the blue among men. 'What I have written, I have written'—if in the Bible we have something thus directly from God, His character as there depicted cannot be called in question in any other court of appeal. But the idea of such divine interpolation will perhaps be more severely disturbed if it shows signs of *inner* incoherence. If the authority attaching to Scripture on this view can resist charges levelled from outside itself, it can hardly ignore charges which have their source from inside itself, without precipitating a situation in which authority itself cannot be saved from collapse and chaos is king. The authority should then at least exhibit thorough self-consistency. But self-consistency of a detailed kind is just one of the things that the Bible, examined verbally, fails to display. Contradictions force themselves on the attention. Examples may be cited from the reported action of God, from the account of His dealings with men, from the laws He is said to impose upon them, and from recorded facts. There is a discrepancy between the divine declaration of punishment of sons and grandsons, 'visiting the iniquity of the fathers upon the children, and upon the children's children, unto the third and to the fourth generation' (Exod. xxxiv. 7), and the affirmation that 'the soul that sinneth, it shall die' (Ezek. xxxiv. 4);[1] between the creation of man before and his creation after the things of nature (Gen. i. 11f. and ii. 8ff.); between the

---

[1] Cf. the parallel contradiction between 2 Sam. xxi. 1-14, David believing God pleased that the descendants of Saul be hanged at Gibeah, and Deut. xxiv. 16, 'neither shall the children be put to death for the fathers'.

imposition and the abrogation of the *lex talionis* (Lev. xxiv. 20 and Matt. v. 38); and Calvin, pointing out discrepancies in the chronology of the Gospels, roundly declares: 'anyone who will consider how little care the evangelists bestowed on pointing out dates will not stumble at this diversity in the narrative'.[1] Such inner incoherence really forbids the conception that in the Bible God precipitates a solid block of inerrant matter into the world of otherwise imperfect things. Even if judgment of the Bible by standards external to itself is rejected, the standard of consistency with itself remains and must, one supposes, be admissible. To attempt to salvage anything out of this view by supposing such discrepancy to be due to scribal inaccuracy in the interests of a hypothetical incorrupt original is implausible and only rests one hypothesis upon another. To suppose 'accommodation' here and suggest that God fits what He has to say to the individual case of the recipient is to make concessions to human conditions which the argument strictly disallows.

There is no alternative but to reject this view of the way in which God works. The authority which He wields, and which through their connexion with Him the Scriptures exercise, is not of this autocratic kind. God's way is not to override or to compel, nor does He triumph by annihilation. The Bible is not an 'inspired statement'; nor does God 'go over the head' of His children when He desires to address them or to speak through them. When He gives us the Scriptures, it is indeed something divine that He bestows; but in their creation He does not simply disregard those to and by whom they come. It is *their* word we have, evoked by and witnessing to *His* Word, and becoming at His will and pleasure *His* Word to us. The Bible is no more identifiable with the Word of God than the Church we know is identifiable with the Body of Christ. But neither is it less so. In the mystery of God's choice and activity, the Bible is always God's Word and the Church always the Body of Christ.

b) *Inspiration of the writers.* The location that may alternatively be suggested for inspiration is the writers, not the written. Thus A. G. Hebert says:[2] 'The alternative when this

---

[1] on Mt. xxi. 10ff.
[2] *The Authority of the Old Testament*, 101.

(that is, the view that regards Scripture as an infallible record of events) breaks down, is to treat inspiration psychologically, as denoting the religious experience of inspired individuals, who are subject to "degrees of inspiration".' It is in this form that the doctrine of inspiration appears when the venerable doctrine of verbal inspiration is discarded. It is safe to say that at least a very large number of Christians today hold that the Bible is inspired in the sense of being written by men who were inspired. It is a view that has much to commend it, having this evident major advantage, that it can accommodate a scientific approach to the Scriptures and accept readily much that the critical study of the Bible virtually compels us to regard as established fact. It is on the whole a recent view, though it has an ancient lineage. It receives classic exposition in the work already quoted, W. Sanday's deservedly famous Bampton Lectures on *Inspiration* given in 1893. The delivery of these Lectures constituted a severe shock to the orthodoxy of their day. 'Concessions were made', writes A. D. White,[1] 'to the newer criticism, which at an earlier time would have driven the lecturer not only out of the Church but out of any decent position in society.' From the same pulpit in Oxford, where some years earlier Pusey had said that Christianity stood or fell by the traditional view of the Book of Daniel, it was now frankly stated that Daniel was not predictive. The lectures created an appropriate stir, but it could hardly then have been foreseen how influential the view which they expounded was to become, and (one may add) how great a service it was to render, at least temporarily, in making compatible for ordinary Christian believers a high doctrine of Scripture with acceptance of the assured results of biblical critical study.

In a sense this view is both the antecedent and the remnant of the view according to which inspiration is applied to what was written. It is antecedent, for it was advocated before scholastic tendencies invested the words with inspiration. The Old Testament readily provided notable examples of men under the influence of inspiration doing unusual, sometimes prodigious and sometimes erratic, things, The study of this belongs to the doctrine of the Holy Spirit in the Old Testament. Sometimes temporarily and sometimes for periods of

[1] *The History of the Warfare of Science with Theology in Christendom*, Vol. II, 357.

greater permanency, sometimes raising capacities already present to a higher degree and sometimes apparently conferring powers not present before, inspiration operated upon an individual and enabled him to do notable works. The Scriptures constitute a record of men thus affected and are written by them. That is, the Bible tells how some men are inspired and is itself written by some of those men. Hence the early reference of *pneumatophoros* to the biblical writers.

Inspiration regarded as applying to the persons or writers is on the other hand also a remnant. When the view that inspiration is to be attributed to the *words* is abandoned, it is still possible to maintain that *those who wrote the words* were inspired. A return is made to an antecedent theory of inspiration. It is this theory, the resuscitation to some extent of an earlier original theory, that is regarded frequently today as a refuge for those who know that the Bible is inspired, but to whom the position that the very words in which it is written are inspired has been denied. There has in fact been a widespread landslide in this direction. The motive is clear: it is thought that by this means something really worth while can be salvaged from the wreck of the verbal inspirationist theory. The writers are credited with being inspired when it is no longer possible to regard the words themselves as being the objects of inspiration.

Sanday's statement of the position is as follows:[1]

> 'Just as one particular branch of one particular stock was chosen to be in a general sense the recipient of a clearer revelation than was vouchsafed to others, so within that branch certain individuals were chosen to have their hearts and minds moved in a manner more penetrating and more effective than their fellows, with the result that their written words convey to us truths about the nature of God and His dealings with man which other writings do not convey with equal fullness, power and purity. We say that this special moving is due to the action upon those hearts and minds of the Holy Spirit. And we call that action inspiration.'

The view is inductive 'because it starts by examining the consciousness of the biblical writers. It inquires what they say, or what they give us to understand, as to the nature of their

[1] *Inspiration*, 127.

own inspiration. It sets out from the mind of the individual writer'.[1] Not that it remains thus individualized; for 'we must needs feel there is more than the individual minds at work; they are subsumed, as it were under the operation of a larger Mind, that central Intelligence which directs and gives unity and purpose to the scattered movements and driftings of men'. This puts the matter clearly: inspiration is by no means merely 'subjective'; it is not what a man thinks up for himself, but something that God sends down. The inspiration of God impinges on the individual, on his heart or his mind or both, who is chosen to this end. The end term of inspiration is religious experience.

There is something else to be added. On the other view, the words are retained intact and are communicable, and hence we may rightly speak of an inspired Bible of which they are the component parts. But what of this individual and transient visitation by the Holy Spirit which results in religious experience? Is it not too subjective for communication? What can inspiration mean to us today, when its object is the religious experience of a dead patriarch, prophet, or Apostle? Those who hold the view are not left without an answer. They will commend the Bible 'because there breathes beneath it a genuine human life, the life of men who though illuminated from on high were yet of like passions with themselves'.[2] The Bible is to be read because it is the record of and about men who were inspired—an account of the remarkable religious experience of a remarkable succession of men, 'religious geniuses', as they are so often called.

Yet the question may be pressed concerning the reason why we should read the Bible. For all that has been said so far only adds up to this, that if we are interested in the religious experience of this remarkable series of men, we should read the Bible, but not, apparently, unless we have this interest. To this there is still a possible answer. It is that where we read of such inspired men, we ourselves become inspired. When we are put in touch with such 'religious geniuses', we are immediately encouraged and inflamed by their example; we are touched by the same flame as they knew and caught up into the religious experience which they enjoyed and which now they communicate to us in and through their writings.

[1] Op. cit., 402.　　　　　　[2] Op. cit., 430f.

'One loving soul sets another on fire', and the record of those who have themselves played the part of religious genius must be influential in reduplicating their experience. 'What has come down to us is revelation, i.e. a number of concrete truths contained in written books on the subject of God and religion. And they are truths because these books are the work of inspired men, so that even through the printed page there speaks the Spirit of God'.[1]

When the answer is given in these terms, an important change has come over the whole picture. The initial question was how the Bible could be interpreted as an inspired book, and the assumption was that in some way the Bible we have in our hands was the vehicle or vessel of inspiration. Now it turns out that the Bible is being recommended, not because it is an inspired book, but because it is an inspiring book. 'They being dead yet speak'; but the object on which inspiration lighted has perished. What is left to us is their inspiring example and record contained in Holy Scripture. This may indeed be all that some people require of biblical inspiration; but it is an impoverished conception. The difference between an inspired book and an inspiring book is very wide. While an inspired book will be inspiring, it does not necessarily follow that an inspiring book is itself inspired. If the Bible is only an inspiring book, we have something of great value, but not of the inestimable value which has traditionally been accorded to it.

What may be said of this view of inspiration and the authority which accorded to the Bible by it? There is no need to quarrel with much of what it says about inspiration or with the phenomena to which, as facts in the case that cannot be disputed, it does right to call attention. If there is a divinely bestowed inspiration, that reaches out to touch a man's heart and mind, there is good reason to try to trace the course of this event. The 'how' of inspiration, the 'mechanics' of its operation, early attracted attention. Philo[2] suggests that inspiration works as if the citadel of the soul were surrendered and then occupied by the Spirit. Again he refers to Gen. xv. 12 as typical of the means usually employed, where 'about the setting of the sun a trance came upon Abraham'. Josephus talks of 'the Spirit of God taking hold of' the prophet, and

[1] *Inspiration*, 430.   [2] See *Inspiration*, 74.

of 'the divine gift passing over' from one person to another.[1] The interest is legitimate and proper, even when inspiration is applied to the words of Scripture. The words even if inspired have to get themselves written; and to enquire about the means by which this takes place is unobjectionable.

Moreover, the view is not tied to the idea that the words come there by means of the 'dictation' of God. Sanday considers the passage Jer. xxxvi. 1-32, where Baruch, after an interval of a year (or perhaps four years), prepares an enlarged edition of a message originally dictated to him by Jeremiah. Two facts in the narrative are evidence against the idea of divine dictation: first, that there is a long delay between Jeremiah's receiving the message and its commission to writing; and secondly, that to the original record there are added 'many like words'. In contrast to Calvin, Sanday[2] concludes that 'the prophets did not feel themselves strictly bound to a literal reproduction of their spoken addresses'. These facts are irreconcilable with the idea that the words of Holy Scripture are what is directly inspired; but they can very well be accommodated by the view which holds that inspiration bears upon the individual person concerned—the inspired man who out of his experience writes down what he must write down.

There is a corollary. When inspiration is regarded as the inspiring experience of a man, it is easy to account for the element of human error. One of the crucial difficulties of verbal inspiration is to account for this element. How can it, without sophistry, be explained that words supposed to be divinely dictated should be inaccurate or false or contradictory? This embarrassment is avoided by holding that it is the writer only who is directly inspired. Then any inaccuracy may be ascribed to the faulty representation of the experience of inspiration. The writer, even if inspired, is not so divinely guided in the record he makes of the inspiration that he is safeguarded from the possibility of error. The interpretation and application of the experience of inspiration may contain error. This represents an important advance on the view of verbal inspiration. The Bible can be regarded as a book both human and divine. There is no need to regard it, as those holding verbal inspiration must do, as though it were an incarnation of the Holy Spirit and so exempt from error.

[1] See op. cit., 77. [2] Op. cit., 238; see Calvin: *Commentary*, ad loc.

But it has still to be asked whether inspiration thus conceived is a sufficient basis for authority. The question raises grave difficulties. For one thing, inspiration has side-slipped from the position accorded to it when the Bible is said to be inspired. Inspiration is now no more than a psychological account of the mechanics of what happens when God wishes to get some truth across to men. Such an account may be legitimate; but it is hardly adequate to explain what is meant by saying that the Bible is inspired. Sanday, drawing attention to the momentous change that takes place when speech gives way to writing, continues:[1]

> 'But in essence and idea the change was a very small one. It was in fact no change at all. The authority of the word written was precisely the same as that of the word spoken, neither more nor less. It was inherent in the person who wrote and spoke, and was derived from the special action upon that person of the Spirit of God. Whether he wrote or whether he spoke made no difference to those who were first addressed.'

It is difficult to be satisfied with this identification of inspiration with authority, especially when we find it regarded as 'inherent' in 'men endowed with special gifts for the discharge of a special mission'. Biblical authority is not in this way firmly enough based. Christians go to the Bible because they conceive it to be in some sense divinely authoritative for them. Something is missing if the reason why they should go is that other men, even those who wrote it, have been authoritatively commanded to speak or write.

Further, inspiration, and in virtue of the identification authority, when thus conceived are to be found only sporadically in the Bible. That the prophets were recipients of inspiration cannot be doubted. At other points in the Old Testament, it is the quality of unusualness that draws attention to inspiration—unusualness whether of physical prowess or spiritual insight. There is no claim in Scripture that the Spirit's manifestations are equally visible throughout. The question then arises: how does it come about that inspiration was conceived as covering the whole of Holy Writ and not merely located in isolated passages? Is it wrong to say that the whole of

[1] *Inspiration*, 226f.

Scripture is inspired? Or have we got the idea of inspiration wrong?

This difficulty is openly admitted by Sanday. He deals with it in two ways. First, he supposes a 'principle of extensions'. By this is meant that the same authority which is possessed by writings obviously determined by the divine *afflatus* is extended to writings which just as obviously are not thus determined. 'That which originally had reference to some particular mode or organ of revelation was extended so as to cover the whole.'

> 'By precisely the same process by which the one term "the Law" or the double term "the Law and the Prophets" came to be used for the whole of the Old Testament Scriptures, the attributes of the Law and the attributes of the Prophets were extended to all the books, and to all parts of all the books, included in the canon.'

The argument does not give much security. Is this really all that is meant when we say the Scriptures are inspired? Is all Scripture rightly said to be inspired if a great part of it is only psychologically associated with what is veritably inspired?

Another explanation is given. It is pointed out[1] that St Paul's letters when they reached the destination for which they were written would 'be treasured in the archives of the Church, in the same chest or cupboard, we may suppose, with the copies of the Old Testament; and they would be brought out and read on special occasions, at first somewhat irregularly, but after a time in a certain order and system'. There is indeed evidence of just this happening, and it is cited by Sanday from Tertullian. Here a principle of assimilation is at work: these writings which almost by accident were placed for safe keeping along with admittedly inspired writings, came through this association to be regarded with the same reverence and qualified with the same authority.—But here questions of the same kind arise. Supposing that this is a correct account of the facts, does it really amount to a justification of the authority which all Scripture is supposed to possess? It may be conceded that it represents one account of the way in which the New Testament as well as the Old Testament came to enjoy authority. But it can hardly rank as full justification.

[1] Sanday: *Inspiration*, 361.

Physical conjunction is no more able to justify authority than psychological conjunction to justify inspiration. One is inclined to look for weightier grounds than the fortuitous storage of apostolic writings in the same drawer as other sacred writings.

Further, the idea that it is the inspiration of persons that is the source of the inspiration and so the authority of Holy Scripture leads to the following important conclusion. The Holy Spirit has not suspended His operations. He still works in the hearts of men, and still 'the wind bloweth where it listeth'. It follows that in the matter of inspiration, we of today stand on an equality with the writers of the Bible. Moreover, in inspiring men, the operation of the Holy Spirit today must be apparently the same as the operation of the Holy Spirit at any other time. We on our side are not as men essentially different from the writers of the Bible; and we bring with us the same human equipment to be employed in our religion. On the other side, the Holy Spirit is after all one with God, as the Son is one with God; and since Jesus Christ is the 'same yesterday, and today, and for ever', the Holy Spirit cannot be essentially different. If then the foundation of the authority of the Bible is found in inspiration, how does it come about that an authority is ascribed to Holy Scripture which is of a different order from that which is accorded to even the foremost of the 'prophets' of modern days? Why is it that the writings of St Thomas à Kempis, of Sir Thomas Browne, or Baron von Hügel are not ranked with the writings of Holy Scripture? It would be hazardous to try to distinguish these writers respectively on the basis of degrees of inspiration, partly for reasons just given, but also because there is no clear criterion by which such a distinction could be made. Yet the fact has somehow to be accounted for, that they are not in practice accorded the same degree of authority. Many people allege that they 'get more out of' one or other of these authors than they do when reading the Bible. Yet few would dream of ascribing to even their favourite devotional writer the same authority as they concede to the Bible. If authority is derived from inspiration, how is this cardinal distinction to be justified? It is not an acceptable answer that we have made a mistake and that in fact we should be putting these and other writers on the same plane as Holy Scripture. Yet just this seems to be the conclusion to which we are driven by the terms of this theory. It looks as if, admitting the undoubted inspiration and inspiring qualities of the Bible, we must look in another direction for the distinguishing mark which separates off the Bible from other books that enjoy similar qualities. We have to look for some other quality than inspiration by which the authority of the Bible is to be guaranteed.

A still more surprising corollary follows. St Paul is one of those who was inspired on any interpretation of the word. He himself claims it, implicitly in the apostolic commission which he holds from Christ, and explicitly as at 1 Cor. ii. 16 where he claims to 'have the mind of Christ'. It follows according to the theory under discussion that what he writes will have the derivative kind of authority which this theory permits the writings of 'inspired men'. Subject to the divine *afflatus* in a pre-eminent degree, what he writes is at least indirectly inspired. But what of the Gospels? The case is more complicated. Their writers (or at least some of them) are recorded in Acts to have been the subjects of inspiration at Pentecost. On this view of inspiration, the suggestion follows that the reason why we read and ought to read the Gospels is because the men who wrote them were inspired men. It may be possible to hold that we read the writings of St Paul because he was inspired. But to suggest that we read the Gospels simply because their writers were similarly inspired men is not even plausible. It is clear that something important has dropped out of place. The fact is that the Gospels are never ordinarily read with this motive or reason, but for a quite different one. We read them because of Jesus Christ; and when we read them for this reason, the fact that the apostles wrote them and that they were 'inspired men' is simply not in our mind.

The conclusion to which this view leads is a very odd one. It is that, while we ascribe to St Paul within the New Testament an authority of the first order, we ascribe to the Gospels authority only of the second rank. Sanday himself admits this.[1] The inspiration of the whole Bible has

'been reached by a simple process of enlargement or extension, properties which the prophets and lawgivers of Israel claimed for themselves in their own proper sphere being

---

[1] *Inspiration*, 400f.

applied to other writers in a different sphere or being applied to themselves otherwise than in their capacity as prophets and lawgivers'.

Hence in the Old Testament the history that is written comes by association to have an equal authority with the properly prophetic utterances. But similarly in the New Testament:

'The preface to St Luke's Gospel breathes a different spirit from that in which St Paul wrote his Epistles. In the one authority speaks, in the other a patient collection of testimony. In the one we see the recipient of special revelations, who had been caught up into the third heaven, and who prophesied and spake with tongues more than all his contemporaries; in the other we see plain human care and research, dealing it is true with sacred things, but dealing with them on the side on which they become visible and tangible; setting down faithfully what had been heard and seen, and having its reward—but a reward appropriate to the gifts exercised and not one appropriate to a different set of gifts to which the writer made no claim.'

The conclusion is really absurd. It is indeed often enough the case that the unity of the Bible is destroyed. But it is to be doubted whether the principle of fragmentation has elsewhere ever been so formulated as to divide the New Testament between the Gospels and the Epistles, to give primacy to the Epistles over the Gospels, and to regard the authority of the Gospels as something derivative and secondary.

It follows that the inspiration of the Bible when commended on these grounds is something essentially different from what it is usually held to be, so that authority can only be ascribed to it in a truncated and ambiguous form. It appears that when the subject of inspiration is made the 'inspired individual', the inspiration does not effectively get past him to illuminate and authorize what he writes. Such authority as does infect what he writes is at best second-hand; and even within this second-hand authority, there are degrees of primacy which involve a surprising reassessment of some of the values usually accorded to different parts of Scripture. It would require very strong grounds indeed to make one think that the usual assessment is wrong and this new view right.

What are the conclusions to be drawn from this part of the argument? That veritable and remarkable experiences of inspiration are recorded in the Bible and connected with its writing need not be doubted. On the contrary, it would be an incredible thing if, when God confronts a man, his mind and heart were not 'strangely moved', and his faculties raised to an unusual pitch of intensity whether of perception or action. We have the record of many of these remarkable experiences in the Bible, and they are particularly evident in the prophets and in the early days of the Christian Church. And further: the Holy Spirit is certainly at work even where His presence is not disclosed by remarkable phenomena. There is a living in the Holy Spirit as well as a being aroused by His operation. In this sense, the remarkable examples of unusual operation are like outcrops of rock that rise above the waves as evidence of the continent hidden below the surface. Of this more tranquil, persistent and pervasive operation of the Holy Spirit, there is plenty of evidence in the Holy Scriptures. Nor can it rightly be denied the name of inspiration, even if it assume no striking form.

But when all this is admitted, it is not an answer to the question whether such inspiration is the real ground for the authority of the Bible. For one thing, this kind of inspiration differs in degree, and only those parts of the Bible in which the Holy Spirit is most powerfully at work would claim attention. For another thing, if it is the presence of the Holy Spirit even in no marked degree that is the basis of authority, then the whole of the Bible is returned to us—but alas! without any real compelling force. The presence of general or particular inspiration in its pages may indeed interest the enquirer, but on the other hand it may not. It may further give him the Bible as an 'inspiring' book. But on this basis there is no injunction and no compulsive reason to read it, if he finds he obtains 'inspiration' more readily elsewhere.

The fact is that there is need to invoke some other element if the authority of Scripture is to rest securely. We must enquire whether it is not something more objective than any experience, even the experience of an inspirational kind, that is to be looked for as the locus and source of authority. Then the Bible will not be commended because it records inspiration as such, or because it is more than usually inspiring; it

M

will be commended because of a more objective quality along-side inspiration and causally determining it.[1]

Full description of what this more objective factor is on which the authority of the Bible rests must await a later chapter. But it may be even now suggested that if we could understand the Scriptures in the sense in which Luther understood them, that they are the crib in which Christ is laid, we should immediately have a most adequate ground for reading the Bible and at the same time a sufficient cause for the inspiration which is both recorded and caused by Holy Scripture.

[1] See K. Barth: *Kirchliche Dogmatik*, I/2, 578: 'The Reformers saw and stated once more the fact that the inspiration of the Bible as inspiration by the Holy Spirit is not just any kind of miracle; nor is it comparable with any other alleged or real inspiration. For it rests on the relationship of the biblical witnesses to the very definite content of their witness. It is indeed this content that inspires them, i.e. which in their speaking and writing gave them a part in the Holy Spirit and therefore makes their writing Holy Scripture. It is not of itself, but—as Luther especially always insisted—of Christ as its Lord and King that Scripture has and again and again acquires for us its clarity as the divine Word.'

VI

Revelation in the Bible

Another reason is commonly advanced as a ground for reading the Bible, and as a basis on which the authority of Holy Scripture can rest. This consideration is that the Bible has to do with revelation, or, as it is often phrased, there is revelation in the Bible. On the one hand, those who claim to be Christians are not likely to contest the statement. The presence of divine revelation can be made out more clearly from the pages of the Bible itself than that of inspiration. Religion involves a relation of men with something other and more than men. In the setting up of this relation, God has some part to play. Even if religion be held to be chiefly discovery on the part of man, the result of intellectual speculation, or the reading off of the evidence afforded by the world around us, God is not necessarily thought of as inactive. He may be regarded as prompting the use of intellect to this end, of sanctioning the discovery of divine things, of leaving traces of His handiwork whose meaning men can read. This activity of God may still be called revelation. Christians hold that in addition to this so-called general revelation there is also special revelation. Special revelation they hold to be communicated by the Bible, and they search the Scriptures in order to appropriate and enjoy it. On the other hand, if there is divine revelation in the Scriptures, this is a strong reason why others who do not confess the Christian faith should read the Bible. The longing for God is indeed strangely compounded with distaste for God; but such as it is, it is not confined to Christians only. The Bible, if it contain divine revelation, may be commended to unbelievers. For both the conversion of the unbeliever and the edification of the faithful, reading of the Scriptures is salutary and commendable.

When the question is raised: what is it that is revealed?, different answers are possible. The Scriptures after all are writing, and writing consists in statements and judgments; and statements and judgments are the devices whereby information is usually conveyed. What more natural then than to suppose that the Scriptures convey information? This information is a certain and quite special kind of information. It is divine revelation that Scripture contains, and the information conveyed will therefore be information about things divine, information primarily about God. A persistent trend running through all Christian theology interprets the revelation contained by Scripture as being of this kind and as having the form of propositions about God. Thus early on, Athanasius says of Israel that it is 'the sacred school of the knowledge of God and of the spiritual life for all mankind'. The statement is satisfactory enough. Israel indeed looks like a school of learners, and the subject matter in which they are being instructed is quite well said to be knowledge of God. But the phrase, 'knowledge of God', is ambiguous. When it is interpreted in the light of the Bible, no objection can be taken. There is no higher end to be attained than the knowledge of God, as Scripture interprets it. 'This is life eternal, that they might know thee the only true God, and Jesus Christ whom thou hast sent' (John xvii. 3). The intention of the Gospel cannot be better summarized than in such words as these. But the knowledge referred to here has a quite special degree of intimacy. It is quite possible to know a whole lot of things about and concerning God, and yet to fall short of this knowledge. It is 'familiar knowledge', as Calvin would say—knowledge that is practically synonymous with communion or fellowship with God. It is the kind of knowledge that the men of the Old Testament have in mind, when God is said to know the way of the righteous, in contrast to that of the wicked.[1]

But it is just as possible to interpret Athanasius' phrase in another way, which the Bible does not so clearly support. Then knowledge in the familiar sense vanishes, and is replaced by a more intellectual conception, in which the sense of communion or fellowship disappears and the relation is between subject knowing and object known. What is revealed in this

[1] Ps. i. 6.

sense of knowledge is truths conveyed in propositions about this object.

Illustrating this conception of knowledge, Harnack[1] writes: 'Take the people of Israel and search the whole history of their religion; take history generally, and where will you find any message about God and the good that was ever so pure and so full of strength—for purity and strength go together— as we hear and read in the Gospels?' Both Old Testament and New Testament for Harnack contain a *message about God*, and it is in this that revelation consists. The best and most reliable information concerning God is to be found in the New. There is irony in the fact that Harnack should write in this strain—Harnack who emphasizes that Christianity fell from grace in early days, when it allowed itself to be pervaded by Greek conceptions. Nothing could be more characteristic- ally Greek than the sentiment expressed in Harnack's words, that the gospel is a message about God, that revelation is composed of statements concerning deity, that what we have in the gospel is a disclosure of eternal verities declared and promulgated by a personality of remarkable powers.

Again, the Roman Church thinks of revelation as primarily composed of propositions, and of Scripture as doctrines neces- sary to salvation.[2] 'By religion', says *The Catholic Commentary*,[3] 'we mean a system of beliefs concerning the divinity and of man's duties in regard thereto. . . . If it is based on knowledge communicated by God to man in some way outside the work- ing of ordinary providence, it is called revealed religion.' The view recurs repeatedly throughout the volume: 'divine Tradi- tion' is 'the body of revealed truth handed down from the apostles through the ages and contained in the doctrine, teach- ing and practice of the Catholic Church'. These statements are typical of Roman theology.

A more general illustration of revelation being regarded as truths expressed in statements may be given.

'The early Christians, the Christians of the Middle Ages, and the Reformers, despite all differences were at one in re- garding Scripture as a revelation in the form of propositions. It entered no one's head to doubt that God's truth was

---

[1] *What is Christianity?*, 51f.
[2] See Chapter IV, and *A Catholic Commentary on Holy Scripture*.
[3] §104b.

revealed to men in a series of guaranteed propositions, literally inspired and infallible.'[1]

The statement is not accurate: it is impossible to class all these Christian believers together as holding one undifferentiated propositional view of Scripture. What is true is that Christians are always in danger of relapsing into this view. The quotation at least bears witness to the recurrent appearance of this propositional view of revelation.

But the biblical interpretation of knowledge of God has overtones which are quite lost when the knowledge is construed thus intellectually. Kittel[2] points out that it is a Greek and not a biblical idea that revelation is connected with 'that which is for all time', namely the eternal verities. The essence of the biblical idea lies elsewhere: revelation is an event.

If revelation does not consist of propositions, of what does it consist? and what does it convey? The other strain which runs side by side with the propositional view, is that revelation consists not in the communication of truths about God, but in the disclosure of God. God reveals Himself, not merely information about Himself. Kittel in the article just mentioned assumes almost without argument that God is the subject of revelation. Revelation is used in the Bible to mean the suspension of God's characteristic hiddenness, and the bestowal of Himself in communion.[3] This amounts to linguistic corroboration of the difference suggested already between the biblical view and the propositional view of revelation. When the biblical writers use the term 'revelation', what they primarily mean is, not that they are made participants of some esoteric information about deity, but that they are taken up into fellowship with deity; not that certain puzzles concerning God's nature are resolved, but rather that the distance between God and men is annihilated and men drawn into communion with God. The biblical conception of the knowledge of God implies a familiar and even intimate relationship with Him.

If it is this that happens when the Bible is rightly used, it is clearly a matter of cardinal importance. How does it happen?

---

[1] John Lowe, in *The Interpretation of the Bible*, 108f.
[2] *Theologisches Wörterbuch zum neuen Testament*, article *kalupto*, A. Oepke, 578.
[3] Op. cit., 575.

What we have or seem to have in the Bible is a record of other people's experience of God. Taking the Old Testament, we have in it the record of the religious experience of the men who figure in its pages. We have accounts of how Abraham felt called by God, of how Moses is commissioned to lead his people out of Egypt, of how in the eighth century a singular succession of men of the greatest personal power and integrity were moved by God to address their people, condemning their faults and pointing out what God required of them. Later the same story is taken up by others, who familiarly speak of the comfort and consolations of God for a people hard put to it to understand the series of shattering blows that had disrupted their national life and bereft them of the homeland in which they and their fathers before them had been accustomed to worship God. What can it mean to us of today that these men enjoyed this remarkable religious experience which is recorded for us in the Old Testament? Similarly, when we come to the New Testament, we find there the record of the birth, life, death and resurrection of Jesus Christ, carefully compiled by the writers of the Gospels. Further, we have in a series of letters the interpretation of this life that had been lived amongst men, and this is applied to the case of those to whom the letters were written. Finally, there is the last book of the New Testament, itself called Revelation, which consists of the record of a religious experience of an unusual though not unique kind, in which the writer tries to convey the meaning of the facts of the Christian faith as it will be finally disclosed when the history of the world is brought to its end and the consummation takes place. Again the question emerges: what can it mean to men of the twentieth century that Jesus Christ lived in the first century a life of unique quality? What is it to us that men found themselves brought into a relation of reconciliation with God by laying hold in faith of this same Jesus Christ? Why should the record of their knowledge of God be anything more to us than a record of what men in a past age experienced concerning the goodness and mercy of God? Merely to read this record is an edifying experience. But is it more? Can the idea that the Bible is revelation make it any more?

It is commonly held that, if there is revelation in Scripture, we find it clearest and most distinct in the New Testament in the life and person of Jesus Christ. There we have 'the fulness of the godhead bodily', as St Paul himself puts it.[1] The testimony of Hebrews is just as clear:[2] 'God who at sundry times and in divers manners spake in time past unto the fathers by the prophets, hath in these last days spoken unto us by his Son.' The dominical words point to the same conclusion, as in the parable of the husbandman in the far country who sends various messengers to his stewards in the vineyard, and finally determines 'they will reverence my son'.[3] Oblique testimony to the same purpose is provided by the practice of Christian believers: if anyone is asked what part of the Bible he is most accustomed to read, the answer is almost invariably that it is the New Testament, and perhaps in particular the Gospels. All this testifies to a real and incontestable fact: it is in the New Testament, or what is the same thing, in Jesus Christ, that we have the clearest revelation of God.

The way in which this is often explained is in terms of 'progressive revelation', and this interpretation of the facts must be examined. Can we find here a solid foundation for biblical authority? It is possible to dismiss one way in which progressive revelation is conceived. G. F. Phillips[4] gives as good a summary of this way as any. It is the interpretation that holds that 'God gave to his prophets one idea (only partly true), then another (rather more true), and then another until the idea of a pure monotheism was reached at last'. This Phillips condemns as an 'absurd suggestion'. And indeed it is so. Similarly, H. H. Rowley[5] notes that 'there are some who would maintain that what is superseded in the Old Testament represents what was the authoritative will of God for men of the particular age and in the particular circumstances at the time when it was given, and who find God to be wholly responsible for every statement found in the Bible. That this is not satisfying is clear from the fact that conceptions of God which fall below the standards of the highest in the Old Testament are found in some passages, and it cannot be that the God who revealed Himself deliberately gave men false ideas about Himself'; and the example is given of how Samuel believed God delighted in the 'wholesale and unprovoked massacre' recorded in 1 Sam. xv. 3. But revelation is in any case wrongly conceived when thought of merely in terms of propositions, as

---

[1] Col. ii. 9. [2] Heb. i. 1f. [3] Matt. xxi. 37.
[4] *The Old Testament in the World Church*, 48. [5] *The Unity of the Bible*, 14.

though revelation was no more than a series of statements, however true, about God. Revelation is not this, but rather the disclosing of God Himself by Himself. On this ground alone, this conception is inadequate. If we reverence the New Testament in a special degree, it is not merely because in it we have the very latest *communiqué* from the council chambers of the Almighty. It is rather because in it more clearly than anywhere else God permits us to enter into the knowledge of Himself.

But progressive revelation is not tied to this intellectual and propositional interpretation of its main thesis. It survives this criticism, to state itself in other terms. Granted that it is God who is the object (as well as the subject) of revelation, we look to the New Testament because there we have the head and crown, the summit and apex of a long process of growth. In the course of this growth, unworthy conceptions of God are stripped away, and the truth of God, or rather the truth that is God, becomes more and more apparent. There is something defective in the revelation of God which makes Him appear as willing, and indeed commanding, the 'slaughter of the Amalekites'.[1] Progressively such ideas of God are shed, and in the prophetic affirmation, that what God requires of men is 'to do justly, and to love mercy, and to walk humbly with thy God',[2] we have a much purer revelation of God. Finally, at the top of the long ascent, we have God revealed to us in Jesus Christ, the Father of His children, who commands them to love their enemies and Himself manifests the same divine quality, and 'while we were yet sinners, Christ died for us'. Here then are three clearly marked stages on the road of advance, and the stages are linked by the idea of progress. It is easy to excuse, if not to justify, the revelation of earlier days. God in revealing Himself must take account of the development of the men to whom He will reveal Himself: *quidquid recipitur recipitur ad modum recipientis*. It is only 'in the fulness of time', which means when men are ready for it, that the final revelation can be made.

Here is a view of the Bible which in modern days has become extraordinarily influential and widespread. It has afforded relief to untold numbers of believers vexed with the apparent difficulty of holding an authoritative conception of

---

[1] 1 Sam. xxx. 8, 17; 2 Sam. i. 1. [2] Micah vi. 8.

the Bible along with the results of critical research. It is therefore worthy of the greatest respect. Whether, however, it really succeeds in guaranteeing an authoritative Bible is more open to question. For the view involves several grave difficulties.

Even when the view has liberated itself from the idea that revelation consists in the communication of propositions, it still works with the idea that revelation is given in a series of instalments. It is not ideas progressively nearer the truth that God gives, but He does lift further and further the veil which hides Himself from men. There is no doubt on any view a difficulty in understanding how it comes about that God's revelation of Himself enters time and takes on the character of a more imperfect and then of a more nearly perfect self-disclosure. Ultimately too this fact must be attributed to God. But to attribute it in the direct way implied in this progressive view of revelation, seems to be very unhappy. It is hardly a worthy view of God which sees Him deliberately disclosing so much of Himself but withholding any more until a future time, pulling back the curtain as it were by inches. Through the enterprise of manufacturing and distributing firms, it has become possible to purchase almost anything by easy payments. But it has been left to the advocates of 'progressive revelation' to suggest that man can have God on the instalment system. If we take seriously the fact that it is Himself that is revealed as the content of revelation, it is the whole of Himself that is the content of revelation. The fact that there is more imperfection and less imperfection in revelation must then be located elsewhere, not in what God does in revelation, but in the apprehension with which men receive His revelation. God is doing always and everywhere all He can, if we may put it so; and it is men in their receiving and recording of the revelation that are at fault. It is men in their finitude, and more exactly in their sinfulness, that introduce perversion into God's self-disclosure, or rather into the record they make of it. If so, it is their record of the revelation that can alone be rightly said to progress, not the revelation itself. Any true view of Scripture must hold that there is both a divine and a human element in it, just as any true view of Christ holds that He is both *kata sarka* and also *kata pneuma*.[1] The imperfection of the Bible is to be located in the human element and not in the

[1] Rom. i. 3f.

divine element, in the human recording of revelation and not in the revelation itself. God is not Himself distorted when He enters space and time in order to disclose Himself, so that later correction has to be made. It is men under conditions of space and time, and especially of human sinfulness, that pervert what He does and says to them.

Further, there is some truth in the rubric that *quidquid recipitur recipitur ad modum recipientis*. But it is easy to misconstrue this truth. It is misconstrued when it is thought that the capacity of the recipient is absolutely determinant of the situation, and that it can ever be entirely suited to what is communicated in revelation. The fact is, and all Scripture bears witness to it, that it is by God that God is known. God Himself must provide the conditions under which He is really apprehended. 'The natural man receiveth not the things of the Spirit of God';[1] this is reserved for the spiritual man— precisely the man in whose heart God has preveniently been at work. 'God through Himself we then shall know', as Charles Wesley's hymn has it.[2] There is no doubt a mystery here. Why does God effectively work in the heart of one man to make of him a believer, and not effectively in the heart of another and thus leave him in unbelief? It is a very real dilemma. But it is not a negotiable way of escape to make the difference depend on the conditions and capacities which a man can bring. Let us suppose that there is real progress in civilization and culture, and in the intellectual and other powers that men possess. It cannot really be supposed that God must wait for this development in order to reveal Himself. It follows that no advance of the things which we rightly suppose are subject to development can ever provide the conditions required for the revelation of God to be more perfectly bestowed. Men bring with them when confronted by God a certain apparatus of capacities and categories of thought. It will be in terms of this apparatus that they will record and apply what happens to them in this confrontation. This record and application of revelation will then progress, if the apparatus itself progresses. But the revelation will remain the self-same revelation of the self-same God. When we are invited to find in the Bible the revelation of God, we are not to look for it in the record and

---

[1] 1 Cor. ii. 14.
[2] From 'Come, Holy Ghost, our hearts inspire', *Church Hymnary*, 196.

application of this revelation, but in the revealing action of God to which both record and application are only the witness and testimony.

But the capital error of the idea of progressive revelation has still to be mentioned. The idea implies positively that more of the same thing is given at the end of the process than at the beginning; and negatively that when the more is given, the earlier and the less is superseded and may rightly be discarded. Progress in other words implies a continuous path of development, along which is strewn all the jettisoned waste of the earlier and less developed. For it is one of the principles of progress that, when the later and better appears, the earlier and worse is simply set aside. Of course, what is thus jettisoned in the march of progress has its own interest—but it is an interest that appeals to the antiquarian, who wishes to reconstruct the path by which the latest and the highest has come about. Applying this to the matter in hand, if the best and highest revelation of God is to be found in Jesus Christ, all that goes before Him, though it possesses this antiquarian interest, is deprived of living reality and relevance. I may indeed turn to the pages of the Old Testament; but they cannot mean anything to me, apart from any incidental interest I may have in the road that has led to the highest and the best. The Old Testament then is relegated to the sphere of *Religionsgeschichte*, and has no intrinsic religious message for us in our day.

In Jesus Christ there is the fullest revelation of God; and it has already been admitted that the believer will turn more readily to the New Testament than to the Old. But the idea of progressive revelation proves too much at this point. It not only accounts for the ordinary man's greater interest in the New Testament, but wholly justifies him in preoccupation with it to the exclusion of the Old. If Jesus Christ is the summit and apex of the process, there is no reason why he should not concentrate his attention wholly upon the New Testament, leaving the study of the Old Testament to those who happen to be interested in the rise and development of Christianity. If this is a just implication to draw, it is difficult to see why the Church reacted so vigorously against the views of Marcion; and Harnack is right when he advocates the dismissal of the Old Testament from the serious consideration of Christians.

If we already have the better, why bother with the worse? It is thus a severely mutilated Bible that survives, and with a much diminished authority.

Something has gone wrong if this is the conclusion to which one is led. It is usually with a bad conscience that Christians admit indifference to the Old Testament. And on this view, it is unintelligible that the Christian Church should have held to the Old Testament as the Word of God as consistently as to the New. Nor is it easy to understand the profound interest which the writers of the New Testament display in relating Jesus Christ to the Old Testament. It is salutary to remember that when a real attack is mounted against Christianity, as in pre-war Germany, one of the first moves in the campaign is to deprecate the Old Testament and its use by Christians.

It is not to be denied that the Bible records a process in revelation. But the process is not from the less to the more developed but from promise to fulfilment. Thus Heb. xi. 39f. says that 'these all, having obtained a good report through faith, received not the promise', that is the fulfilment of the promise; 'God having provided some better thing for us, that they without us should not be made perfect'. Time for the Bible is not a continuum in which through progress an earlier and worse is succeeded by a later and better. However true this may be in some fields, it is not true of the revelation to which the Bible witnesses. Time is rather the order in which God grants fulfilment to promise, realization to prophecy. If there is 'some better thing' which we have and the men of the Old Testament lack, it is not simply the final stretch of the road along which they went. Promise does not develop into fulfilment; fulfilment is a different thing, though, of course, it has relation to what has gone before. Nor does prophecy simply become realized by development or progress; it must wait till fulfilment and realization is accorded to it. The 'better thing' which the New Testament gives to Christians is not just more of the same kind as before; it belongs to a different category.

Revelation is then in two chapters, and the first chapter does not simply develop into the second. Could we then say that, despite this, there is in fact a parallelism between the process of progress and the process of promise-fulfilment? Could we affirm that as men advanced God's revelation is eventually

realized and fulfilled? Apart from what has already been said
about the inability of any advance on man's part to fit him
for the further revelation of God, there is another insuperable
difficulty. This would be to try to fit what is a series of distinct
actions on to a supposed continuity, and anything like exact
coincidence in such a case is impossible.

The fact is that when we talk of progressive revelation we
are trying to naturalize God. We so bring Him into the natural
process, that we deny Him sovereign intervention. The Old
Testament does not simply become the New Testament. Two
actions of God are rather to be recognized: God gives the
promise, and to that promise He also gives fulfilment. Both
actions are moments in the whole process of redemption. But
they are each entirely real moments, so that the earlier does
not simply merge imperceptibly into the later by means of
progress.

Further, the distinction here implied means not that the
New Testament abrogates the Old, but that each constitutes
a relevant reality in its own right and of its own kind. There
is no fulfilment in the Old Testament, and there is no promise
(of the Old Testament kind) in the New.[1] Each is of its kind
complete and perfect; and neither therefore can be superseded
by the other.

There is of course a uniting bond between the Old Testa-
ment and the New. Jesus Christ is the uniting bond. This is
to anticipate what will later have to be said. The men of the
Old Testament have Jesus Christ in promise; the men of the
New Testament have Jesus Christ in fulfilment. God reveals
Himself in the Old Testament; and if He does so at all, He
does so savingly; and if He does so savingly He does so as
Jesus Christ, for all that it is Jesus Christ as pre-incarnational.
God reveals Himself differently in the New Testament, though
not of course without relation to the Old Testament, in the
incarnate Jesus.

There is a residual question. If progressive revelation does
not stand up to the criticism that can be urged against it, does
anything remain of the thesis? It has to be allowed that *something* progresses, even if this something is not revelation as such.
What then is it? The answer is that progress belongs to the

---

[1] This is a very summary statement; but it may stand until the last chapter
is reached.

record of and witness to revelation in which the Bible consists. Here record must be taken in a wide and comprehensive sense. The fundamental conception is that God keeps up a sustained pressure upon men. This does not vary in progressive fashion, though it does include the two distinguishable moments of the old and the new covenants. 'Saving history is God's institution of revelation, which takes human development into account, but is not itself the product of development.'[1] But close by there is the variable and progressive factor. What does vary is the way in which men upon whom the pressure is brought to bear have responded to it. The revelation seen through the prism of this factor does display a 'divine economy'.[2] Here is the sphere in which it is possible[3] to distinguish between 'child-like' and 'mature' elements in the Scriptures.

This response is compounded of two distinguishable factors, though the distinction between them is not always easy to make. These factors consist of the way in which men have *understood* the pressure of God's revelation and the way in which they have *applied* what they understood.[4] One or two examples, taken almost at random, may clarify the situation. First, men's understanding of the revelation: the whole Bible records a remarkable insight into the character and qualities of God. Among these God's righteousness (meaning by this in the present context, God's perpetual and implacable concern for men's being right with Himself) is constant and outstanding. But there is alteration—or, one may say, progress— in the way in which this righteousness was understood by the men on whom it impressed itself as an inalienable characteristic of God. The man who not only urges God to remember the savagery of his enemies, but even allowed himself the outburst: 'Happy shall he be, that taketh and dasheth thy little ones against the stones' (Ps. cxxxvii. 7, 9), knows a good deal about God's concern that His children be right with Him; but he represents it in a form supplied by the bitterness of his soul, and so interprets it differently from the writer of Isa. liii. The

---

[1] Brunner: *Revelation and Reason*, 291.   [2] Op. cit., 134.
[3] As Eichrodt, qtd. op. cit., 292, n.34.
[4] The importance of the idea of application is suggested by Sanday: *Inspiration*, 396, etc. 'Religion consists not only in the knowledge of God and of His will, but in the realization of that knowledge in the heart and conscience, in its effect upon conduct, and in its recognition by acts of worship and praise.' It is this second component to which he gives the name 'applied revelation'.

writers of the Old Testament rightly apprehend this chief characteristic of God that He is a God who saves. But their interpretation of this insight is not uniform, and the covenantal relations involved in Exodus are expressly contrasted with those implied by the 'new covenant' of Jer. xxxi. 31-33.

Secondly, men's application of the content of revelation: changes of a relative kind take place in the way in which the men of the Bible apply what they know and learn in the act of God's revelation of Himself to them. In the cult, for example, the ark that served them well in the days of nomadism is replaced by a temple at Jerusalem soon after the people take up a more settled manner of life. It is not an unimportant thing that such variations as this should be present in the Bible: they witness to the fact that God's revealing activity is not suspended as one age succeeds another, and this is true even when the pre-scientific age gives way to the scientific age, or the atomic era supervenes on the pre-atomic. The circumstances may alter, but the activity of God remains fundamentally the same. A similar kind of identity in difference is to be observed in connection with the worshipper himself. There is a sense in which men of every age are basically the same, for all the differences that superficially catch the eye. Whether in the twentieth century B.C. or the twentieth century A.D., they bring a certain basic equipment to the business of living which does not alter much as the years pass. This is true in the case of religion, as in more material matters. Here too they bring with them a certain basically unchanged apparatus which they employ in their religious activities, whether it be in the time of Abraham or that of nuclear fission. It is an apparatus further which those who stand within the *Heilsgeschichte* represented by the Old and New Testaments, have in common with the men of other religions. But this same apparatus is differently employed. There is identity and there is difference between the ritual of animal sacrifice, the primitiveness (or more probably the retrogression) of human sacrifice, and the offertory at Christian Divine Service. Within the Bible itself, there is identity and difference between what Solomon did (2 Chron. viii. 4f.) at the dedication of the temple and what Micah demands should be offered (Mic. vi. 8). The forms in which religion appears in these examples differ. The later may be said in some sense to be an advance on the earlier, and so to constitute an absolute advance. But there is little ground here on which to base the idea of progress in revelation.

There is also a development which may be regarded as absolute, in the sense that, once it is achieved, there can be no return to the earlier form without spiritual or moral defect. The application of God's saving purpose is seen to be in process of extension in the course of the Bible. It is idle to suppose that the declaration of the splendid range of God's salvation as made by Isaiah (xlv. 22): 'Look unto me, and be ye saved, all the ends of the earth; for I am God, and there is none else', could have been made by Moses as he extricated Israel from the clutches of Pharaoh and led them towards a 'promised land' whose occupants were to be forcibly extruded. But it is just as idle to suppose that it is the purpose of God that thus achieves extension. Men's understanding of the purpose and their record of it, but not the purpose itself, is the subject of development.

Similarly too it must be allowed that there is a real intensive advance observable in the Bible, as the moral demands implied by revelation unfold themselves. The men of the Bible find themselves obliged to apply their religion more radically to their personal and social life. Thus Amos's demands for personal and social justice achieve a new level of urgency just as they reach an unprecedented degree of intensity. The right interpretation of what is happening here cannot be that God is for the first time making these demands upon His people. Nor even can it be true that they have a quite unprecedented character only now being made plain to men. The situation is in fact more complex. What happens is rather that the pressure of the presence of God already carries with it an obligation of at least an incipiently moral character, that men fall and know that they fall short of even what they know to be required by Him of them, that the prophet is himself recalled, and in turn recalls his people, to a realization of their wrong, and that in so doing he achieves a new degree of insight into the application of the implacable demands made upon those who have to do with God. It is in this way that progress takes place. That God is at work here cannot be doubted. In a wide sense it is true that God is ultimately responsible for the *modus recipientis*. But His responsibility is personal responsibility and so permissive and evocative of man's own responsibility. The two are distinguishable and God may not be drawn down into and identified with the progress observable in human response. No point to point correspondence is possible between what God does and what man does in response, so long as man continues to be a sinner.

Yet without the pressure that God maintains, there could be no advance at all. Here the biological analogy is more appropriate than often: God seeking communion with His children and exposing them to the ceaseless pressure of His presence, constitutes an environmental factor which does not fail to elicit some kind of response. God evokes what progress there is. The spirit of man is sufficiently transcendent of what simply is, to know, when two ideas compete with one another in the mind, which is the higher and the better. This is indeed no guarantee of obedience to or conformity with the higher and the better. There is a certain appreciation of what should be; the defect manifests itself elsewhere, in a 'collapse in the hour of performance', to use Gladstone's famous phrase. Even here we have to remind ourselves that 'it is not to be supposed that development was brought about by the unfolding of the human spirit through the mere passage of time. There is no automatic spiritual growth of mankind'.[1] What is thus precariously gained may with dreadful ease be lost.

One cannot resist the conclusion that the fundamental misunderstanding of those who advocate progressive revelation lies in the fact that they identify revelation with the Bible. Then it becomes inevitable that the progress which they rightly discern in the Bible should be immediately ascribed to revelation. But the Bible is not simply and directly revelation, but only the witness to revelation, which God for His purposes takes to be the instrument for revealing Himself anew. Abraham is called not by a God who has only parsimoniously revealed Himself, but by the same God and Father of our Lord Jesus Christ, who then operates under the dispensation of promise, and now under that of fulfilment. If Samuel thinks God pleased with actions that now seem plainly immoral, it is not because God bestows an erroneous revelation of Himself, but because Samuel interprets the undoubted righteousness of the same God in accordance with principles

[1] H. H. Rowley: *The Unity of the Bible*, 7.

that belonged to the wild and savage time in which he lived. And turning to the other term in the relationship of revelation, there is indeed an advance in revelation, and a very real advance it is. But its nature has to be understood. The difference between Abraham and Samuel on the one hand and St Peter and St Paul on the other is not a difference between lower and higher degrees of revelation; it is the difference between a dispensation of promise and one of fulfilment. This is effected not by the bestowal of the latest instalment of revelation, but by the decisive action of the ever-revealing, ever-saving God. The record, the application and the intellectual receptivity of revelation may progress; but it is not in the power of such progress to contrive an incarnation.

For us of today this has an immediate relevance. The whole process of salvation is constituted by promise and fulfilment. I find the promise in the Old Testament, and I find this promise's fulfilment in the New. The promise is not to be found except in the Old Testament, nor is the fulfilment anywhere but in the New Testament. Hence for the exposition of the whole redeeming activity of God, both Old Testament and the New are necessary. But for this redeeming activity, it is not the process of the revelation that is of great importance, but chiefly and indeed solely the object that is revealed. And this is Jesus Christ.

VII

The Theology of the Word

I. BARTH

In the Preface to the 1st edition of his *Kirchliche Dogmatik*, I/1,[1] Barth says:

> 'If I look back at the way I have travelled, I seem to be like someone groping his way up the steps of a church tower, who clutches, instead of the stair rail, a rope, which happens to be the bell-rope; and to his alarm, he and others also hear the great bell above audibly struck. He had not wished to do this, but he neither can nor wishes to undo it. Greatly moved by the occurrence, he continues his ascent.'

What is it in Barth's theology which aroused such marked and unexpected attention? We should not be far wrong in saying that it was the new seriousness with which it deals with the Bible. The theology of the Word is appropriately named, if only because it attempts with unusual strenuousness to elicit from the Scriptures what they contain, and to base upon them what it ventures to say. But this is not the only reason. Barthianism has by no means attracted everyone. If we are to take seriously what Barth himself says, it is not attractive even to him. A recent expression of this appears in the Preface to Weber's useful compendium of the *Dogmatik*:[2] 'If there are "Barthians", then I am not one of them.' But a great many people will gladly allow that Barth and Brunner have done much to restore the Bible in its greatness, and, in contrast to much prevalent thought, have made what it says appear more

---

[1] ix.
[2] Otto Weber: *Karl Barth's Church Dogmatics*—an introductory report on Vols. I/1-III/4, Preface to the German edition, 9.

likely to be true than false. This, at a time when there was so much loose thinking about the Bible, and when even the best work of the critics seemed rather to diminish than enhance its authority, has been an immense and signal service to theology.

Barth sets forth his view of Scripture and scriptural authority in two long sections in the *Kirchliche Dogmatik*, I/1, ch. 1, and I/2, chh. 3 and 4.[1] Each section makes its approach to the subject in its own way, and the difference of approach is significant. In the first section, the Bible is treated almost incidentally. The Word of God assumes three forms: the Word of God as preached, the written Word of God, and the revealed Word of God; and the Bible is the second of these three forms. Throughout the chapter, it is the Word of God that is really the theme, and since it is the same Word of God that appears in all three forms, what is said about any one of the forms throws a light on the other forms. None of the three forms is independent of the others, and all are for the sake of the Word of God whose forms they are. The Bible does not stand alone in any sense, but subserves the Word of God. It is one of the means or organs by which the Word of God operates. In the second section, Holy Scripture is treated directly, but only after a chapter entitled 'The Revelation of God', in which three parts deal in turn with God as triune, the Incarnation, and the gift of the Spirit. This represents a notable departure from the tendency especially evident in Calvinism to set the doctrine of Holy Scripture prominently in the forefront. Barth's presentation makes it clear from the start that a clean break has been made with the tendency in Protestant Orthodoxy to identify revelation with Holy Scripture.

The written Word of God is flanked by the Word of God as preached and the revealed Word of God. By beginning with the Word of God as preached, Barth follows Luther in insisting that the Gospel is primarily proclamation. The Word of God implies a commission, 'God's positive behest' (100). From this follows a proclamation, that is 'man's language about God on the basis of an indication by God Himself fundamentally transcending all human causation, and so devoid of

---

[1] References to *K.D.*, I/1, are given as in the English translation, to *K.D.*, I/2, as in the German.

all human basis' (101). It implies further an object or datum;
for proclamation is a 'proclamation about something, a relevant assertion or proclamation of a real object' (101). This
real object is God's own self-objectification which is real 'solely
in the freedom of His grace, in virtue of which from time to
time He wills to be the object of this language, and is so
according to His own good pleasure' (102). The Word of God
further implies a judgment. It carries its own criterion with
it, and the assurance that it is true. Finally, the Word of God
is 'the event itself, in which proclamation becomes real proclamation' (104).

The divine character of what happens as the Word of God
becomes the event in which God speaks, however, by no means
obliterates the humanness of the proclamation. On the contrary, 'as Christ became true man and also remains true man
to all eternity, so real proclamation becomes an event on the
level of all other events' (105), and can only in this way be
seen and heard. Characteristically Barth makes the point that
to set the human over against the divine as though they were
competitors and rivals and what is given to one is automatic-
ally stolen from the other is to misconstrue the situation. 'Between God and the true service of God there can be no rivalry.
The service of God need not be omitted in order that God
Himself may come to honour it' (105). The man who proclaims brings into the act himself, his volition and all his
faculties, and the execution is wholly his; yet God of His free
grace does not disdain to make that which is humanly and
hence ambiguously done His own Word. Proclamation 'through
the new robe of righteousness thrown over it' thus becomes 'in
this its earthly character a fresh event, the event of God speaking in the sphere of human events' (106). 'Real proclamation
as this new event, in which the event of human language
about God is not set aside, but rather exalted, is the Word of
God.' Man's speaking about God becomes that 'in which and
through which God Himself speaks about Himself'.

Two features of the Word of God as preached characterize
also the Word of God as written. Holy Scripture is distinguishable from the Word of God and subserves it. It too, like
proclamation, is the occasion on which the event-of-the-Word-
of-God occurs. Moreover, just as the human character of proclamation, so far from being lost, is necessarily retained, so

with the Bible: room is not only allowed for the humanness of Holy Scripture; the fact is that the Bible cannot become the Word of God by leaving out its human character, but only by bringing its human character into the service of the Word of God and thereby constituting the double-sided event which occurs when God Himself speaks of Himself.

The place and nature of this written Word of God, however, is further defined in relation to proclamation. The enterprise of proclamation is ventured upon only in recollection of past revelation and in expectation of future revelation (110). Not that this basis is dual, for of course revelation whether recollected or expected is the same revelation of the same God. This is the form in which the Bible affirms that insight into a discernible pattern is basic for the understanding of Holy Scripture and its authority. That there has been revelation is the essential lynchpin in the whole structure. The question arises concerning the nature of the recollection of this revelation. It might have been, Barth says, laid up for us, as it were, within human nature itself, and so taken the form of a 'timeless essential state of man himself, namely his relationship to the eternal or absolute'. Proclamation would then have been a process of anamnesis: by 'heart-searching', a neglected or hidden part of human nature would be rediscovered and forthwith unfolded. But in fact the matter has been contrived differently. For the recollection which lies at the basis of proclamation, the Church has to turn not inwards upon the hidden depths of man's nature, but outwards to something quite distinct from human nature, in which nevertheless the Church finds its proper being, namely to Jesus Christ its heavenly head. As the Church looks outwards to the transcendent (if also immanent) fact of Jesus Christ for its true being, so its proclamation is correlated to an objective fact or entity different from itself and superior to it. This entity is Holy Scripture (113). This Scripture is 'the bolt here actually thrust home against the Platonic anamnesis'. And as it excludes 'heart-searching', so too it regulates what the proclamation is to be: 'simply, in the first place, by being there and telling us what God's past revelation, which we have to recollect, already is', it offers a canon or rule.

It is to be noted how closely Holy Scripture and proclamation are here linked. Scripture is 'proclamation in writing'

(114). Of course, Scripture is also from another angle a 'historical document'; but its essence consists in the fact, not that it is an ancient relic of past days, but that it is a 'Church document' and declares in writing the same thing as proclamation declares in speech. And Scripture and preaching are

'entities that stand side by side within one genus: there Scripture as the beginning, here the preaching to be carried out today, as the continuation of one and the same event; Jerusalem and Paul at the beginning, the preacher of the Gospel today at the end of one and the same series' (114).

Luther is quoted[1] in a passage that declares that 'we parsons and preachers are to our time what John the Baptist was to his. We let John the Baptist's finger point and his voice ring forth: "behold the Lamb of God, that taketh away the sin of the world".' There is a fundamental likeness between what Scripture does and is and what preaching does and is: both witness to objective fact. There is also a fundamental unlikeness, since in the series there is a succession and hence a priority or hierarchy. It is a dissimilarity not of preaching or proclamation from Scripture, but rather of the proclamation preached or written by the prophets and apostles from all other human words. Barth thus links the prior and uniquely normative role of Holy Scripture with the prior and uniquely normative role of prophet and apostle.

Holy Scripture thus offers a standard for all succeeding proclamation. It is norm, as the antecessor has priority in the series over the successor. Hence the necessity for the proclamation of the antecessor to be fixed in writing. In this way, 'he being dead yet speaketh', and his written word exercises free power over the Church (117). It is true that the norm or standard might have been given to the Church by God in the form of an oral tradition, passed from mouth to mouth and from spirit to spirit without the intervention or aid of a written document. A spiritual-oral tradition might quite well have been providentially preserved within the life of the Church. It is further true that this has sometimes been supposed to be the case. Papias is cited, in a phrase which marks the beginning of this deviation, as declaring the superiority of the 'living and lasting voice' over books. This is taken up in the second century:

[1] Serm. on Matt. xi. 2f., E., I. 159.

'the "aliveness" is now no longer sought and found in the written word of the apostles themselves, but in the "voice" of such contemporaries as had themselves known the apostles, and this "living and lasting 'voice' " is now already given the advantage over the "books", i.e. the apostolic writings'.

Karl Adam is quoted as fulfilling this line of thought, when he contrasts the 'dead Word' of the Bible with the 'vitality' of Church tradition, as we have already seen. The fact, however, is that the normative function is allotted to no such contemporary voice discernible in ecclesiastical tradition, but to a written word. As such Holy Scripture confronts and addresses the Church as an 'inexorable authority'. There is indeed place for spiritual-oral tradition within the Church; but it represents the Church 'engaged in dialogue with itself', and lacks accordingly the objective authority of Holy Scripture.

A warning is issued against another not dissimilar way in which the authority of Scripture is always being menaced. Scripture is a 'concrete authority', a free power, and a 'norm which magisterially confronts the Church'. Scripture has, however, to be understood, and hence must always be expounded. It is by means of exegesis that Scripture is 'in a process of continual incorporation into the life, thought, and language of the Church'. But herein lies a danger, that the exposition which incorporates Scripture into the life of the Church should annul its normative character. 'All exegesis may become predominantly an imposition instead of an exposition, and to that extent deteriorate into a dialogue of the Church with itself.' In this way once again, the only result would be that Holy Scripture would lose its objective authority, and the voice with which it speaks would be smothered and not expressed by what the Church was saying. The Church, attempting to control the Bible, in fact silences it. The remedy Barth suggests is that 'Bible exegesis should rather be left open on all sides, not, as this demand was put by Liberalism, for the sake of free-thinking, but for the sake of a free Bible' (119).

There remains a further decisive question: how does it come about 'that the prophetic and apostolic Word in particular takes up this normative position over against the Church and its proclamation' (120)? The same question is put when it is asked: 'What makes the Bible of the Old and New Testaments

in particular into the canon?' At this point the only answer
that Barth gives to this most important question is that 'the
Bible constitutes itself the canon. . . . The Bible is the canon
just because it is so.' To specify any more closely what it is in
the Bible that gives it this unique and authoritative place
would be to act as if 'we had a measure in our hands with
which we were in a position to measure the Bible'. Again putting the matter slightly differently, Barth allows himself to say
that the Church's experience operates here:

> 'the Church's recollection of God's past revelation has
> computed (*ausgerechnet*) that the Bible is its object, because,
> as a matter of fact, this and no other object is the promise
> of future divine revelation, which can make her proclama-
> tion a duty upon the Church and give her the courage and
> the joy of this duty'.

This is simply a roundabout way of saying that the Church
has found that God makes the *record* of past revelation the
occasion of present revelation.

It is difficult to assess this definition of what in the Bible
constitutes it an authority. The argument is circular, but it
cannot be rejected for this reason alone. In a sense the Bible
must always bring with it its own 'universe of discourse', and
by the standards it supplies it demands to be judged. But the
circle suggested here is unduly narrow. It is true that the
judgment of the Church is the determining factor in the fix-
ing of a canon and the recognition of its normative authority.
But some more objective factors are also at work, for example
real or supposed apostolicity, and they supplement substantially the formal verdict that the 'Bible imposes itself as norm'.

What Barth goes on to say carries the matter further, but
hardly strengthens the position. The content of Holy Scripture must be taken into account. What distinguishes the Bible
from the Church engaged in dialogue with itself is its objective content: 'the prophetic apostolic Word is the word, the
witness, the proclamation and the preaching of Jesus Christ'
(121). This is of course incontestably true. But there are other
books that also speak about Jesus Christ and witness to Him;
and as preaching is the continuation of proclamation, and the
preacher of today of the series begun by prophets and apostles,
so these books are a continuation of the process of the written

Word. The first term of the series has a certain uniqueness. But when the question of the nature of this uniqueness is raised, we get here no clear answer: for it is no answer simply to fall back upon what was earlier said.

'Thus it is in virtue of this its content that Scripture imposes itself. Scripture of this—really this—content is, in contradistinction to other scriptures, Holy Scripture. Where the Church heard this word—it heard it in the prophets and apostles and nowhere else—it heard a magisterial, a final word which it could never again confuse or place on a level with any other word.'

But both the Epistle to the Hebrews and the Epistle to Diognetus speak about Jesus Christ; why then does the canon include one and exclude the other? Scripture has not been marked off clearly enough from other written proclamation by appealing solely to the 'experience' of the Church; and we have to wait till later for definition of what it is in the 'content' of Scripture that gives it authority.

The consideration of this second of the three forms which the Word of God assumes ends by emphasizing again that 'the Bible is God's Word so far as God lets it be His Word, so far as God speaks through it'; and real proclamation is the Word of God in 'exactly the same sense' (123). The emphasis falls here upon God's freedom in action. Barth decisively breaks with the view of Protestant Orthodoxy at this point. Lutheranism, Calvinism, the Schwenckfeldians and Quakers, he says, hold a doctrine of the *efficacia verbi divini etiam ante et extra usum*, 'to the effect that a divine power belonged to the Word of God proclaimed and written, whatever its effect upon the hearer or the reader might be' (124). Barth reclaims for God Himself in the freedom of His grace this power and virtue. Against Quenstedt, he maintains that the Bible is an *instrumentum* requiring *novo motu et elevatione nova ad effectum ultra propriam suam naturalem virtutem producendum*; and against Hollaz, that the Word of God is not a *vis* or *potentia*, but rather an *actio*. 'The Bible therefore becomes God's Word in this event, and it is to its being in this becoming that the tiny word "is" relates, in the statement that the Bible is God's Word' (124).

This is one of the most significant merits of what Barth has to say about Scripture and its authority. God does not delegate even to Holy Scripture the virtue which He Himself exercises in making proclamation or the Scriptures His own Word. In this way the door is effectively shut against all bibliolatry. The Bible can never take the place of God. On the contrary, God retains in His own hands the *actio*, however regularly the Bible is taken by Him for His instrument. Men when they deal with the Bible are dealing with God if and as He wills that it be so. God is taken out of the deistic prison to which Protestant Orthodoxy consigned Him. This restored insight can no doubt be traced to the influence of the new personalist note which has affected both theology and philosophy since Kierkegaard. It is, Barth says (124), 'the Word of God who is a person'; and this is further emphasized in what follows (cf. 152f., 157).

Barth's treatment of the third form which the Word of God takes, as the revealed Word of God, may be more summarily dealt with. The Bible is attestation or witness, pointing away from itself and the experience of those who take it upon themselves to make the record of revelation, though the record does indeed contain a great deal of 'religious experience'. The Bible 'is not itself and in itself God's past revelation, just as the Church's proclamation also is not itself and in itself the expected future revelation. But the Bible speaking to us and heard by us as God's Word attests the past revelation'. It is 'not itself and in itself God's past revelation, but by becoming God's Word it attests God's past revelation and is God's past revelation in the form of attestation' (125). The writers of the Bible write about 'something else'. 'It is not themselves, and not, emphatically not, their own special experience of and relationship to God, that they wish to present to and urge upon the Church, but that something else by their own agency'. And here Barth uses the now famous illustration of the pointing finger of St John the Baptist in the Isenheimer triptych by Grünewald (126).

It follows that the Bible 'claims no authority for itself'; 'its witness amounts to letting the something else be the authority, itself and by its own agency' (126). 'Therefore we do the Bible a poor honour, and one unwelcome to it, when we directly identify it with this something else, with revelation itself.' The Bible and revelation *become* one in an event. *Deus dixit* and *Paulus dixit* are two different things, yet they *become* one thing.

'Precisely because, where the Word of God is an event, it is not two different things, but becomes one, we must maintain that it is not self-evident or intrinsically the same thing, that revelation is to be regarded primarily as the superior, the Bible primarily as the subordinate principle' (127f.).

Following Augustine, Barth compares the biblical witnesses with those 'hills from which, according to Ps. cxxi, cometh our help: not from the hills as such, but from the Lord who made heaven and earth'. Hence 'revelation is originally and immediately, what the Bible and Church proclamation are derivatively and mediately, God's Word'. They are God's Word by from time to time, in the freedom of God's grace, becoming God's Word; whereas 'revelation signifies the Word of God itself, the act of its utterance' (133). And again: 'revelation does not differ from the Person of Jesus Christ' (134).

The section goes on to emphasize the unity of the Word of God in the three forms which it assumes.

'The revealed Word of God we know only from the Scripture adopted by Church proclamation, or from Church proclamation based on Scripture. The written Word of God we know only through the revelation which makes proclamation possible, through the proclamation made possible by revelation. The proclaimed Word of God we know only by knowing the revelation attested through Scripture, or by knowing the Scripture which attests revelation'. If an analogy of the relations thus set forth is sought, it can be found in only one place: 'in unfolding the concept of revelation—the doctrine of the three-in-oneness of God' (136).

'For revelation, Scripture, and proclamation, we can substitute the divine "Person"-names of Father, Son, and Holy Spirit, and vice versa. But it is a unity of relation, not a unity of identity. The Reformers had a true insight into the dynamics of the mutual relationships between the three forms.'

In Orthodoxy, this insight is lost and its place taken by a 'freezing up of the connexion between Scripture and revelation'. This results in no real action taking place today. It is this tendency that has already been observed, noted and deplored.

The subsequent paragraphs of the chapter under review add several important points. First, 'God's Word means God speaks' (150). The term 'speaks' is not a mere symbol. Nor is it an intellectualization of something which in itself has really a different and perhaps unintelligible content.

> 'We might very well be of the private opinion that it would be better and nicer if God had not spoken and did not speak with such deliberate "intellectualism" and that it would be more appropriate to God if "God's Word" meant all sorts of different things, apart from the meaning "God speaks".'

But the facts of the case are different. 'The form in which reason communicates with reason, person with person, is language; so too when it is God's language' (152), though of course in this case it is 'divine reason that communicates with human reason, the divine person with the human person' (152f.). 'The Word of God—we should not evade the concept so much *tabu* today—is a rational and not an irrational event' (153).

Those who complain that Barth's theology is simply an example of present-day irrationalism, and also those who know his theology at first hand chiefly through the controversy with Brunner in the now-famous *Natur und Gnade—Nein!* interchange, must take account of what is said here. Barth is not to be ranked with the anti-intellectuals of the day. He expresses surprise at the 'extraordinary polemic which it has been the fashion in recent years to wage against the so-called intellect of man, his powers of comprehension and thought as a centre of possible religious experience of the Word of God' (231). Taking the other side, he declares that the communication of God's Word to man, since it is quite literally language, 'must at least involve a claim upon the intellect, and the experience of it must at least involve the co-option of the intellect'. Turning the tables upon the anti-intellectualists, he suggests that their thesis may indeed be a wrong-headed attempt after holiness which cannot succeed (231). 'The idea of the *sacrificium intellectus* is but a last desperate attempt to make of the knowledge of God a work of man, to have a human possibility correspond to what is the sole work of God' (283). The 'knowability of the Word of God is really an inalienable affirmation of faith'. Certainly it involves a miracle, but it is a miracle worked by Christ passing the closed doors of a man endowed with intellect. The Bible is thus a witness to the knowability of the Word of God. Barth has here significantly departed from the conception of the vacuum (*Hohlraum*) which so perplexed and offended readers of his earlier *Römerbrief*. A man has certainly not to empty himself, or even be emptied, in order that the Word of God may address him. On the contrary, it is the man as such and as a whole who is addressed. Again the point Barth really makes in the *contretemps* with Brunner is not that God addresses man in independence of intellect, but rather that there is no special faculty in man which can constitute the point of contact between man and God. We must not feel 'bound to claim, or to discover and assert any sort of unusual or recondite anthropological centres in order that a man may experience the Word of God' (232). 'If our aim is to investigate the content of the divine spirit in the consciousness of man, is it not with us as with the man who wanted to scoop the reflection of the fair silver moon out of the pond in a sieve? What shall we find there to fix and to investigate?' (247). The real ground for our knowing God in His Word is shifted from any inherent possession or quality in man to the action of God Himself upon the whole man equipped as he naturally is (261). Once again there is returned to God what should never have been alienated from Him.

Two corollaries follow. The speech of God, like any other speech, has its correlates in 'hearing, understanding, and obeying' (153). Barth quotes from Luther:[1] 'Christ's Kingdom is a hearing kingdom, and not a seeing kingdom. For the eyes lead and guide us not thither where we find Christ and get to know Him, but the ears must do that.' Speech demands reply or response. Whenever we depart from the primary meaning of the Word of God as speech, we begin to think naturalistically. Then it is very easy to slip back into the sphere in which 'there is no longer speech and answer, knowledge and decision, but only movement, pressure, and impact' (154). Here is restored the insight of the Reformers, who knew something of the fact that the relation of Holy Scripture to the Word of God implies an event, and if an event then something which really happens between two distinguishable entities: the

[1] Sermon delivered in Merseberg, *W.A.*, 51. 11. 25.

subject addressed and the subject addressing are the two poles
between which the event, the flash of contact, occurs.

The second corollary is that God's Word in Holy Scripture
or elsewhere is personal. This truth is already safeguarded by
the concept of speech. But speech is the means whereby ideas
are conveyed in propositions. God's Word, however, is not an
idea. 'It is not "a truth", not even the very highest truth. It is
the truth because it is God's person speaking' (155). 'God
always utters a *concretissimum.*' God certainly 'reveals Himself
in propositions by means of language, and human language at
that, to the effect that from time to time such and such a word,
spoken by the prophets and apostles, and proclaimed in the
Church, becomes His Word' (156). But it is always He who is
thus revealed, and not some abstract truth about Him but also
apart from Him. On God's side it is thus a personal Word.
But on man's side too, it partakes of this personal character.
We have here to acknowledge the 'relatedness or pointedness'
of God's Word, 'its character as an address' (158). Indeed,
'the only way we know it is as the Word directed to us, coming home to us'. The point is that, even if God's Word takes
the form of propositions, the propositions are not like Euclidean
timeless truths to which a man must bring only his intellect
if he is to understand them. God speaks with men as in conversation, addressing them. In Scripture when it becomes
God's Word, we hear this address, carrying with it the authority
of the speech of God Himself.

This personal response-provoking character of God's Word
in Scripture may be stated in terms of calling and decision.
'Where the Word of God is heard and proclaimed', this happens in relation to 'election', 'calling', and 'setting apart' (168).
Calling is dependent on God's good pleasure, and for this
reason resists implacably all necessary relation with or involvement in the natural-historical order. On the other and human
side, it is constituted by 'an act of God which happens *speci-
alissime*, in this way and in no other, to this and that particular
man' (181). Or again, the relation between revelation and Holy
Scripture is said to have the quality of *contingency*, resting as it
does upon a 'contingent *illic et tunc* from the standpoint of
God who speaks', and also on a 'contingent *hic et nunc* from
the standpoint of the man who hears' (169). We may put
Barth's point in this way: calling or election seen from this

angle is simply God seeing to it that His communication is correctly addressed to the individual for whom it is meant. Decision is involved as correlate. Specially addressed, the individual must specially respond: 'as election and calling, the Word of God becomes operative on and in a decision of the man to whom it is spoken' (182), and this because 'this "God with us" is spoken to *me*, because *I* hear it'. The content of this decision is faith and obedience or, of course, on the other hand unbelief and disobedience; but in either case they are mine, and then 'I exist' either according to the Word of God or in contradiction to the Word of God (183f.). 'In one way or the other it is I—so that it is my, my extremely responsible decision'. The relation of calling and decision is summed up in the lapidary if rather cryptic sentence: 'In virtue of God's decision I am by my own decision a believer or an unbeliever' (184).

The second contribution which this later part of the exposition makes to the understanding of Scripture and its authority helps to fill up the lacuna noticed at an earlier stage in the argument, where no specific answer seemed to be given to the question of the essence of the uniqueness of the scriptural witness as compared with other written witness to Jesus Christ. Barth holds that, however the case may be with other words and acts in general, God's Word is not to be distinguished from God's act, but rather is always God's act. God's Word therefore is both 'the utterance of a person' and also 'an active participation in history'. Barth sees in this involvement in history a fact of great importance—of such great importance that it differentiates 'times'. There is first the 'time of the direct, original utterance of God Himself in His revelation, the time of Jesus Christ (which, according to John viii. 56, was also and already the time of Abraham)—the time of that which prophets and apostles heard in order to attest it'. Secondly, there is 'the time of this testimony, the time of prophecy and the apostolate, the time of Peter upon whom Christ builds His Church, the time when the canon arose as the concrete counterpart in which the Church receives its norm for all times'. Finally, there is still another time—'this or that time of the Church itself, the time of derivative proclamation, related to the words of the prophets and apostles and regulated by them' (164). This principle regarding the times serves to

o

make the distinction required between the Bible and other books, and between the men of the Bible and other men who also witness and whose words may well 'from time to time' be made the Word of God itself. It thus offers a definition of the uniqueness which the Bible requires if it is to be regarded as authoritative. In all three times, the utterance of the Word of God is 'by the mouth of man' (165): Jesus Christ no less than the prophets and the apostles was a man, and the prophets and apostles no less than we. Any order of precedence between these three classes therefore depends not on human qualities which they all manifest, but upon some other characteristic. This characteristic Barth finds in the fact that each belongs each to its appropriate time. Jesus Christ in His time (which stretches before and after the Incarnation) stands absolutely as Master and Lord, and the prophets and apostles in their time, as also we in ours, submit to the absolute precedence of His utterance. But we in our time make a submission which is indirect to His utterance, since this utterance is mediated to us by that of the prophets and apostles in the Bible. We may alternatively say that the submission we make is double: both to the utterance of Jesus Christ, and also to the utterance of Holy Scripture. It is this that makes the prophets and apostles 'stand in their office as witnesses, in an utterly unique and peculiar position in the Church compared with all the rest of us'. Barth insists on this dual absolute difference, that between the prophets and apostles along with ourselves *and* Jesus Christ, and that between ourselves *and* the prophets and apostles. A difference in degree here will not account for the distinction. For then the Word of God is bound to be humanized: we no longer are in the position of necessarily 'letting ourselves be told something' (167).

Must we then regard ourselves as simply in receipt of a second-hand story, of merely reiterated tidings? The written character of the biblical witness would no doubt keep the repetition in perfect good order; but it would be preservation by refrigeration. Barth apprehends this question, states it in his own way, and finds a reply to it. The question really concerns how, despite the absolute distinctions that have been set up, Jesus Christ can be contemporaneous with the prophets and the apostles and also with ourselves, and how too the prophets and the apostles can be contemporaneous with us.

It is from the historical point of view quite impossible to achieve contemporaneity, and hence the question cannot be solved by an understanding of history or a special interpretation of history. The answer Barth gives is, as might be expected, that Jesus Christ in His own time becomes contemporary with all other times, and the prophets and apostles in their time become contemporary with us in the time that follows theirs, in virtue of the free act of God (158).

This distinction between the time of the original utterance, the time of testimony, and the time of the Church, is the material ground of the uniqueness of the Bible. It is not merely dependent on God's volition. The 'miracle' is located at a certain place: at the point where human words become the Word of God. The uniqueness of the prophets and apostles and of the Bible they wrote, and the thing in which resides their authoritative character, is the proximity of the writers to what they testify. It is they who first tell us something. Nor is it a dead report; for as they tell it, this something is made ours.

The third contribution to our understanding of the Barthian view of Scripture is made in a subsequent section, entitled 'God's Language as Mystery'. The Word of God is 'worldly', a term which is to be taken in the sense that it is involved in the world. This worldliness of the Word of God is a principal way in which its mysteriousness appears (188). 'When God speaks to man, this happening is never so marked off from the rest of what happens, that it might not promptly be also interpreted as a part of what is otherwise happening.' 'We do not possess the Word of God otherwise than in the mystery of its worldliness.' Barth illuminates this statement with several examples. Theology as surely as it makes use of human speech, 'is also a philosophy or a conglomerate of all sorts of philosophy'; the Church is also a sociological entity and might quite well be mistaken for this alone; the sacraments are symbols, dissimilar indeed from other symbols, but with a dissimilarity very easily overlooked; preaching is also simply describable as an 'address'. So too with Jesus Christ, who 'in fact is also the rabbi of Nazareth, historically so difficult to get information about, and when it is got, one whose activity is so easily regarded as a little commonplace alongside many later representatives of His own "religion" '. Even the miracles 'do not burst these walls of worldliness; from the moment

they took place they were interpreted otherwise than as proofs
of the Word of God, and admittedly they may ever again be
interpreted in a very different sense'. Finally, 'the Bible in
fact is also the document for the history of the religion of a
tribe in Nearer Asia and of its Hellenistic offshoot'. In other
words, we always have the Word of God 'in a form which as
such is not the Word of God as such, and moreover does not
betray that it is the form precisely of the Word of God'. Two
things are being said here. It is stated first that the Word of
God may remain hidden even in the Bible. This again reveals
the firm hold that Barth has upon the truth that Bible and
Word of God are always distinguishable. It is said secondly
that the Word of God is only known in the Bible or some other
similar form. The form as such possesses no inherent power of
revelation. Barth says, rather too stridently, that 'it as little
has in it the capacity of revealing God to us as we on our part.
have the capacity of knowing God in it. If God's Word is
manifest in it, it happens, of course, "through it", but in such
a way that this "through it" means "in spite of it" ' (190).
The form is never a mirror, but always a *larva*, or mask.

One chief element in the worldly form the Bible provides
for the Word of God is its humanness, with all the error,
ignorance, misdeeds, misjudgments and false statements that
this includes. It is therefore of some importance to see how
Barth handles this worldliness to which the Word of God is
always tied. Barth opposes the view of those who deal with
the matter apologetically and only if its recognition is forced
upon them. 'We ought not', he says (192), 'to conceive of the
worldliness of the Word of God as, so to speak, a disagreeable
accident.' It is not a temporary inconvenience which will
eventually be removed. 'Revelation means the incarnation of
the Word of God', and 'incarnation means entry into this
worldliness. We are in this world, and are ourselves thoroughly
worldly. Were God to speak to us in a non-worldly way, He
would not speak to us at all.' The prime demonstration of this
is the incarnation of Jesus Christ: 'to get round the worldliness of His Word would be to get round Christ'. Thus so far
from worldliness being accidental and dispensable, it is essential: 'the facts are not that God was veiled from us by some
unfortunate disturbance and then unveiled Himself by remov-
ing this veiling. . . . The facts are that God Himself veils

Himself and in the very process—which is why we should not dream of entering into the mystery—unveils Himself.' Further, it is good for us that it is so, for a direct and unveiled approach would mean not greater love, but rather the end of the world. The worldliness of the Word of God is not only excusable but altogether necessary.

It is by this principle that Barth understands the 'imperfections' of the Bible. His view is of course not the only view possible when the way of apology is repudiated. Orthodoxy, identifying revelation and the Bible, attempts the *tour de force* of divinizing the very imperfections. Or again, the late 'Calvinism' of B. B. Warfield alleges that every step in the preparation of the Scriptures is the result of the direct providential ordering of God, so that even the 'discoloration' which results as the Word is communicated through the stained glass of the personality is divinely designed with express purpose, if only to demonstrate the futility of human reason. Barth takes neither of these ways. One does not have to explain away the weariness of Jesus, and there is no call to blush for His tears. These are the manifestations of a real humanity. Similarly, Holy Scripture is written by men and represents the involvement of real divinity in real humanness; yet the humanness is neither obliterated nor divinized. Fundamentalism represents the attempt to stand faithfully by the words; but this results in making the worldly form into an idol. Liberalism essays the distillation of a divine content for which the worldly form is vessel; but the result is an arbitrary eclecticism. Barth is true to the position of the Reformers in affirming an essential relatedness between the two, grounded upon the free action of God.

The second large section in which Barth discusses particularly Holy Scripture and its authority occurs in the *Kirchliche Dogmatik* I/2, Chapter 3, 'The Holy Scriptures', and Chapter 4, 'The Proclamation of the Church'. There is a good deal of repetition as Barth now amplifies the outline already given, with some illuminating and suggestive detail.

a) *Holy Scripture as witness*. The fundamental proposition concerning the Bible is that 'the Bible is the witness to God's revelation, and this itself is based solely on the fact that the

Bible really gives an answer to our question concerning God's revelation and sets the sovereignty of the triune God before our eyes' (511). That the Bible is a witness implies a restriction, for 'thereby we distinguish the Bible from revelation' (512). A witness is always different from that to which it witnesses; in the case of the Bible, 'we come upon it in human language and written by men, and we have in these words and by their mediacy hear of the sovereignty of the triune God'. But this restriction does not constitute a separation or imply any incompatibility between the Bible and revelation. Quite the contrary: in its very humanness the Bible says something specific; it is a word that indicates a thing or object (513). We have therefore 'to hear what the Bible as human word has to say, to understand it from the standpoint of what is said, and to expound it in its relation to what is said' (516). And 'what is said is precisely God's revelation, that is the sovereignty of the triune God in His Word through the Holy Spirit' (519). 'Revelation can only be made in the Bible through revelation, and can only be heard as the thing that the Bible says' (ibid.). Thus the distinction between the Bible and revelation is compatible with the unity of the Bible and revelation. There *may* be a distinction, but there *can* be a unity. This possibility is fulfilled not by anything we can either bring or do, but by the free grace of God. Barth adds with emphasis that no special hermeneutics is required in the case of the Bible. The distinctiveness of the Bible depends not on a special hermeneutics, but on the special thing that the Bible says.

b) *Distinctions within the human witness.* The status of those who write the Scriptures is next considered. The distinction between the three 'times' of the Word of God is now amplified. Old Testament and New Testament are related by both distinction and unity. In distinction, the Old Testament witnesses to the coming Messiah, and the New Testament to the Messiah who has come. In unity and wholeness, on the other hand, Old Testament and New Testament each contain both law and Gospel (as Luther affirmed). There is distinction: the Old Testament witnesses to Him who has not yet appeared, while the New Testament witnesses to Him who no longer has not yet appeared. But the distinction is relativized by the fact that the object of both Old and New Testaments is the same.

Between the witnesses themselves, there are all the differences
that distinguish men of strongly contrasted individualities. Yet
there is a wholeness and a concord between even such different
witnesses (534). But it should be remembered that it is not any
kind of system that they concordantly propound. Looking from
outside the Bible, we therefore observe diversity unified into
a whole; looking from the Bible to the outside, on the other
hand, there is differentia sufficient to mark the Bible off from
the other writings of world literature. This differentia is its
theme; and its theme and 'decisive centre' is the resurrection
of Jesus Christ from the dead to which it testifies (537f.).

This witness is borne by men. If the question be raised:
Why should we listen to these men?, the answer must be that
these men are quite 'special men' (539): they are these namely
'who over against the once-for-all contingent revelation have
the essentially correlative function of being the once-for-all
contingent first witnesses'. Their existence is necessary if there
are to be any second and third degree witnesses. For this reason
alone, that they occupy this initial place, they are 'special
men' and must be reckoned with as such. If we overlooked
these men, we should overlook the once-for-all event to which
they witness. Barth can even say: 'The existence of these
certain special men is for us and for all men the existence
[*Existenz*] of Jesus Christ' (539). He further points out that the
setting of these men in this special initial position is something
deliberately contrived by our Lord, who, according to Mark
iii. 14, 'ordained twelve that they should be with him, and
that he might send them forth to preach', a passage which,
according to Barth, has a meaning proleptically referring to
the resurrection. Nor is their being with Him to be separated
from their writing the record of what there occurred: 'Between
God and these certain special men something occurred once-
for-all, and they confront us in what they wrote or what had
been written as living documents with that once-for-all occurrence.'

This quite special position imposes on the men who occupy
it a passive and an active function. Passively, they are quite
distinguished from us and all who follow by the once-for-all
events they saw and heard. Actively, they are quite distinguished by the fact that they are enjoined to proclaim that
which they themselves observed by hearing and seeing. It is

of great importance that it is in this and in no other feature that the 'greatness' of these men consists, as also the claim that they make upon us that they be heard by us. 'This they do, not as thinkers, or religious personalities and geniuses, and not as moral heroes, though all these in a rightly understood sense they also were.' The function they specially discharged is discharged of course by means of any such qualities they possessed, but not because of their possession of them in exceptional degree (544). It follows that the distinction between form and content at this point is inadmissible (545). We cannot have *this* witness except in *this* form. Nor may we free ourselves from this witness as though it were dispensable and we could come into direct relation with the object to which it witnesses. For both these reasons we have to hold faithfully to the texts we have, and give ourselves to recollection and expectation of the revelation to which they bear testimony. It is this character which raises Scripture to the position of critical and authoritative norm over against all that Church or Christian history or personal taste and inclination might propose as an alternative standard (551).

Scripture has then this unique priority. But as the original and legitimate witness to God's revelation, it also *is* the Word of God itself (557). This originality in and by itself is not enough to constitute the Bible the present Word of God. To suppose this would be to slip again into the ways of Orthodoxy, and seek, for the ostensible honouring of Scripture, to incorporate in it something whose real place is elsewhere. But as thus original it has a uniqueness which is not locked up in the past but is bestowed upon it by God in His freedom, determination and power in the present and for the future. Once again,

'round this matter of *event*, the whole problem of Holy Scripture turns, as does also that of dogmatics, preaching, sacraments and proclamation. In the reality and truth of this event, there is nothing already past or only future, nothing that is pure recollection of pure expectation. In this event this original witness is the Word of God' (558).

c) *Inspiration of Scripture.* For the right understanding of inspiration, Barth recognizes the decisive importance of 2 Tim. iii. 14-17. Two points are made at the outset. First, the word *theopneustos* is literally to be understood as (on the one hand passively) infused, filled and governed by the Spirit of God, and (on the other hand actively) breathing, diffusing and making recognizable the Spirit of God. The second point is that the relation between God and the Scriptures which is affirmed in verse 16 is to be referred to the disposition, deed and decision of God, and that more is not said about this reference is simply because it belongs to the sphere of the mystery of the free grace of God, where our access is restricted. It is the same with the other decisive passage, 2 Pet. i. 19-21. It too has a 'decisive middle phrase'. The prophets are linked to Scripture, but not by the will of men. It is the deed of God.

Barth makes two observations here (560). First, these biblical passages themselves speak necessarily of the men concerned; but they speak of them strictly in their relation to God and the Spirit of God. There is no reference to spiritual exercises or religious genius or the like, but only to men who are sent and empowered. In other words, the men referred to here are *auctores secundarii*. It follows secondly: if the *secundarii* has to be emphasized on the one hand, on the other the *auctores* has also to be remembered. In other words, there is no suggestion that the men concerned are deprived of humanity in any way or that they are relieved from the necessity of using their human faculties. 'Their act is like all human action, their own.' Hence just at the point where the Bible relates Scripture and its writers to God, and where the concept of inspiration makes a transient appearance, there precisely we are called on to see men who have been chosen and called to obedience, and engaged in the discharge of the special duty laid upon them. Barth will not permit the idea of inspiration to be side-tracked into the shallows and employed merely to furnish a psychological account of how the Bible got written. At the same time, this delivers him from the need to lock up inspiration into a golden age in the past: by this definition, the idea conveyed by *theopneustos* refers us to the present, and more explicitly, refers us to the event in virtue of which we can say that the Scripture has priority and the Scripture is God's Word (561). It refers us to it, Barth makes clear, but it does not itself occasion the event.

The way is now clear for defining what the idea conveyed by the term *theopneustos* means. It is 'the act of revelation, in which the prophets and apostles in all their humanness became (the witnesses) they were, and in which alone they in all their humanness can become for us (the witnesses) they are' (563). Expounding further the distinction between the inspiration and divine infallibility of the Bible and its human fallibility, Barth observes that its writers by no means possessed a Salomonic compendium or divine knowledge of all things in heaven and earth. On the contrary, they are assailable by reason of their characterization by the culture of their time and place, and the resulting offence cannot be evaded. Their capacity for error must be admitted (564). 'Even the religious and theological contents of the Bible are assailable; and of this in recent times we have become more aware because of the growing insight into the world view which they in common with their contemporaries held' (565). Moreover, it is not just some background or other from which the Bible comes, but specifically a Jewish background: of the men of the Bible it may be said *quod potuit homo dixit*; but it must be added that it is a *homo Judaeus* who has spoken. In this assailability the case of the Bible may be paralleled by that of Israel itself, which, though always assailed in the political world of its day by enemies, was nevertheless God's witness. In both cases, the indefectible thing is not infallibility but the divine choice (566f.). There is no indefectibility of the kind sometimes supposed, because the incarnation is real and the Bible is a human writing. The defects are there, and cannot be removed; but to be offended by them is anti-Semitism. It is in virtue of the miracle of the Word and of faith that 'the offence falls away, the perversion is overcome, the anti-Semite in us all is banished and the human word which is the Jewish word of the Bible heard as God's Word, and comes home to us' (568). Here we come very near to the heart of the problem of authority: the assailability or inappropriateness of the human word in the Bible is really beside the point. Just as no indefectibility could give it the authority of the Word of God, so no defect or imperfection can deprive it of this authority. For the ground of its authoritative character lies safely elsewhere: not in itself, and particularly not in any of the fine qualities it possesses, but finally and quite securely in the fact that it is the means elected by God's free grace for the operation of God's free grace. But if the ground of the authority is found in that it is the accredited and elected instrument of God, this authority may be said to work itself out and to come into exercise through a *graphe theopneustos* and the reality this idea connotes. This human word must remain merely human, unless as elected 'the same Spirit which created this witness as such, gives to the men who are its hearers and readers witness of its truth. This self-disclosure (of God) in its totality is what *theopneustos* denotes; it is the inspiration of the word of the prophets and the apostles' (573).

d) *Verbal inspiration.* In view of what has already been said about verbal inspiration, it is worthwhile noting what Barth has to say about this contentious idea. He counts it as one of the striking things about early Christian theology that the wider idea of the inspiration of the writers narrowed down to the inspiration of the words the writers used in a grammatical sense. Here Matt. v. 18 played a fateful role from Clement of Alexandria[1] to Gregory of Nazianzus.[2] And indeed, Barth warns us, we must be careful to take this text quite seriously (574). If we do not, then inevitably we treat only certain elements of the Bible as inspired, according as they appear important to us. But this means the replacement of a genuine inspiration of the Bible by a notion of 'inspirationism', and what is said of the free grace of God becomes 'inspirationism understood in a naturalistic sense'. The distinction Barth here makes between inspiration and inspirationism is definable as the difference between an inspiration which God retains in His own hand and effects by His own act, and an inspiration imparted as such to the words of the Bible. Of course it is true, Barth declares, that God says what His witnesses say. But this depends on a mystery which remains with God. The idea of dictation (introduced in Barth's opinion by Augustine), however, works against real inspiration. This idea follows a baleful course, in which the Holy Spirit is said by Athenagoras[3] to use the mouths of the prophets as His organ, or, as Pseudo-Justin,[4] to breathe through them as through a reed, or, as Hippolytus,[5] to play on them as on a zither or harp. This amounts to a stabilizing of the human word as the Word of God. It seems indeed to secure an impregnable authority for

[1] *Protrepticus*, IX. 82. 1.   [2] *Orat.*, 2. 105.   [3] *Leg. pro Chr.*, 7, 9.
[4] *Coh. ad Graecos*, 8.   [5] *De Antichristo*, 2.

the Bible, but the price is too high. The mystery in which
God contrives that the Bible becomes His own Word is reduced to a mere marvel, the *Mirakel* to a *Wunder*. This is a
secularization of the concept of revelation. As Docetism robs
Jesus Christ of His real humanity, so this secularization robs
the Bible, and thereby also the Word of God, of its humanness
(576). It runs counter to the insight of the Reformers, who
clearly saw that inspiration rightly conceived serves the glory
of God, not the dignity of the Scriptures as such. To think of
it in the latter sense infringes the sovereignty of God (579).
The ground for the authority of the Bible then transfers itself
from God to the Bible itself. The Bible becomes independent
of and divorced from Christ and the Spirit. It becomes a
'paper Pope', entirely delivered into the hands of the expositors. In contrast to this, the Romans have at least the advantage of a living Pope (573).

Finally in this section, Barth criticizes Calvin for bringing
forward 'secondary grounds' for the authority of Scripture. It
is, he says, as though Calvin were nervous lest the subjective
operation of the Spirit was not strong enough to guarantee its
authority. When this happens, then the role of the Holy Spirit,
in commending Scripture and warranting it to us as authoritative, becomes a 'luxury' for the believer (596f.). Barth repeats
again that all we can really say here is that 'Scripture becomes
known as the Word of God, because it is the Word of God'.
When we say that it becomes so 'through the Holy Spirit', we
simply mean that it becomes so 'through God in the free and
gracious action in which He turns to us' (597). If the Achilles'
heel of the Protestant system is the question, who guarantees
the divine character of the witness? it may be said that the
recognition of the authority of Holy Scripture is a matter of
confession, and that when this is realized, this very weakness
is also its greatest strength (598).

e) *The authority of Holy Scripture*. Barth affirms that when
we speak of authority in the Church, we imply that there is
in the Church a court of appeal, which has a closer relation
to the basis and essence of the Church than any other. This
authority is Holy Scripture (600). Its position as the 'historically oldest document' in the possession of the Church, itself
gives Holy Scripture authority. Scripture does not deny that

there are other authorities in the Church; but none of these other authorities has the character of a document, let alone the character of the oldest document (601). This character which Holy Scripture possesses would suffice alone to give it a particular authority, but an authority also which would be only relative. Authority implies obedience. If there is authority in the Church, then the Church must be simply obedient to itself, or it is obedient to something other than itself. If we are to avoid the error of Rome, the truth must lie in the second alternative. Authority implies one that imposes and another on whom the imposition is made: one authority and one obeying the authority. The prophets and the apostles themselves, however, are in the position of obedient servants. If it is they who constitute the authority, authority in the Church would simply be brought down again into the Church; and then the Church would no longer be the Church of Jesus Christ. 'The existence of the Church stands or falls by the fact that in it obedience is rendered as it was rendered by the prophets and the apostles' (604). The position in which the prophets and the apostles stand for rendering their obedience is an unrepeatable position. Our time and theirs are different times. Yet this position must be reconstructed, if the Church, like the prophets and apostles, is to render obedience. 'This authentic reconstruction of the revelation and this authentic example of obedience rendered to it is the content of the witness of the prophets and apostles in Holy Scripture' (605). The Church cannot make appeal directly to God and to Christ and to the Holy Spirit, and so bypass Scripture. Scripture is that in which and through which it renders obedience to authority. Apart from Scripture, the Church would be only a human society accustomed to a beautiful memory and intended to perpetuate this memory (606).

'The evangelical Church—and this is the only true Church —stands or falls by whether it understands the proposition: The Bible is the Word of God, exclusively, and accordingly does not claim an immediate, absolute and material authority for a third court of appeal or for itself' (607).

The fault of the Roman Church is precisely that it claims authority for itself. The fault of the 'Enthusiasts' in the Protestant Church is that, bypassing the Scriptures, they claim access to a revelation directly granted to the Church; and in fact, without guidance by the norm of Scripture, they resort to some more convenient court of appeal. Decision must be made between the two alternatives: either a self-governing Church or a Church obedient to an authority over against itself. The right decision is of course clear: the character of being self-governing belongs to God only; and in any case the Church is an *ekklesia*, an *evocatio*, and as such is called to obedience to an authority which is not merely immanent (659). On the other hand, a Church which pretends to be self-governing relapses into a Church engaged in a monologue with itself (651). Against this relapse, there stands the Bible, through which, in the witness of the prophets and apostles, the Church is called to obedience to the only valid and legitimate authority.

This valid and legitimate authority in the Church has its correlate in the freedom of the Church—but a freedom only under authority, i.e. under the Word given in Holy Scripture. Here again there are two representations which must be avoided. Roman Catholicism submits itself to clericalism determined arbitrarily and solely by itself, and this infringes the authority of God's Word. On the other hand, the 'Enthusiasts' within Protestantism surrender to the tyrannical authority of the god in their own hearts. True authority is not hostile to but rather creative of freedom. It is the freedom of the Word. It is the power that meets us in Holy Scripture, and 'the truth is that Holy Scripture in its insignificance has more power than the whole world put together' (760).

This power of Scripture is a hidden power, and a superior power, and it has its location in the Church. The Roman Church, in regarding Scripture as a *depositum*, offends against two of these principles, and complies with the third only by changing the meaning of the terms. The true conception of the Word sees that it is constantly creating freedom in the Church and thus creative of the Church itself. It thus becomes the 'bearer of Church government', and it follows that all human Church government is under the concrete dominion of Scripture. In the freedom thus bestowed on believers, God's Word comes to men, and they are thereby constituted, not self-knowers and not not-knowers, but co-knowers (*conscientes*) (796).

Granted this freedom, believers exercise it in undertaking responsibility for the exposition and the application of Holy Scripture (797), and the Church undertakes the proclamation of this Word. The Word of God suffers no weakening or dilution when it comes by way of the prophets and apostles through Holy Scripture to us. They are the first witnesses who, under Him, witness to Him. We are under and dependent on them. But the same Word is operative both in them and in us, since the Word is really an incarnate Word. That God's Word should be in men's mouths is certainly an astonishing thing. But the proclamation of the Church is not the proclamation of human ideas, but the proclamation of the Word; and this God acknowledges as proclamation of Himself. To speak about God is indeed impossible, for if men speak of Him it is not He of whom they speak. Nevertheless, it is this that becomes possible by God's recognition of men's proclamation. In this way, men say what God says; and when they speak in this way, then *haec dixit Dominus*. Precisely this assailable human word is, since God's promise stands, in 'indirect identity' with God's own Word, while retaining its humanness.

In standing before Holy Scripture, we do not stand before authority itself. Rather we stand before that in which, as we hear it, we hear God Himself speaking. The authority of Holy Scripture is not a possession of Holy Scripture, not even a gift bestowed by God Himself. Holy Scripture is authoritative because God Himself takes it and speaks through it.

2. BRUNNER

Brunner is the other chief expositor of the variety of modern thinking that has come to be conveniently known as the theology of the Word. So much is there in common between him and Barth, that it was a matter of perplexity and regret that the two should even seem to fall out over points of detail, however important. It is a new view of Scripture that has precipitated the theology of the Word. It is a recovery of what was rediscovered at the time of the Reformation, only to be lost again with tragic speed; but the rediscovery is supplemented by the contribution which the recent years of critical study have made. There is indeed a good deal of difference

between the external appearance of the work of Barth and
that of Brunner; as one turns to the latter, something of the
difficulty as well as of the excitement goes out of the argument.
Brunner presents his views—and this is true of his views of
Holy Scripture as well as of other matters—as the calm statement of conclusions from which the sound and fury by which
they were achieved has died away. What does this difference
amount to? It has been alleged that Brunner's work is less
profound and searching in its analysis of the matters discussed,
that the profound waters emanating from Barth have run out
into the shallows, where, if they acquire clarity, they lose depth.
On the other hand, I recall a remark of John Oman about one
of the works of Barth as the stream flowed from his hand
through the press, that it was the kind of material a man gets
together before he begins to write a book. There is truth in
both observations. But discounting the difference in method
and presentation, when Barth and Brunner speak about Scripture and its authority, they are found to be saying the same
thing. But emphases of course differ, and at some points clearer
expression is given by Brunner. At all events, some things are
so firmly stated by him, and form such important and characteristic features of his theology of the Word, that they deserve
mention.

a) *Personalness.* The most characteristic word in all Brunner's
theology is the word 'encounter' (*Begegnung*). It is this that is
the centre of revelation and forms its substance. For revelation
is an event in which God makes Himself known or communicates Himself to man and in this manner encounters him.
Further, just as 'our communication takes place through
words', so 'the "Word" of God is the way in which God communicates Himself'. 'God's self-communication takes place,
ultimately and finally, in the Person and the history of His
Son' (*Revelation and Reason*, 119). Brunner insists just as much
as Barth that when we say 'word' here, we are saying something real and not something merely analogical or symbolic.
'Word', that is to say, is not merely the best metaphor of which
we can think. Indeed, so little is Word as applied in the case
of God a metaphor and a shadow of the real thing only, that
it is in fact the really full thing itself. Thus 'while our words
are always only signs, which *suggest* what we mean, God's

Word is the actual *meaning* itself: it is "communication" as well as "that which is communicated"—or, rather, not "that which is communicated" but "the One who communicates Himself" ' (ibid.). Thus moving from the standpoint of encounter, Brunner passes by way of Word to establish that it is God Himself that is communicated. He reaches the same conclusion when, in setting out the Christian position in his *Dogmatik*, he begins with the Word. 'The prophetic word is the standard and characteristic form of [God's] revelation' (*Dogmatik*, I, 26). When the prophet, however, says that 'God laid His words on his tongue', Brunner connects this with the idea of the Word of God (quoting Eichrodt: *Theologie des alten Testaments*, II, 21ff.). When again the New Testament supplements and fulfils the Old Testament, what God gives is no longer a mere word, but a person—Jesus Christ. 'A person is, however, not a spoken word [*Rede-wort*], but a speaker [*Redender*], who is also not merely a speaker but a doer [*Handelnder*], a living active subject' (ibid., 28). We have to do with a God who communicates Himself by means of His Word.

The next step is to affirm that when a Word thus comes to men, it evokes a response. This response is the 'interior word of faith' (*R.&R.*, 120). This occurs when Peter makes the great first confession: 'Thou art the Christ' (Matt. xvi. 16); or when St Thomas cries: 'My Lord and my God' (John xx. 28); or when St Paul can testify: 'It pleased God to reveal his Son in me' (Gal. i. 16). Speech elicits and evokes speech. The first form of this responsive speech is pure confession. But a second stage supersedes when it is necessary to proclaim Christ to others. It is only the man who has first said: Thou, who can go on to this second stage. When he does so go on, he says no longer Thou but He. 'He now speaks *about* God, about His Lord Christ; God is now the object of his proclamation' (ibid.). The attempt is made to persuade and convince another. 'This effort of his can succeed only if God permit it to succeed; that is, if God uses the spoken word to reveal Himself in the heart of the hearer, addressing him, and evoking from him the answer of faith' (121).

This is the principle that determines the place that the Bible must have. First it is to be noted that God's revelation is capable of translation into words, just because He Himself reveals Himself in the Word He addresses. But it is, of course,

not the word of translation itself that can convey God, but
only when it is made the vehicle for this purpose by God's
permission and action. Speech about God can fittingly become God's speech, only if it is made so by His activity.
Further, this speech about God which is proclamation may
be either spoken or written. Whether it is a prophet or an
apostle speaking, or the Bible which is written—both are proclamation, and both may become the vehicle of God's self-
communication.

The danger, Brunner insists, that is always present is to
conceive that the speech about God is itself the object of belief.
Then revelation is equated with doctrine, and faith with *assensus*.
An intellectualism of revelation takes place. This error is made
both by the Roman Church and by Reformed Orthodoxy.
But in rejecting such intellectualism, it is not necessary to reject the intellect: 'We only come to the knowledge of [God]
where definite words and statements about Him are made, and
expressed, and understood' (151). 'God's Word is more than
can ever be confined within human language, but it does not
come to us apart from human words.' 'The word is the way
in which mind communicates with mind, subject with subject, will with will' (*The Divine-Human Encounter*, 47). 'Since
the Word became *flesh*, proclamation of Jesus must be made,
and telling about Him is the primary witness; since the *Word*
became flesh, the teaching witness must go alongside of the
proclamation' (*Dogm.*, I, 44). This leads to Brunner's drawing
at a fresh point the familiar distinction between religion and
reason, between revelation and theology. 'All utterance about
God, no matter how much personal earnestness it may have,
has always the abstractness of theology' (*The Philosophy of Religion*, 19). '*Toute traduction est une trahison*' and '*traduttore—tradi-
tore*'—yet the hazard has to be undertaken (*Dogm.*, I, 83).
Thus proclamation itself is an intellectualization of revelation.
The Thou of confession has already given place to the He of
statement. The important distinction is not between the Bible
as revelation and the theology that expounds the Bible. The
Bible is witness, and theology is the reiteration and translation
of this witness. But both point to the revelation, to God speaking, and both are therefore distinct from this.

No less than Luther and Barth, Brunner insists that, when
God makes Himself known, an event takes place in which the

believer is caught up. 'Revelation is no objective thing by itself, but a transitive operation: God makes Himself known to someone' (I, 34f.).

'Only where Jesus Christ has revealed Himself to an apostle has the divine revelation reached its goal; the circuit is now complete. Had there been no apostle on whom this perception dawned, then the story of Jesus would not have become a revelation to humanity; it would not have become the Word of God. It would have echoed and re-echoed, like a sound which passes unheard in a primeval forest. It would have been like a bridge which had been begun from one side of a river, but which never reached the other side' (*R.&R.*, 122).

But again it is not Scripture in itself that is transitive in this sense. Only the Holy Spirit can make it transitive. 'The *testimonium Spiritus sancti* means the Spirit-given understanding of the word of Scripture, that is of the witness of the apostles already become a human word' (*Dogm.*, I, 34). And further, this operation of the Holy Spirit is the work of God Himself, and is not effected by any Spirit locked up within Scripture itself by a kind of 'inscripturation'.

b) *The primacy of the scriptural witness.* The Bible is proclamation, and preaching is also and no less proclamation: 'Where there is knowledge of Jesus Christ through the Holy Spirit, there is correspondingly no distance between apostles and Church members, and also no difference between the apostles and the Christians of later generations' (I, 38). In what then consists the authority of Holy Scriptures? and what is the quality which makes it, among many testimonies, uniquely authoritative? Brunner's answer is quite clear. The Holy Scripture is uniquely authoritative, not because it is written by apostles, but because of the position which the apostles occupy. 'An apostle is one to whom the primary knowledge is entrusted, not mediated by the intrusion of any other human being, apart from which Jesus Christ would not have been the revelation to humanity' (*R.&R.*, 123). 'The Bible confronts the Church as the apostolic primitive witness to the revelation which has taken place in Jesus Christ' (130). 'The Scripture has this authority because it is the primary witness of the revelation of God in Jesus Christ' (*Dogm.*, I, 53). It is this historical priority that is the distinctive mark of the apostle. The case of the Old Testament is a little different. Its distinctive mark is that it is preparation for the revelation which it fell to the apostles to attest. Of this more will be said.

Alongside the historical priority of the apostles, Brunner sets a further characteristic. Since the first alone cannot be the ground of its normative value, a second quality is distinguished. They enjoy a factual pre-eminence (53), which is thus defined:

> 'This pre-eminence is based on the fact that the original witness possesses a special dignity, since it itself belongs to the event of the revelation of Christ. The honour that belongs to the apostle above all later teachers of the Church is that he as first recipient, one may say as first participant, of the historical revelation of Christ, has a special measure of the knowledge of Christ. In contrast to all who come later, he is eyewitness of the resurrection, as he is eyewitness of the earthly history of Jesus' (54).

The phrase 'special measure of knowledge' which the apostles possess is perhaps unfortunate. It does not mean a special degree of spirituality or even a special measure of intimacy with the risen Christ. Brunner himself suggests that a later Christian might quite well by this standard be ranked above an apostle. Besides, he is much too appreciative of the work of Kierkegaard to fall into the trap of supposing that apostles reap a special personal advantage in knowing Christ, because they stood in a unique temporal proximity to Him. Their pre-eminence consists in something more objective—something they possess in relation to the Church and those who succeed them. It consists in their having been eyewitnesses, and from this position being able to proclaim the Gospel to others who cannot occupy this position. Barth has something to add to what is said here, when he points out that in fact the books of the Bible are not all written by those marked with the character of eyewitness. In principle, however, Brunner too concedes this, when he allows that the canon, being the decree of the Church, is 'not final and infallible' (*R.&R.*, 131), and that the right and duty remains with the Church to re-examine and revise it.

The apostles therefore occupy a special place and exercise

a special authority. There is a difference between them and us. Both they and we enjoy the Holy Spirit, and therein they and we are alike. The apostle has a special significance 'not in virtue of the What, but in virtue of the How: that is in virtue of the way in which we, in contrast to the apostles, receive the Holy Spirit and thus the knowledge of Christ' (*Dogm.*, 138f.). They have these gifts directly, we through the intervention of the medium of Holy Scripture. 'This form, the written Scripture, is the medium in which the Word of God comes to us, since it alone contains the apostolic word of revelation' (*R.&R.*, 126).

c) *The human element in Holy Scripture.* Brunner admits the presence of a human element in Holy Scripture and employs it for the demolition of the doctrine of verbal inspiration. The apostolic writings, Brunner declares, do not themselves claim any such verbal inspiration or the infallibility it implies. Nor are the facts compatible with any such doctrine. Thus so far is St Paul from claiming God's dictation as the source of his writing, that

'on the contrary, he permits us to see quite plainly the natural, human way in which these letters were written. He wrestles with problems of expression in language, he breaks off sentences, he corrects himself while he is writing; the divine revelation seems to be something which is freely appropriated in a natural human activity' (128).

Again, the research which St Luke conducted for the compilation of his Gospel 'excludes automatic dictation and verbal inspiration, with its claim to an oracular divine infallibility'. The 'early tradition was also a product of human research and selection, and, therefore, it is not verbally inspired. . . . No one today who keeps his eyes open to facts and fails to be aware that this tradition has certain errors and inconsistencies.' 'The apostles who, in the "Council of the Apostles", first of all strove with one another before they could come to a common decision, are also in their accounts of events not free from inconsistency and error' (128f.). Again, the same is true of the doctrinal element in the apostolic message. Brunner points out that when St Paul speaks of the time 'when it pleased God to reveal his Son in me', he does not mean that he was given a 'ready-made system of Pauline theology. Rather, the apostle needed a long and intensive spiritual and mental work of appropriation—a word of which we gain glimpses in his letters—before he was able to say what he did in his latest letters' (ibid.).

These plain facts, however, are not incompatible with inspiration, but only with the view of inspiration formulated as verbal inspiration. Of course, there is inspiration: 'How could that which hands on the divine revelation that has been received be lacking in divine inspiration?' 'Human research . . . does not exclude inspiration.' 'Not only the writings of the apostle Paul, but also his speech and action flow from this source, that is, from his life "in Christ", and the Holy Spirit given by Him.' The doctrine of inspiration with which these facts are compatible is different from that propounded in the form of dictation. What we have is 'human testimonies, given by God, under the Spirit's guidance, of the Word of God'. From inspiration in this sense these writings derive their authority: 'they have a share in the absolute authority of the Word, yet they are not the Word, but means through which the Word is given'. Since this is so, it is possible to distinguish between a 'central point' and a 'circumference'. The criterion offered here is Luther's own principle, *was Christum treibet*: 'the Scripture is unconditionally authoritative, in so far as in it the revelation, Jesus Christ Himself, exercises authority' (*Dogm.*, I, 57). Since Scripture is not merely inspired but inspired witness, the criterion between what is and what is not Scripture is to be found not subjectively by distinguishing between degrees of inspiration, but objectively by observing the content of what is written.

d) *The place of the Old Testament as preparation.*

'The Bible is binding upon us not by reason of any quality resident in itself, whether 'by nature' or by impartation, but because God is finally authoritative and in the Bible God, so far as He chooses, makes known the mystery of His will, of His saving purpose in Jesus Christ' (*R.&R.*, 135).

But the roles played by the Old Testament and the New Testament respectively are different. Certainly they both have the same subject and theme: the revelation of God, Jesus

Christ Himself. 'We have the revelation in no other way than in the whole Bible' (*Dogm.*, I, 57). But the Old Testament and New Testament deal differently with it. They do not say just the same thing; they witness to the same thing from different standpoints. This difference can be denoted by the differentiating terms promise and fulfilment (*Dogm.*, II, 239). It may also be designated as the difference between 'preparatory and final revelation' (*R.&R.*, 134). Brunner takes the idea of preparation very seriously. Thus:

'God could also have sent His Son into the world without any preparatory revelation, but He did not will to do so, nor, in actual fact, has He done so. God's mighty acts do not overshadow or constrict the historical process; the story of the way in which God educated His people, transforming these wild and nomad tribes into a "people", with a strict piety, controlled by His Word, shows us that the historical fact of revelation and the sphere of education are not so far apart as an orthodox, intellectualistic theology would have us believe. It was only in a people which had thus been prepared that the Christ could be born and understood. The Old Testament revelation is the preparation for the revelation of the New Testament' (*R.&R.*, 134).

The concept of preparation here proposed refers perhaps chiefly to the prophetic element in the Old Testament in virtue of which expectations were aroused which found their satisfaction in the coming of our Lord. But the definition proposed is wide enough to include also a more 'natural' development, in which preparation of an intellectual, social and psychological kind is not excluded.

'Just as the history of revelation itself is disclosed as a divine economy, or a kind of education, so is it with the record of the revelation. God Himself moved with His people Israel from the primitive stage to the higher forms of belief and worship, and finally to the highest of all, and this "divine economy" is visible in the Old Testament' (133f.).

Irenaeus is cited in support:

'It is one and the same father of the household [*oikonomos*] who lords it over the whole house, giving an appropriate

rule to the slaves and uneducated, but to the freemen and
those justified by faith communicating introductory writings
suitable, and unlocking the inheritance to the children . . .
namely, the Word of God, our Lord Jesus Christ';[1]

and also Calvin, who talks of the '*paterfamilias*' who 'instructs,
rules and treats his freemen differently in boyhood, adolescence
and manhood'.[2]

Other views have, of course, been taken of the relationship
between Old Testament and New Testament. Brunner distinguishes two other groups: that which sees a fundamental
difference between Old Testament and New Testament to the
point of contradiction; and that which affirms their unity to
the point of complete identity. Each is open to a characteristic
peril: 'If only difference is seen, the Old Testament is no longer
God's revelation; if the unity alone be emphasized, revelation
becomes timeless doctrine' (*Dogm.*, II, 241f.). The more significant and historically important of these groups is the second.
The Church has officially been more alert to the error of
disparaging the Old Testament in favour of the New,
than of the more subtle error of so reading both together that
the Old Testament surrenders its distinctive witness. In fact,
the only way in which this view could be made plausible is
by the use of the method of the allegorical interpretation of
Scripture.

> 'In its insistence on the unity between the two Testaments,
> the Church has been mistaken, and has caused a great deal
> of confusion by undervaluing the difference between them.
> It has gone astray when it has made artificial attempts to
> harmonize the two, trying to prove, by an excessive use of
> allegorical interpretation, a unity of doctrine which is in
> direct opposition to God's wise and loving method of edu-
> cating mankind' (*R.&R.*, 135).

But the employment of the allegorical method of interpretation
is in fact no improvement on a position which should not have
been occupied at all. It itself lies open to the strongest of objections. These are chiefly two. Unless a firm and clear standard
of some kind be adopted, the method (as it early did in Origen)
permits anyone to read what he pleases into the sacred texts.

---

[1] *Adv. Haer.*, 14. 14. 2.   [2] *Insts.*, 2. 11. 13.

The criticism of the 'wax nose' is applicable much less in the case of those who sit loose to the letter of the text and allow themselves to be taught by the Holy Spirit, than of those who pretend to hold to the letter of the Scriptures, but have to find relief by seeking under the letter some fanciful interpretation to make it plausible. Each man, then, Brunner says (*Dogm.*, I, 56), becomes his own pope. It is not, however, in this way that Holy Scripture can exercise an authority which is either recognizable or useful.

e) *Scripture as authoritative.* Brunner's answer in brief to the question of how Scripture is authoritative or wherein the authority of Scripture lies, is that, just as revelation itself becomes a norm by means of Scripture, so Scripture becomes authoritative because it witnesses to the revelation. The revelation of Jesus Christ and Scripture are not identical, but as what is witnessed to and what witnesses they have an unbreakable relationship. Orthodoxy in fact was unable to see and answer the question raised here. For it, the revelation of Jesus Christ and the biblical witness are not distinguished, and the theory of verbal inspiration precluded any attempt to prise apart what had thus been fused together. 'When Scripture becomes simply identified with the Word of God, the axiomatic authority of scriptural doctrine and its unconditionally normative character become self-evident and require no basis' (*Dogm.*, I, 53). Scripture, that is, has not to go outside itself for the source of its authority, which has in fact, divine as it is, been incorporated within itself. Then it is true, as has so often been said, that the Romish pope is simply replaced by a 'paper pope'; 'quite unnoticed the position of dependence on the Word of God is usurped by the appeal to pure doctrine' (*The Divine-Human Encounter*, 22). But Luther's principle that Christ is *dominus et rex Scripturae* can be turned not only against the Roman dominance of Scripture by the Church, but also against the Orthodoxy which erects Scripture into an absolute authority on its own account. The authority of Scripture is then seen to be not inherent, but strictly eccentric. 'What treats of Christ is apostolic'; and what is apostolic is authoritative because it treats (and, as has been shown, treats in a unique way) of this Christ. 'The real norm, then, is revelation or Jesus Christ Himself, who witnesses of Himself to us through the Holy Spirit, and who also avails Himself for this self-revelation of Himself of the witness of the apostles.' This is the core of the matter, and regulates the sense in which Scripture is authoritative.

Two things are to be noted. The first is that Scripture has authority as the unconditionally necessary means of absolute authority.

'Since we are bound in an unconditional sense to the witness of the apostles as the medium and means of revelation, we are bound in only a relative sense upon the authority of this witness. The unconditional authority is Jesus Christ Himself, whom we have solely through the report and doctrine of the apostles; but He whom we have by their means alone stands above them. Their witness is valid and unconditionally binding, so far as it really witnesses to Him' (*The Divine Imperative*, 55).

The other thing is that this conditional-unconditional authority which Scripture exercises operates only within a specified field.

'So far as the Bible speaks of the objects of secular knowledge, it has no kind of doctrinal authority. Neither its astronomic-cosmological or its geographical world picture, nor its zoological, ethnographical or historical affirmations, are binding for us, whether in the Old Testament or the New Testament. . . . In these parts, Scripture remains the one source of our knowledge of revelation to which we are unconditionally directed, but it is in no sense a norm for our knowledge and teaching' (57).

Brunner means that the revelation is given in a situation that is characterized in a certain way; but the furniture of the situation is not to be confused, let alone identified, with the revelation. Putting it in his own words, the presentation of revelation to us requires an alphabet; but this is no excuse for interchanging the alphabet with the message; we have to distinguish without separating.

Brunner sums up the matter thus (*Dogm.*, I, 63):

'The theology of the Reformation was right in setting the doctrinal authority of Scripture above that of the Church as its norm; but it was wrong when it made the Bible a final court of appeal, since then it simply identified the word of the Bible with the Word of God.'

In fact the Bible has its authority in no such easy form, but in and by the action of God Himself as he uses it to communicate Himself to the believer.

VIII

The Authority of the Bible

The title given to this book is *The Authority of Scripture*. Yet up till now no definition of the term authority has been attempted. If this is regarded as a defect, it is one which there is no intention even now of remedying at any great length. For the purpose here, we may begin with a simple question: Why should I read the Bible? Or again, what kind of recommendation can be given for reading it? Several answers can be suggested which, though valid in themselves, fail to present the Bible as the bearer of authority in any strict sense. Some of these answers offer obviously adventitious grounds for reading it. It is no doubt possible and in some sense right to read the Bible because of the excellent literary qualities which the Authorized Version possesses, and this was certainly one of the early reasons given to us when at school. The claim of the Bible upon our attention would then not be different from that of Shakespeare or R. L. Stevenson, and genuine authority belongs to neither of these. Moreover, this ground has little internal warrant from Scripture itself, and any such commendation will at best be purely extrinsic, as if one should advocate buying a Hoover on the ground that, with certain adjustments, it can be made to cut the grass. At the other extreme, it can be answered that the Bible ought to be read because it is true: 'Jesus loves me! this I know, For the Bible tells me so.' Yet this alone will hardly suffice. Truth does indeed command assent with authority. But it must be apprehended as truth—one must see it to be true; and this involves grounds on which one deems it true. Thus the question again arises: Can the Bible be so commended that its truth is made apparent?

At this point an external guarantee may be proposed.

Calvin[1] asks what Augustine meant when he wrote:[2] 'I should not believe the Gospel, unless I were influenced thereto by the authority of the Church.' The Romans answer the question in one way, declaring that the Bible's commendation is the authority of the Church, and this interpretation Calvin rejects. Here we need only say that, if this is the right answer, the Bible enjoys an indirect and second-hand authority, admitted by those alone who recognize the primary authority of the Church. This is to shift the locus of authority to something external to the Bible itself. We cannot then speak rightly of the authority of Holy Scripture as such. Even C. H. Dodd's definition in the Preface to his book, *The Authority of the Bible*,[3] seems to support an external conception of authority: 'I assume that the function of authority is to secure assent to truth'. But the distinction made between authority and truth is a little awkward, and prompts the question what would happen to truth if the authority which secures assent were withdrawn.

The question: Why should I read the Bible? would be fully answered if it can be shown that the Bible is authoritative. But the authority with which it is credited will have to be carefully defined. It will have, for one thing, to rest on something other than internal but trivial characteristics or impressive but external guarantee. It will have further to be *permanent* and not merely introductory and so eventually dispensable, *simple* and not esoteric, *universal* and not merely suited to certain interests and tastes, *categorical* and brooking no evasion, and *acceptable* in the sense that, while independent of the person upon whom it imposes itself, it secures the assent of that person.

Here a brief warning should be given. Authority is often confused with immediate applicability. It is then thought that every word and command in Scripture is forthwith obligatory for faith and conduct. This is a conception imposed upon us by that fragmentation of the Bible which has been already noted and deplored, which is foreign to the Bible itself,[4] and which criticism has done so much to encourage. The Bible is not authoritative because it is verse by verse immediately em-

---

[1] *Insts.*, 1. 7. 3.   [2] *Contr. Epist. Fundam.*, 5.   [3] 2nd edn., xiii.

[4] So C. H. Dodd: *According to the Scriptures*, 127: 'the appeal in the New Testament is to whole contexts rather than to particular proof texts. . . . The proof text kind of argument was frequently used by Christian apologists at a somewhat later period.'

ployable. The example of our Lord in matters of hygiene[1] is not authoritative, yet this does nothing to impair the authority of the incarnation. It is rather to be expected that the authority of the Bible will consist in the intrinsic quality of the whole. This must now occupy attention.

a) *The Bible is the book about Jesus Christ.* That Jesus Christ is a phenomenon of importance in the story of mankind is a statement requiring no explanation and no defence. For Christians the fact is admitted and self-evident: the faith they profess is called after Him; the freedom they have from the past is of Him; the life they live in the present is in Him; and the hope they have for the future rests on Him and on the work He accomplished and will accomplish. Jesus Christ is central to their faith; He stands with a lonely splendour and eminence among, or rather out from, the other members of the human race. But in some measure and degree, the same admission is made by those who do not profess the Christian faith. Far beyond those from whom Jesus Christ wins full recognition for the claims He made, He evokes an admiration and a reverence, which, stopping short of the highest honours, is none the less a remarkable tribute to His greatness. What relation does the Bible have to these facts? The Bible is a book about this individual; and His importance imparts an importance to the book which is the record of His life and work. The book which tells us about this personality may be said to have some kind of authority.

But more: the Bible not only is concerned with Jesus Christ, but is the only book of its kind. It is safe to say that no such accurate recording of what any man was and did had ever appeared before. Acquaintance with Jesus Christ evidently evoked in men the overwhelming conviction that others must be told; and it was to the execution of this task that the Gospel writers dedicated their records. A new and unprecedented interest was aroused in those most nearly concerned with Jesus Christ in this portion of history; an individual became the focus of their attention, and they felt compelled first of all to declare orally and then to set down in writing the 'things which are most surely believed among us'.

This book about Jesus distinguishes itself with sufficient

[1] E.g. John ix. 6.

clarity also from the books which follow. Unnumbered books have since the day of the compilation of the Gospels been written with Jesus as their theme. They are comparable with the Bible as having the same subject matter. Yet there is a distinction between these later works and the writings of the Bible. The latter form a fairly close unity in virtue not only of their theme but of their authorship and compilation. This unity has as its core the evidence of eyewitnesses; and round this core there are associated other writings which are those not of eye-witnesses but of men who stood next to these eye-witnesses and whose writings could for the most part be checked by their memory. It may indeed be impossible to separate decisively the books of the Bible from others contemporary with them, since the differentia is not merely earliness of composition. But it remains true that in the Bible we have a group of works manifesting a combination of qualities which together distinguish them sufficiently from other works: qualities of integrity, authenticity, and proximity to the subject of their writing, together with at their centre the hard core of eye-witness record. The Bible must be accorded at least all the authority proper to a work of this kind.

It may seem that what has been said applies to the writings of the New Testament but not to those of the Old. The Old Testament is not a book about Jesus Christ in the same sense as the New Testament is. The acts of Jesus Christ could not be recorded before His advent, and the record of the Advent begins with the New Testament. Yet if position is taken up within the New Testament itself, it is impossible to disregard the Old Testament, and to ignore it is to fail to follow the lead of the New. The fact is that the New Testament throws out grappling irons which make the Old Testament fast to itself. There is a variety of such ties; but it is sufficient here to mention one kind only. Since it has been said that the Bible is a book about Jesus Christ, the question can appropriately be asked whether Jesus Himself was at pains to make connexion with the Old Testament. The answer is quite certainly affirmative. When in His sermon in the synagogue of Nazareth (Luke iv. 21) He reads the passage from the prophet Isaiah, He uses the idea of 'fulfilment' to connect the Old Testament with what the New Testament is recording. Similarly (Luke xxiv. 27; cf. xxiv. 44f.), on His appearance on the Emmaus road to

the two disciples, He acts as His own expositor, 'and beginning at Moses and all the prophets, he expounded unto them
in all the scriptures the things concerning himself'. For the
understanding of Himself, He turns to the pages of the Old
Testament. Hence the Old Testament at least throws light on
the New Testament; and if the theme of the New Testament
is manifestly Christ, this is true in some sense also of the Old
Testament. The Bible as a whole is about Jesus Christ.

From this alone it follows that the Bible can rightly claim
to be authoritative. Since it exercises the uniquely important
role of telling us about Jesus Christ, it is not unreasonable to
give this as reason why people should read the Bible. If, however, this were all that could be said, Scripture would be left
with only the function of effecting an introduction of Jesus
Christ to those who had not heard of Him. Once this introduction had been effected, Scripture could then be simply discarded. One may safely say that it has never been thought to
be this merely introductory function that gives Scripture its
authority.

b) The next step must therefore be to examine more carefully *the relation of the Bible to Jesus Christ*. The Bible is
'from cover to cover a book about Christ'.[1] This is true equally,
though not identically, of both the Old Testament and the
New Testament. W. Vischer[2] suggests a right way of ex-
pressing this fact. The Bible, in presenting Jesus Christ, is
composed of two semicircles of witnesses. Jesus Christ standing as it were in the middle, on this side there is a semicircle
of witnesses and also on that side. On that side stand the
writers of the Old Testament. They point forward to the
future. They are not in the least interested in themselves. On
the contrary, they bid those who read their works or listen to
their words look away from them: Look rather, they say, into
the future; an event will take place—*the* event. They do not
indeed clearly see the precise nature of the event, nor is what
they variously say quite compatible with itself. But while they
are hesitant and sketchy in the detail suggested, they are quite
sure about the framework. Pointing into the future, they bid
men look for God to act. On the near side stands the other

[1] Alan Richardson: *Preface to Bible Study*, 39.
[2] *Das Christuszeugnis des alten Testaments*, 29.

semi-circle, the witnesses of the New Testament. They also point, but this time point back. Directing attention away from themselves in whom they have as little interest as the Old Testament writers in themselves, they declare: Look there; the event has happened. The event stands in the middle of these two semicircles. It is the event of the incarnation; it is the coming of Jesus Christ. From one side, this event belongs to the future; from the other it belongs to the past. Each side witnesses, but witnesses in the way appropriate to it, the one prospectively, and the other retrospectively. Continuing the quotation made above: the Bible is a book of 'testimony, first of the prophets by way of promise, then of the apostles by way of fulfilment'.[1]

Taking first the New Testament, the truth of what has just been said is evident. The witness of the New Testament is borne by men some of whom were actual eyewitnesses of the event, and by others associated with them who stand in temporal proximity to them. 'That which we have heard, that which we have seen with our eyes, that which we beheld and our hands have handled concerning the word of life—that which we have seen and heard declare we unto you, that ye also may have fellowship with us' (1 John i. 1-3). In the New Testament we have the testimony of witnesses who have seen and heard.

There is one complicating circumstance which has to be reckoned with. The most extensive single contributor to the writings of the New Testament is St Paul. One of the unresolved puzzles of the New Testament is whether St Paul ever saw Jesus in the flesh or not. 'Henceforth', he says (2 Cor. iv. 16), 'know we no man after the flesh: yea, though we have known Christ after the flesh, yet now know we him no more' —is St Paul here referring to himself and his own experiences, or is his 'we' meant to indicate others who could claim to have seen Jesus in the days of His flesh from whose number he is himself excluded? Did he claim himself to have had visual contact with the incarnate Christ, or is this a privilege which he allows others but knows himself to have been denied? The question has a wider scope. It is not the case that all the other writers of the books of the New Testament were eyewitnesses of Jesus in the flesh; not even all the Gospel writers can claim

[1] Richardson: *Preface to Bible Study*, 39.

this. It is therefore necessary to conceive of the witness offered by the New Testament as having a wider basis than direct visual or tactual contact. The witness of the New Testament is still entirely directed to Jesus Christ, but not only to the incarnate Jesus Christ. It bears witness also to the Jesus Christ who rose again and is ascended. The real connecting link here is the witness of those who undeniably had been eyewitnesses —the apostles belonging to the twelve, who made it their business not only to record the acts of the incarnate Christ, but also the acts which that same Christ now ascended still performed. It is a continuous course of events to which they bear witness, one which runs through incarnation where the eye can see, into the ascension where the eye is no longer witness. To this latter phase in the whole course of events belong those other New Testament writers who cannot claim to be eyewitnesses, and especially St Paul, who (probably) without physical contact witnesses only to the continued acts of the same Jesus Christ. The record of the course of events would have been prematurely closed, unless, organically connected with the witness of the acts of Jesus Christ incarnate, there were set the record of the work of Jesus Christ risen and ascended. Thus the witness completes itself: the full character of Him to whom it witnesses is now evident. There is no more to be said: He will continue to act, 'as it is written of him',[1] down to the end of time.

But a chapter closes when Jesus has thus been presented. He will continue, and His acts will continue; but He will not be other, and His acts will not be other, than they are presented in the New Testament. In principle all that requires to be said has been said, and the New Testament is thus normative for Christianity. Here too is the distinction between the books of the Bible and subsequent writings that also witness to the Christ. They witness to the continued activity of Christ; but they do not add anything decisively novel to what is said in the New Testament. All they do is further to exemplify what is there originally and completely and thus also finally expressed. 'Succeeding ministers', as Calvin says,[2] 'have no other office than to teach what is revealed and recorded in the sacred Scriptures.' They may even do so with a superior degree of clarity or spiritual insight. Brunner[3] says that

[1] Mt. xxvi. 24. [2] *Insts.*, 4. 8. 9. [3] *Revelation and Reason*, 127.

'it is, of course, quite possible that a witness to Christ of the sub-apostolic period may have a degree of knowledge of Christ which compares favourably with that of an author of the New Testament, and at particular points might even surpass it. We cannot deny *a priori* or *a posteriori* that certain writings of later teachers and preachers may even excel in the depth and richness of their knowledge of Christ. But such writers would be the first to admit that they owe all their knowledge of Christ to the Holy Scriptures.'

Luther is cited as example, who declared that he 'might have made as good a New Testament as the apostles wrote', but declared that 'we must learn from them and humbly drink from their fountains.' It is not extraordinary spiritual power or evangelical effectiveness that invests the apostles or their writings with their unique authority, but their proximity to Him to whom they and all who follow them bear witness.[1] A. G. Hebert argues similarly, and concludes: 'The Bible ends at the point where Church history begins. It is not hard to see why it should end at this point.'[2]

An important corollary follows. The characteristic by which the New Testament commends itself to us is the fact that it is the work of those who were either eyewitnesses or at least proximate witnesses to Jesus Christ, first in His life and then in His exaltation. This is a character which is not transferable. A wide and insurmountable difference distinguishes those who thus originally witness to Jesus Christ whether in incarnation or in exaltation, and those who follow them in witnessing: the latter cannot be the first to do so, for this place is already exclusively occupied. On this fact alone, the hypothesis that the apostles transmit an identical office to others who succeed them comes to grief.[3] This is not to deny that something is

---

[1] The formal ground of the authority of the Bible is simply the fact of the temporal-spatial proximity of the witnesses. The substantial ground is of course the impact of Christ upon them. This may be expected to evoke from them an 'inspired' response, though even in this 'inspired' appropriateness the marks of humanness are all too clearly apparent.

[2] A. G. Hebert: *The Authority of the Old Testament*, 49f.

[3] Dom Gregory Dix (see *The Apostolic Ministry*, 262) does not hold that the office into which the apostles admitted or assumed their successors was identical with the apostolic office. He holds that the differentia consists in the fact that, while the *leitourgia* of the apostles included the right of appointing their own successors, that of the bishops appointed did not. Not only, however, does this distinction appear most unlikely (see *The Historic Episcopate*, edited K. M. Carey,

transmissible and actually transmitted by them to their successors. But by the nature of the case it is impossible that they should admit others to the status of first and proximate witnesses which they alone enjoy. Others, however exalted and authoritative their office and function, can only witness to that which has already been attested: they can only witness to that same activity of the same exalted Lord occurring in their own experience and the experience of their contemporaries, to which already complete and sufficient witness has been borne. It is a great pity that A. G. Hebert, who clearly sees and rightly appreciates the place the New Testament occupies here, should fail to draw the implication of his thesis.[1] The original and primary scriptural witness comes to an end, and later writings cannot take their place alongside of it, though, of course, they have an indispensable function as secondary proclamation. Similarly, the ranks of the original and primary witnesses thin and at last empty; other later witnesses cannot fill them up, though of course they have an indispensable part to play as secondary witness.

The inalienable and intransmissible characteristic of the New Testament writings is that they are the proximate witness to Jesus Christ. There follows from this the essentially contingent character to which reference has already been made, both of the New Testament itself and of the canon in which the writings crystallized. It is always dangerous to speak or think in terms of what God *must* do. Yet with all reverence certain things may be considered essential to the witness the New Testament bears—two things at least: it is essential that witness should be borne to the life and work of the incarnate Jesus; and it is essential that witness should be borne to the further work and activity of Christ exalted. Only in this way, so far as we can see, is the whole scope and significance of Christ declared. That we have a complete witness of this kind in the New Testament writings is simply a fact. We might in a manner of speaking have been granted a more abundant witness of these two kinds; we might conceivably have been

43f.); preoccupation with matters of order treated in isolation blinds him to the far more important difference that exists—the fact that the apostles are the original witnesses, and this status no successor can either usurp or share. Cf. E. L. Mascall: *Corpus Christi*, 19: 'our Lord's institution of the Apostolate, which is continued in the universal Episcopate'.

[1] See his contribution, 'Ministerial Episcopacy', in *The Apostolic Ministry*.

granted rather less, provided that the two kinds of witness are at least represented. Speculation of this kind is as idle as wondering whether the birth of our Lord might not have been a year earlier or six months later. The Gospel, since it deals with space and time, has this air of contingency, and the witness to the gospel is similarly characterized. The perception of an absolute distinction never necessarily depends upon ability to trace the precise line along which it first emerges.

In the case of the Old Testament, different considerations have to be taken into account. The function of the Old Testament is in general the same as that of the New: it is that of witness. But the Old Testament and the New Testament occupy each its own point of view, and the witness is appropriate to the point of view. The hard core of eyewitness characteristic of the New Testament is not a feature of the Old. The event to which it witnesses still lies in the future, and must wait upon time to unfold before it makes its appearance. Yet it is true that the Old Testament does witness to Christ. It may even be said, as will be seen later, that Christ is present in the Old Testament. The obvious fact has already been mentioned that the New Testament makes contact with the Old Testament, so that standing within it one is forced to conclude that it could not have been written so, unless the Old Testament had preceded it. Now the complementary fact has to be observed. Standing at the other end of the relation, it is just as plain that the Old Testament throws out into the future ahead of it connecting lines which are caught up in a remarkable way in the New. The conclusion is forced upon us that, unless the Old Testament had found a concluding instalment outside itself, it would give the impression of essential incompleteness, of a story whose narration has been prematurely broken off, of a puzzle without solution. The Old Testament awaits something like what is provided in the New Testament as a crime and detection story awaits its final chapter. This inherent incompleteness of the Old Testament is so obvious that it calls for little comment here. H. H. Rowley[1] has fashioned it into a modern 'argument from prophecy' which has its own impressiveness. He argues that the reader of the Old Testament cannot but be aware that what he is

[1] *The Unity of the Bible*, 95-121.

reading 'continually looks forward to something beyond itself'.[1]
Conversely of the New Testament: 'we have here the fulfilment of something that was promised in the Old Testament,
and something that by promise and fulfilment binds the two
Testaments firmly together'.[2] It might, of course, have happened that the incompleteness of the Old Testament was never
in fact made good, that the promises remained dead letters,
that the various connecting links thrown out into the future
simply dropped into space, that the cheques the Old Testament writers make out upon the future have payment declined.
The facts, however, are different. There is discernible between
Old and New Testaments a correlation which is noteworthy.
This correlation is in the main general, but it does not exclude
certain particular and detailed instances. 'There is', says H. H.
Rowley,[3] 'a broad correspondence, though not a detailed correspondence, with the promise of the Old Testament, a correspondence that is significant and impressive, and one that is
unique in history.' But there are also points where more detailed correlation is noticeable. It may be true that 'so far as
the Virgin Birth of Christ is concerned, it is neither proved
nor disproved by reference to Isa. vii. 14'.[4] But at the same
time, as the same writer declares,[5] 'of no other than Christ
can the terms of the fourth Servant Song be predicted with
even remote relevance'. On this basis, Rowley bases his conclusion:[6] 'to ignore [all these elements of response to promise]
and to dismiss the Old Testament as a human document in
which no hand of God is to be seen seems . . . impossible'.
Quite properly he repels the suggestion that what he offers
here is a rational 'proof': 'to show that faith is reasonable is
not to destroy faith; nor is the establishment of its resemblance
to be confounded with "proof" '.[7]

The argument leads on to much more profound considerations which must soon occupy attention. In the meantime, it
indicates the way in which the Old Testament from its own
standpoint witnesses to Christ as really as does the New. It is
the witness of expectation, not, as in the New Testament, of
affirmation. Further, the writers of the Old Testament share
in a way appropriate to them in the characteristics of proximity and contingency which belong to those of the New

[1] Op. cit., 95.   [2] Op. cit., 106.   [3] Op. cit., 108.   [4] Op. cit., 120.
[5] Op. cit., 106.   [6] Op. cit., 118.   [7] Op. cit., 120, n.3.

Testament. In their case indeed proximity has not quite the same sense. They do not require to stand next in space and time, because Christ has not yet entered space and time. It is enough if they stand before Him and point forward to Him. Yet there is a kind of spiritual proximity which is striking. It belongs as has been said, not indeed to the revelation as such, but to the interpretation and reception of the revelation, that there is 'progress' to be observed. Moses does not so clearly and unmistakably witness to Christ as does Isaiah in ch. 53 or Jeremiah in ch. 31. It is this high plane that is reached before the Old Testament closes. The spiritual associates of the writers of these passages figure as persons in the New Testament narrative—John the Baptist, and Simeon who is numbered with those who were 'waiting for the consolation of Israel' (Luke ii. 25). That there is contingency here too is equally clear. Why, if Isaiah and Jeremiah constitute the summit of spiritual advance in the Old Testament, should they have preceded by so long a time the advent of Him whose coming they declared? Daniel at least survives from the years that intervene, and the role of his book in determining the Messianic conception is important. Yet why should the contribution of the years immediately preceding the advent be so meagre? As in the case of comparable questions raised about the New Testament, it is neither possible to say nor right to speculate too inquisitively. In the books of the Old Testament there is at least fulfilled a condition which as far as one can see is necessary. A sufficiently clear witness to what will be is there found, which at the incarnation finds ratification.

c) *The biblical pattern.* It is now necessary to go deeper into the question of the relation between the Bible and Jesus Christ. There is already prospectively in the Old Testament before the appearance of Jesus Christ in the flesh something that at least resembles the lineaments of Jesus Christ when He comes, a 'correspondence' that is 'quite unique in history'.[1] The question that must now be raised concerns the character of this remarkable relation which issues in a correspondence in which an event of startling magnitude on any assessment also impresses its form, as it were, upon ages that preceded its occurrence.

[1] Op. cit., 108.

The Old Testament singles out one event and accords it pre-eminent and dominant importance. This event is the Exodus. Here six things are to be noted about it.

(i) First, as anyone can easily see, it is an event of extraordinary importance for all the story related in the Old Testament. It constitutes the historical beginning of Israel as a people. It is, of course, true that much is said about times long before the day of Moses. Apart from reference to the beginning not only of Israel but of mankind and the universe in which man lives, a good deal is said about the patriarchs. God becomes known as the 'God of Abraham, and of Isaac, and of Jacob'. But, if the categories of myth, legend and history be applied to the Old Testament, the first figure to spring with hard edges from the background of intermixed fact and fiction is Moses; and the event in which he is portrayed as being engaged is that of the Exodus. If one takes history in one of its customary meanings, as the narration of what happens, Israel steps on to the stage of history as a people in course of being delivered from slavery in Egypt. But the Exodus has a no less important place if history be taken in the other sense, as the happenings that are recorded. The thing which really sets Israel on the map of the world, the event in which the nation is seen really biting into the course of history, is again the Exodus. From the time that this happened Israel is a recognizable and historical national entity, which is in fact to prove, for certain assignable reasons, remarkably tenacious of its identity.

(ii) Secondly, the Exodus has not only an importance, but an importance recognized by the people who found in it their historical beginning. This nation continually returns and is always being enjoined to return in grateful remembrance to this event. Here one or two examples must suffice. At the time of the event itself, Moses is recorded as solemnly enjoining the people: 'Remember this day in which ye came out of Egypt, out of the house of bondage' (Exod. xiii. 3); and the writer of the story is moved himself to give added emphasis to the injunction: 'It is a night to be much observed unto the Lord for bringing them out from the land of Egypt: this is that night of the Lord to be observed of all the children of Israel in their generations' (Exod. xii. 42). The concluding scenes of this act are recorded in song, ascribed variously to Moses (Exod. xv. 1ff.) and to Miriam, Aaron's sister (Exod.

xv. 21ff.): 'I will sing unto the Lord, for he hath triumphed gloriously: the horse and his rider hath he thrown into the sea.' Illustration is again found in the Psalms, and more especially in the great series of Psalms of praise and recollection (Ps. ciii-cvii). Here, after declaring the excellence of God in His works of creation, the Psalmist turns to the history of his people, and recalls in glowing terms the events leading up to and subsequent upon the Exodus (Ps. cv-cvii). Further, the prophetic mind is similarly aware of the initiatory importance of the Exodus, as when Hosea (xi. 1), speaking for God, declares: 'When Israel was a child, then I loved him, and called my son out of Egypt.'

(iii) Thirdly, as some of the quotations have already shown, the writers of the Old Testament are not only aware of the secular importance of the event of the Exodus. They are conscious that it carries also a religious significance. The form which recollection of this event regularly takes is a grateful song of praise to the God whom they discern to have been at work in the event. In this mighty act of deliverance they see the 'arm' and the 'right hand' of God operating for their salvation. No feature in all the Old Testament is of greater moment than this. In the event in which the people is constituted a national entity, they espy God to be at work savingly. This is something which though frequently obscured and forgotten is never quite lost, and to its realization the people are again and again recalled. God is 'their saviour, which had done great things in Egypt' (Ps. cvi. 21). This fact about God and His activity is interpreted both positively and negatively. Positively, God works for the deliverance of Israel, and this despite their repeated disobedience and forgetfulness.

> 'Our fathers understood not thy wonders in Egypt; they remembered not the multitude of thy mercies; but provoked him at the Red Sea. Nevertheless he saved them for his name's sake, that he might make his mighty power to be known. . . . And he saved them from the hand of him that hated them, and redeemed them from the hand of the enemy' (Ps. cvi. 7, 8, 10).

Negatively, God works for the destruction of those that stand against Him. This is interpreted as involving the removal of those who oppose Israel. Hence the song of triumph at the destruction of the pursuing Egyptians. Hence too the declaration of another psalm (Ps. xliv. 1f.); 'We have heard with our ear, O God, our fathers have told us, what work thou didst in their days, in the times of old; how thou didst drive out the heathen with thy hand.' But the negative principle is also interpreted as applying to resistance within the chosen people itself. Thus: 'they forgat God their saviour, which had done great things in Egypt. . . . Therefore he said that he would destroy them, had not Moses his chosen stood before him in the breach, to turn away his wrath, lest he should destroy them' (Ps. cvi. 21, 23). The Psalmist has already learnt the lesson, emphasized so powerfully by Amos, and later in the New Testament, that 'God is no respecter of persons' (Acts x. 34).

(iv) Fourthly, the Exodus constitutes the initiation of Israel as a people; but it is also the initiation of a series of events which have the same saving character. Other events follow which are also deeds of deliverance and salvation. The re-iterated form into which the Book of Judges throws the history of the times recorded has frequently been noted. Stages follow one another to compose great acts of deliverance: disobedience; defeat and oppression by the enemy; supplication and repentance; and finally deliverance by the strong hand of God. Similarly, too, and on an even more shattering scale, there follows the historical event of the captivity in Babylon. It is a remnant of the people that survives to have even this ignominy thrust upon it; and it is an even more exiguous remnant that finally emerges from the fires of this discipline. But a remnant does emerge: a deliverance is once more effected; the saving God is seen again to be in action. The story would be incomplete if the last and greatest act were not here mentioned, though it is one that takes us beyond the reach of the Old Testament, and throws us up on the shores of the New Testament. Here too God the Saviour, God the deliverer, is at work—this time to redeem and deliver 'not from Egypt, nor from Babylon, but from Satan, sin and death'.[1] In other words, the events which constitute the history of Israel and the record of the Bible are contrived according to one pattern, and this pattern is a saving pattern.

(v) The fifth observation follows: the Old Testament sees in

[1] A. G. Hebert: *The Authority of the Old Testament*, 52.

these events not merely the pattern of a nation's history. Since God is discerned to be at work in these events, the Bible sees in them the pattern of the divine behaviour. When God acts, and whenever He acts, what is done displays a salvific character. When Israel remembers and celebrates the Exodus, it thinks not primarily of a nation being born, but of a God at work, and, recognizing God at work, it is compelled to acknowledge the redeeming and delivering character of the work and the redeeming and delivering character of God Himself. The God who meets them in history is not only one who acts, but one who when He acts does so savingly. His deeds bear the stamp of salvation, and their doer the character of a saviour.

We must not think that the knowledge of this character of God is based on a deduction from observed things and events. It is not by inference that Israel comes to a conclusion that God is a saving God. A more immediate process is at work. God confronts men in the acts which He accomplishes among them and they know Him in these acts; just as we know a man in and through his body, and not merely by some kind of hazardous inference based on observation of how his limbs act and his tongue moves. No one[1] really supposes that the body of a person comes between us and him, either by way of obstacle which must be overcome or disregarded, or by way of premise on which a conclusion is based. On the contrary, it is the medium by which the person is conveyed, communicated and known. In much the same way, the acts which Israel delights to recollect and in which it boasts do not come between it and God, either as obstacle or as premise. They are the medium through which He is known.

This then is what, for want of a better phrase, may be called the biblical pattern, so far as it expresses itself in the Old Testament. 'The main story', says A. G. Hebert,[2] 'with which the Bible is occupied is the story of God's dealings with Israel, from the time when it became a nation, under Moses.' The testimony of Rowley[3] is similar: 'The fundamental concept of the divine election of Israel sprang out of the events of the Exodus. . . . Here, once more, we find a thread that runs all through the Old Testament, at least from the time of Moses, and that gives a unity to its thought.' In fact, it appears that

---

[1] *Pace* John Wisdom: *Other Minds*, and others of the same school.
[2] *The Authority of the Old Testament*, 50.　　　[3] *The Unity of the Bible*, 26.

the saving character of God is the thread, and that election is the instrument employed to effect the saving purpose of God. 'The most significant things that are taught about God's character are deeply stamped on the Bible as a whole, and they all spring from Israel's experience of God in the period of the Exodus.'[1] So too R. A. Knox:

> 'the history of the patriarchs has a significance of its own, but *at the same time* it is full of types, and images, pointing forward to the truths of our redemption. And was this, as it were, accidental? Could we, if God so willed, have found types just as adequate in the legends of paganism? (So St Paul, I think, has Pandora's box in mind in Rom. viii. 20.) Is it a mere resemblance that links the escape from Egypt to the resurrection? For St Paul it is not that; the same pattern is somehow working itself out'.[2]

Another Roman writer is also aware of the truth of the matter. Dom Ralph Russell writes:[3]

> 'The history of God's liberation of His people from captivity in Egypt and later in Babylon and the bringing them to the land of promise attains in the prophets and Sapiential Books a universal spiritual significance. This already shows that the "spiritual sense" of the Bible rests on events, on things, on God's whole design for the world's salvation, rather than upon words in particular passages.'

(vi) A further, sixth fact has now to be observed. This remarkable insight into the character of God and the quality of His actions and deeds is not only speculatively apprehended. It lies also at the basis of the prophetic element in the Old Testament. Coupled with the recognition and appreciation of events in the past, at each stage in the nation's history there is an expectation and a hope of saving events in the future. This expectation and hope is not grounded on the belief that 'history repeats itself'. Here one might be tempted to quarrel with John Marsh's view,[4] or at least with his expression of it. The book forcibly presses home the importance of the Exodus

---

[1] Op. cit., 65. [2] *The Sunday Times*, 14th February, 1954.
[3] ' "Humani Generis" and the "Spiritual" Sense of Scripture', in *The Downside Review*, 1951, 4.
[4] In *The Fulness of Time*.

event both as *fait accompli* and unfulfilled promise, and as the key to the understanding of what is going on in the Bible. For the Old Testament, we are told, 'time was not a chronological continuum, but a theological series', and this is no doubt true, if it mean that time is regarded not merely as chronological sequence but one interpenetrated by the activity of God. But to say that history has, as its substratum in virtue of which it possesses unity and simultaneity of before and after, an identity of here and there, seems to foreshorten what is really involved. It is not so much a simultaneity of this kind that supplies the unity, but rather the same God whose work manifests an identity of pattern. It is not that 'in the declarations of the prophets the future is not simply descried but becomes an effectual part of reality now'; but rather that prophets divine the future in virtue of that true insight which they have been given into the nature of God and of His operations with men. Again we read: 'in the period which we now chronologically call B.C. there were "islands" of theological time which in faith anticipated the events and situations that were once and for all consummated in history at the incarnation'.[1] But time does not as it were contain the potentiality of anticipating itself. What does happen is that the men of the Old Testament discern in past and present the character of God and the pattern of His action, and assured by this they are bold to foretell the future.[2] And, further, as we shall later see, they are themselves meantime nourished by the saving God Himself, until they are taught to 'call his name Jesus, for he shall save his people from their sins' (Matt. i. 21).

As the divine saving pattern is the link between prophecy and fulfilment, and insight into this pattern constitutes the ground of prophecy, so it is this same pattern that constitutes the ground and criterion for legitimate typology. It is quite true that the Old Testament is a *typos* and a *figura* of the New. This means, for example, that in some sense the anointing of

[1] *The Fulness of Time*, 157.

[2] A. G. Hebert agrees with this view when he summarizes the history of Israel in phases, each with its characteristic 'confession of faith', and each of these confessions containing a recorded event in the past and an assured hope for the future (see *The Authority of the Old Testament*, 51). Similarly, K. Barth (*K.D.*, I/1, 111): 'Church proclamation must be ventured upon in recollection of past, and in expectation of future revelation. The ground of expectation is thus obviously identical with the object of recollection.'

Christ with the Holy Spirit is antitype to the anointing of Aaron and of Solomon. But direct relationship can be set up between them only at the expense of the earlier term and by the sacrifice of its historical reality, so that it may function as a foreshadowing of what is to be. In fact there is a *tertium quid* in which the two terms find their true relationship. This *tertium quid* is the saving work of God with its reiterated pattern. It is on these grounds not unnatural that His dealings with real persons separated by a period of time should bear the same character. The relation is not merely of shadow and reality, of representation and represented, but of equally real historical characters, in dealing with whom God's work assumes the same pattern. The principle may be used even more widely. Since the same God operates throughout, the same pattern can be traced in His work both before and in the incarnation; but the same pattern is also observable in the work which follows the incarnation. As Aaron is by Moses anointed to a priesthood in the chosen people, and Christ at Jordan to a priesthood for all the world, so Christians at baptism are anointed into membership of the Church and a priesthood of all believers.[1] There is a right kind of typology which is not mere fantasy, just as there is a real kind of prophecy which is not merely 'inspired guesswork'; and both rest securely upon an understanding of the reiterated pattern of God's saving work.

The Bible itself provides the evidence for what has just been said, and detailed illustration is dispensable. Two striking illustrations must here suffice. The first is to be found within the Old Testament itself. Isaiah in a noble passage (ch. 45) declares that Cyrus is appointed as the instrument of God: 'For Jacob my servant's sake, and Israel mine elect, I have even called thee by thy name: I have surnamed thee, though thou hast not known me' (xlv. 4). But the range and scope of this magnificent conception is even wider. In God's purpose are comprehended not only Israel but all nations: 'Look unto me, and be ye saved, all the ends of the earth; for I am God, and there is none other' (xlv. 22). Whenever other peoples are seen to fall under the sovereignty of God, they are conceived as coming within the salvific operation of God. In other words, God manifests Himself as the saving God not only at all times

[1] See Gustav Hök: 'Luther's Doctrine of the Ministry', in *The Scottish Journal of Theology*, Vol. 7, 36f.

but also to all men. When the final extension of His sovereignty is apprehended, the pattern of God's action is still the same, and all His children become equally beneficiaries of salvation, or of course by their rejection of the benefits they incur lasting loss.

The second illustration will serve to show the intimate connexion that exists between the Old Testament and the New. When Jeremiah is stirred to prophetic utterance, he foresees a new covenant. But this new covenant is specifically linked to what has already taken place at the Exodus. Thus (xxxi. 31f.):

> 'Behold, the days come, saith the Lord, that I will make a new covenant with the house of Israel, and with the house of Judah: not according to the covenant that I made with their fathers in the day that I took them by the hand to bring them out of the land of Egypt.'

Is this bold prophecy of a new covenant, with its implied connexion with and also difference from that implicit in the Exodus, really fulfilled? The answer is: to the letter. When the Last Supper is celebrated and the new covenant is no longer a matter of prophecy but of fact, the celebration takes place in the context of the annual memorial of what happened at the Exodus.

> 'We are not concerned [says H. H. Rowley[1]] with the controversy as to whether the Last Supper was a Passover meal or whether our Lord died in the hour when the Passover lambs were being slain. Whether His death is associated with the death of the Passover lambs, whose blood sprinkled on the doorposts was a reminder of the ancient deliverance, or whether His death, like that of the firstborn of Egypt, followed the eating of the Passover, matters little for our present purpose. In either case the death of Jesus is related to that ancient deliverance by the time at which it took place.'

Few illustrations could make plainer the identity of pattern observable, not only within the Old Testament, but throughout the whole of the Bible.

d) *Jesus Christ in the Old Testament.* If it is correct to describe

[1] *The Unity of the Bible*, 112.

in these terms what may be called the biblical pattern, the full significance of this pattern must be appreciated and exploited. There is more here than a mere subjective interpretation of history. Such an interpretation can of course be imposed by anyone who is willing to manipulate and force facts and events into designs which originate in his own mind. This is not what is offered in the Bible. There is no need—nor is it possible—to give an absolute guarantee of the historical accuracy of every detail recorded in the Old Testament. History never achieves demonstrable certainty, but it may be modestly stated, with the assurance which the subject matter allows, that the Bible records the events of the story of Israel with sufficient accuracy.[1] The pattern, then, which they manifest is not merely a matter of interpretation. It will not necessarily be observable to the casual eye. But it is really there in the events themselves, objectively grounded on the fact that God is a saving God whose action therefore falls into a salvific pattern.

Hitherto the concern has been to show from the evidence the Bible provides how its writers were compelled to regard the course of history and the shape of things that were and are. Attention has now to be directed to the objective ground behind the pattern they discerned. The question can be put in this way: What does it mean that the men of the Old Testament were, and knew that they were, both observers and beneficiaries of the activity of a saving God? Can it mean anything else than that there were in some real sense in contact with Christ and that therefore Christ is in a certain manner present in the Old Testament?

How may we conceive or represent this? It may be easier to answer the question if a certain type of wrong answer is first rejected. A certain strain of christological thought, which persists throughout Christian theology from the earliest times to the present day, insists that Christ is so simply and literally present in the Old Testament that the difference between it and the New virtually disappears.[2] In the early days of the

---

[1] For corroborative evidence, see A. G. Hebert: *The Authority of the Old Testament*, 56, 59; W. J. Phythian-Adams: *The Call of Israel*, 64, *The Fulness of Israel*, 36f.; W. Neil: *The Rediscovery of the Bible*, 117: the Bible contains 'a substantially reliable record of events during a specific period of world history'.

[2] Cf. what Brunner says, *Dogm.*, II, 241f.

Church, Irenaeus,[1] commenting on John v. 48, 'Moses wrote of me', says that this is

> 'no doubt because the Son of God is implanted everywhere throughout his writings: at one time speaking with Abraham, when about to eat with him, at another with Noah, giving him the dimensions [of the ark]; at another, enquiring after Adam; at another, bringing down judgment upon the Sodomites; and again, when he becomes visible, and directs Jacob on his journey, and speaks with Moses from the bush.'

Recently there has been a recrudescence of this typological interpretation, and with it a number of attempts to reassess the relation of Christ to the Old Testament. Most extreme of these attempts is that of Wilhelm Vischer.[2] Vischer has much of great value to say about the promise-fulfilment relation in which Old and New Testaments stand to one another; and one valuable passage has already been cited in the present chapter. But he allows the argument to carry him further than common sense would advise or other considerations permit. An example of Vischer's christology occurs[3] in his exposition of Gen. xxxii, where Jacob engages in strife with an angelic stranger at the ford Jabbok. 'Who is this man?' asks Vischer. His answer is unequivocal. Quoting Luther, he declares: 'Without any contradiction, this man was no angel, but our Lord Jesus Christ, who is true God and was yet to become a man whom the Jews would crucify. He was', continues the quotation, 'very familiar to the holy Fathers, often appeared to them, and frequently spoke with them.' Vischer adds: 'Jesus Christ is then the concealed name of this man; and we must further say with Luther, that Jesus Christ in that night when He came upon the patriarch in his solitude assumed a *larva* or mask.' Jesus Christ is really already there—disguised and under a veil, no doubt; but then, it is argued, in the incarnation too He is disguised and veiled. On this, N. W. Porteous comments[4] drily: 'this is certainly very muddled theology'. It is indeed. Living *post eventum* we may certainly interpret Jacob's encounter in some such way. But what we then do has to be

---

[1] *Con. Haer.*, IV. x. 1; see Hebert: *The Authority of the Old Testament*, 267.
[2] *Das Christuszeugnis des alten Testaments*.
[3] *Op. cit.*, 187f.
[4] In *The Old Testament and Modern Study*, edited by H. H. Rowley, 338.

R

carefully distinguished from the *sensus litteralis*. Otherwise interpretation of this kind does violence either to time and history or to the significance of the incarnation. On the one hand, if events recorded in the Old Testament are to be understood as symbols of what only later becomes historically real, their own historicity is imperilled. The persons who appear in the Old Testament exist, not in their own right, but as figures of others in the future. The Old Testament as a sufficiently accurate historical record disappears. On the other hand, if this violation is to be avoided, it must be held that Christ is present in the Old Testament in the same sense as He is in the New. Then it is impossible to conserve the significance of the incarnation. This significance is based upon the occurrence of something entirely unprecedented, though not of course unheralded, and it is this that is incompatible with a view that holds Him to be present in the same sense in both Old and New Testaments. It is perhaps specially significant that the suggestion that Christ is thus present in the Old Testament is supported by an identification of the veiling in the New Testament with a hypothetical veiling in the Old. The modes in which Christ is present in the two Testaments are thus even more closely assimilated to one another. This is to undermine the reality or the uniqueness of the incarnation.

The error in which this mistaken view of the presence of Christ in the Old Testament originates is a wrong view of the witness to Jesus Christ which the Old Testament bears. Old and New Testaments witness to Christ in the same or in too similar a sense. This is not the view of the Bible which maintains the distinction between promise and fulfilment as differentiating the Old and New Testaments. It is therefore this that must be remembered if a better account of the relation between the two Testaments is to be offered.

The witness of the Old Testament to Christ is not identical with that of the New. On the contrary, while the former is primarily to the future, the latter is primarily to the past. The Old Testament is a witness of promise. Jesus Christ to whom it witnesses is not yet. More strictly, Jesus incarnate is not present in the Old Testament. Yet this does not imply that He is in no sense present in the Old Testament both to the writers and to the people whose history they record. The Bible itself supplies evidence showing that Israel is and knows that it is in contact with the saving God. In the New Testament, it appears that God is the God and Father of our Lord Jesus Christ. Of course as such He is not a different or another God, distinct from Him whom the men of the Old Testament knew. Otherwise it was Marcion that was right and the Church that was heretical. How then should the God and Father of our Lord Jesus Christ save except by Jesus Christ?; and if He save in the days of the Old Testament, how again except by Jesus Christ already present in the Old Testament? That a real and unprecedented event takes place in the incarnation is certainly to be maintained. Yet God does not become binitarian at the Advent, any more than He first becomes trinitarian on the first Whitsunday. The same God and Father of our Lord Jesus Christ is identical throughout, both before the incarnation and after it, though the reality of the incarnation demands that this identity be not interpreted as undifferentiated homogeneity. If God saves in the time of the Old Testament, Jesus Christ is there, by whom He saves. It is indeed a Jesus Christ not yet incarnate, not yet recognizable, not yet identified as a person. The pattern has been discerned, but the Person in whom this pattern receives final exemplification has not yet appeared. When, however, this occurs, it bears the name of Jesus. To put the matter another way, the term Messiah is current in the days of the Old Testament, but only as a functional and official title; with the advent, the title becomes a proper name and is linked with Jesus of Nazareth.

God if He saves does so by Jesus Christ—not indeed the incarnate Jesus Christ of the New Testament, but by Jesus Christ appropriately present in the Old Testament. This is corroborated when the matter is looked at from the other side. Jesus Christ does not begin His career at the advent. The New Testament testifies that Christ is He by, from and through whom all things are made. At this point all the problems of trinitarian theology force themselves into the foreground, and it is impossible to deal with them in any detail here. But three facts at least seem undeniable: that Christ's career does not start with the incarnation, that Christ is 'the same yesterday, today and for ever', and hence that, where Christ is, there salvation is under way. It must at the same time be maintained that the incarnation and the human life and work of Jesus do inaugurate something fresh. The way in which these two sets of facts seem most capable of reconciliation is to suppose that Christ existent prior to the incarnation is indeed present in the Old Testament for the saving of God's people, and that the same Christ, now incarnate, crucified, risen and regnant, is also, with a difference appropriate to the circumstances, present in the New Testament and in the age which the New Testament inaugurates. How could Christ who is the agent of creation be, prior to incarnation, quite cut off from the world which is thus dependent on Him? And if He be not cut off, how can He be present to it without being savingly present?

It has been said that the Old Testament is the witness of promise. It can now be added that there would not be even promise were not Christ already present. He is not there as person, not even as the unrecognized personal stranger at the ford Jabbok or at any other place: the incarnation has not yet occurred. But the men of the Old Testament did achieve or were granted insight into the pattern of God's saving work. It is this that constitutes the promise and the ground for the expectation which the promise aroused. When the final disclosure of the pattern is made, it becomes personalized, and the Saviour finds a name; and the person and the name is Jesus. Both for God and for men, there is novelty and identity here. God's saving purpose is identical throughout, though before the advent it is not incarnate. It is manifestly not the case that at the advent God shifts the responsibility for salvation and the whole redemptive burden on to shoulders other than His own, and begets Jesus for this purpose. The truth is that Jesus Christ is already at work wherever the work of salvation is going on. On the other hand, men are not left entirely in the dark until the birth at Bethlehem, nor are they faced with something entirely unexpected at the cross. They have already detected the pattern and known the power of God's saving activity. They have even in moments of exaltation dreamt that this pattern might be personal, as in the Isaianic Suffering Servant.[1] The men of the Old Testament have themselves found and experienced salvation. It is presumptuous to suppose that because 4,000 years separate him

[1] So H. H. Rowley: *The Unity of the Bible*, 59: 'It is hard to avoid the feeling that in this Song the writer has an individual in mind, and to this scholarship has inclined increasingly during the last half-century.' And, op. cit., 147: 'In the Old Testament the Suffering Servant was a concept; in the New a figure of history.'

and us, or even because the incarnation lies between, that therefore Abraham is further off from the source of salvation than we today. Here the parable of the eleventh hour labourers (Matt. xx. 1ff.) has a lesson to teach. None of the labourers hired early or late get any reward until at the end of the day they are all called in; and then their reward is in every case the same. In the divine assessment, Abraham, St Peter and the latest twentieth century believer are ranked as equals and stand equally near the source of salvation. The saving pattern is identical throughout, but not till Jesus comes do men come to know personally Him of whom even in pre-advent times they were not quite bereft.

What is said here bears some resemblance to typological theology. Yet it is sufficiently distinct and, it may be hoped, does not suffer from the same defects. Rowley also works with the idea of a biblical pattern, though he does not venture to carry the argument so far as is done here. He states[1] the distinction between pattern and type clearly.

> 'In finding the same pattern of revelation here and in the Old Testament we are not resorting to typology, and arguing that the old revelation was a foreshadowing of the new. . . . The old revelation had a reality and a validity in its own right. The new, too, had a validity and a reality in its own right. If both were revelations of the same God, as they claimed to be, then in the common pattern of the revelation, . . . where neither could explain or control the other, we have the signature of God.'

Typology errs when the reality of the type is imperilled in order to supply a *figura* of the antitype.[2] It is indeed not surprising that agents and events, retaining their distinct and independent reality, should manifest traces of the divine saving pattern. When the sun draws lesser bodies into its orbit, it communicates to them a similar circular motion; yet they remain distinct from it. Similarly, God draws into the service of His saving plan agents who remain relatively independent, and whose actions, though displaying the same kind of pattern, remain distinguishable from His. But the saving work of God in the Old

---

[1] *The Unity of the Bible*, 98.

[2] This is true of even certain biblical usages, e.g. Matt. ii. 14, referring to Hos. xi. 1. The principle of the relation between New Testament and Old is rightly discerned, but it suffers from a too scholastic application.

Testament attests not only the presence of Christ there but also the reality of them who appropriately knew and enjoyed Him.

e) *The attitude of Christ to the Old Testament.* The thesis that has been outlined can be tested against one piece of evidence which will be recognized as crucial. Is the view put forward here congruous with what the New Testament represents its writers as thinking concerning the Old Testament, and above all, is it congruous with what they represent as our Lord's thought in the matter? The questions are in the nature of things not clearly distinguishable from each other. Several things may be taken for granted without argument or illustration. The immense interest of the writers of the New Testament in the Scriptures of what is now the Old Testament and their intimate familiarity with them will be conceded right away. One may suppose that the synagogue had done its work for those in the early Church who were Jews, and the Scriptures were known with all the retentiveness of memories not dulled by easy resort to the printed page.[1] For those not Jews, interest in the Scriptures was considerable and widespread, as the case of the Ethiopian eunuch (Acts viii. 27ff.) testifies. Besides, there is the concrete evidence of the New Testament writings themselves and the reiterated reference in them to what is contained in the Scriptures. Further, the relation of the gospel to the Scriptures is conceived in terms of fulfilment. The frequent 'as it is written' and 'that it might be fulfilled which was spoken' puts the thing beyond doubt. As to our Lord's attitude, there is every reason to suppose that it was similar to that of His contemporaries at these points.[2]

The attitude of our Lord to the Scriptures must, however, be more precisely defined. From the New Testament it may be gathered that the reference which, implicit or explicit, He makes to the Old Testament falls into two classes.[3] There is

---

[1] See E. Nielsen, *Oral Tradition,* 12f., 33.

[2] For a more detailed account of our Lord's attitude to Scripture at this superficial level, see R. V. G. Tasker's *The Old Testament in the New Testament.*

[3] W. Sanday (*Inspiration,* 419) distinguishes a third class: 'Is there not what we might perhaps call a *neutral zone* among our Lord's sayings? Sayings, I mean, in which He takes up ideas and expressions current at the time and uses without really endorsing them. There were many matters which it was the will of God to have altered some day, but "the time was not yet". And the Son entered so far into the mind of the Father as to leave these matters where they were, and to forbear from making any change in reference to them.'

a class of sayings (or actions) in which He improves upon what is written in the Scriptures He knew, and another where He endorses what is there.

Taking first the cases where He improves upon Scripture, we find the most obvious examples in St Matthew's account of the Sermon on the Mount. 'Ye have heard' is here repeatedly offset by: 'But I say unto you.' Our Lord supersedes what is written by an injunction made on His own authority in which the original is reformulated and in the process also transformed. Unbelievers join with believers in acknowledging here a supreme ethical insight which discerns the spiritual core of the older formulation and expresses it in terms which are categorical and final.

But this supersession is quite different from cancellation. Our Lord solemnly denies the destruction of the law and asserts its fulfilment: 'For verily I say unto you, Till heaven and earth shall pass one jot or one tittle shall in no wise pass from the law, till all be fulfilled' (Matt. v. 18). In the very act of superseding the law as formulated, He asserts its profound and lasting majesty. Here is something that calls for consideration. What is the nature of this magisterial authority which in this manner 'fulfils' the law while at the same time exalting its lasting significance? Must it not be an authority equal to the authority on which the law itself was given? Must it not indeed be of the very same nature as this original authority? If this is the case, we are certainly carried far beyond the conception of mere ethical discernment of however supreme a kind. We are face to face with what is indistinguishable from that supreme original authority itself.

Gore, giving some account of 'Our Lord and the Scriptures',[1] says roundly: 'He insists upon the ethical quality of the Scriptures as primary.' This may serve to exemplify a certain view of our Lord's attitude to the Scriptures. According to it, our Lord regards the Old Testament as a quarry out of which there may be extracted by judicious selection a large number of edifying principles and rules of conduct, and He Himself gives to these principles and rules a final formulation. There is of course an element of ethical improvement in the work of our Lord. But it is quite another matter to suggest that our Lord sees the Old Testament only as something to

[1] In *The Doctrine of the Infallible Book*, 19.

be improved. The writers of the New Testament 'did not confine their interest to those passages in which the revelation of God's nature most approximated to that given in the teaching of Jesus, or to those moral precepts which could be most easily taken over as part of a Christian ethic'—the statement of R. V. G. Tasker[1] is to be approved without reservation. The truth is that alongside of the cases in which our Lord improves earlier statements in Holy Writ, there is a second class in which He endorses what is written.

The most obvious examples of this class are marked by the words: 'that it might be fulfilled' or their equivalent. It is true that this phrase is usually the comment of the writer of the Gospel himself and is not put into the mouth of our Lord. It is true also that some instances occur where the express concurrence of our Lord in its use is in the nature of the case unlikely or impossible; for example, John xix. 36, where the exemption of our Lord from the harsh measures taken to accelerate the death of crucified malefactors is regarded as 'done, that the Scripture should be fulfilled, A bone of him shall not be broken'. What is quite unlikely, however, is that the discernment of a similarity and parallel between the life of Jesus and statements made long before in the Scriptures of the Old Testament is simply an invention of the evangelists— a hypothesis to whose demands they may be conceived as manipulating the whole story in order to conform. It may then be taken for granted that if the records indicate a certain general, and at points detailed, correspondence between the life of our Lord and the Old Testament, it is one that has foundation in the mind of our Lord Himself and in the teaching in which that mind was expressed.

The question must now be asked: What is the nature of this correspondence? There is one type of answer which is quite unsatisfactory. It holds that the correspondence is adequately accounted for by remembering that our Lord was influenced by the Old Testament and what stood written there, as indeed, steeped in the knowledge and love of it as He was, He could not fail to be. Two examples may be selected to illustrate this type. R. V. G. Tasker[2] is chiefly concerned with the attitude of those who record the Gospels rather than

[1] *The Old Testament in the New Testament*, 12.
[2] *The Old Testament in the New Testament.*

with our Lord Himself of whom the Gospels are the record. But, as already said, the distinction is not absolute, and for the purpose here may be discounted. The disciples think in this matter as their Lord. A correspondence is found in the New Testament writings between the final acts of Jesus' life and what appears in the Scriptures of the Old Testament. Reference is made to the Exodus and other redemptive acts, and the statement follows, that it was 'natural that early Christian teachers should regard the death and resurrection of Jesus as their New Testament counterpart'.[1] It may be that this statement is capable of bearing a more profound meaning than appears at first sight. But in fact it says no more than that there is a certain external resemblance between the life of our Lord and the Old Testament, to which as it happens the writers of the New Testament could not very well be blind. Again, speaking of the Virgin Birth, the writer states that 'these traditions are greatly influenced by the Old Testament'. The plain meaning of this is that knowledge of the Old Testament is not merely illuminating the facts concerning Jesus as they are known, but actually moulding the record of these facts. External influences of various kinds of course did put pressure upon the writers of the New Testament Scriptures, and these must be conceived as influencing the formation of the record. But it is another thing to allege that the Old Testament is among these external influences, or, more exactly, no more than one among them. In fact, it is quite unlikely that the Virgin Birth is constructed in order to 'square' Old Testament prophecy. The case seems rather to be the other way round: the Old Testament is being strained to supply predictive statements.[2] If this is so, the New Testament is not being written to provide correspondence with the Old. Rather, so strongly is the conviction held that this correspondence really and already exists that it is supposed even where it is not certainly to be found.[3]

The other example is provided by G. F. Phillips,[4] who enquires how the writers of the New Testament regarded the

[1] Op. cit., 83.

[2] See article, 'Virgin Birth', in *A Theological Word Book of the Bible*, 276a.

[3] At other points, the book is more satisfactory, e.g. in its emphasis that 'it is the same God with whom [the men of the Old Testament and Christians] have to deal'.

[4] *The Old Testament in the World Church*, 58-66.

relation of the Gospel to the Old Testament. Our Lord being
'steeped in the language of the Old [Testament]', 'His poet-
mind' 'saw deeps in it never perceived before'. A 'poetic fitness
of word to action' is contrived.

'It was His own sure conviction that the key to His life
and ministry lay in the Old Testament rightly understood. . . . So He ordered His ministry, and went to His
death, consciously in order that the Scripture might be
fulfilled, or in other words, that the will of God might be
done. The illustration most easy to observe is the final entry
into Jerusalem, which He deliberately planned to be in its
detail so obvious a fulfilment of the promise in Zech. ix. 9,
that it must challenge Jerusalem to faith in His Messiahship
or rejection of it.'

Next, the 'author's mind' behind the record is considered: it
finds the Old Testament suggestive. Matthew does not indeed
seek 'for artificial verbal "fulfilments" of ancient prophecies;
rather is his mind so saturated with the Scriptures that each
happening concerning Jesus as he tells it recalls some familiar
ancient word, and draws from it a deeper meaning than ever
it had before'. He 'quickly saw the parallel between the two
situations' in Matt. i. 22 and Isa. vii. 14.

In all this, there is no suggestion that anything deeper than
literary association is at work. H. H. Rowley shows how inadequate this is. He points out[1] that there is some kind of analogy
between the relation of New Testament and Old and that of
Milton and classical mythology. The analogy, however, is only
partial: Milton is not understandable without reference to
classical mythology; but, while classical mythology is not at all
dependent upon Milton for its understanding, the Old Testament
is precisely so dependent on the New. It looks as though something more profound than literary association were here involved.

The view of the Old Testament held by our Lord is similarly trivialized. The suggestion is that, taught by the Old
Testament, Jesus sees much that is suggestive and useful for
the purpose He accepts for His life, and He brings His life
into external conformity with it.[2] The author rightly says that

1 *The Unity of the Bible*, 94.
2 Cf. even H. H. Rowley: *The Unity of the Bible*, 104f.: 'our Lord was much
influenced by this passage' of the Suffering Servant.

the Old Testament contains the key to an understanding of our Lord's life. Sometimes too there certainly is a deliberately contrived imitation, as in the entry into Jerusalem. But there is an essential weakness in thinking that either our Lord or the evangelists understand the Old Testament as no more than an earlier model which requires to be copied by the Saviour of the world when He comes. The view certainly retains for the Old Testament the real historicity of which it must not be deprived; the ideas and persons are real—the idea of the Suffering Servant and the hard-edged historical character of Moses. But the external and artificial relation of example and copy greatly impoverishes the connection traditionally supposed to exist between Old and New Testaments.

Nor does it represent the full biblical understanding of the matter, as examples show. Luke's Gospel (xv. 14) recounts the appearance of our Lord in the synagogue at Nazareth, His reading from the Scriptures, and the words with which He begins the sermon. The words are significant: referring to the passage of Scripture just read from Isaiah, He declares: 'This day is this scripture fulfilled in your ears.' Again, in the same Gospel occurs the story of the post-resurrection appearance to the disciples on the road to Emmaus (Luke xxiv. 13ff.). The record declares that after a rebuke for their spiritual dulness, 'beginning at Moses and all the prophets, he expounded unto them in all the scriptures the things concerning himself'.[1] There is similar evidence from another source. In the Fourth Gospel, our Lord is recorded as saying: 'Search the scriptures; for in them ye think ye have eternal life: and they are they which testify of me' (John v. 39). Again (John viii. 53ff.), when the Jews invoke the case of Abraham, our Lord is reported as taking them at their word and following their lead: 'Your father Abraham rejoiced to see my day: and he saw it, and was glad. . . . Verily, verily, I say unto you, Before Abraham was, I am.' There is still another source of evidence. St Paul (1 Cor. x. 3f.), referring to the patriarchs, declares that they 'did all eat the same spiritual meat; And did all drink the same spiritual drink; for they drank of that spiritual Rock that followed them: and that Rock was Christ'.

Expression could only have been given to such statements on the basis of a conviction that the relation between Old

[1] Cf. also Luke xxiv. 44.

Testament and New is something much more profound than that of model and imitation. When this evidence is heard, it is difficult to resist the conclusion that our Lord looking into the old Testament finds there, not an edifying model, but Himself. In other words, the connexion between Old Testament and New is not psychological and associative, but ontological and real. No doubt, since our Lord is human, there are stages in the growth of His understanding of the Old Testament and of what it contains; and no doubt as an account of this growth a good deal of what the two books examined have to say is acceptable. But it is not right that a psychological account should be accepted as the whole story. Behind the psychology of the thing, there either lies or does not lie the reality. Something of great moment for the understanding of the Christian faith is at stake here. It is one thing if our salvation rests upon the brilliant insight of a spiritual genius into the significance of lessons contained in sacred books, and his remarkable ability in contriving a facsimile and imitation. It is another thing if it rests on the basis that, wherever and whenever there is salvation, it is God that saves and it is Jesus Christ who is the Saviour—and it is a far better thing. And if Jesus Christ is thus by His own testimony to be found in the Old Testament as well as in the New, the whole Bible has an integral unity which is the strongest basis for authority.

The importance of this unity has recently been freshly realized.[1] St Augustine, in a nicely balanced phrase, writes:[2] 'As much injury is done to the New Testament when it is put on the same level with the Old Testament as is inflicted on the Old Testament itself when men deny it to be the work of the supreme God of goodness.' With even greater authority, another wrote of 'God having provided some better thing for us, that they without us should not be made perfect' (Heb. xi. 40). There is, of course, a difference between the Old and New Testaments; yet the story is one, as Christ pre-existent, Christ incarnate, and Christ risen and regnant, is one. In this sense, St Paul takes up the Jewish legend that the rock which Moses smote followed Israel in all their nomadic wanderings and gives it Christian meaning—'and that Rock was Christ' (1 Cor. x. 4). As R. A. Knox has said:[3] 'Already (or should

---

[1] See H. H. Rowley: *The Unity of the Bible*, 1 *et passim.*
[2] *On the Proceedings of Pelagius*, 15.   [3] In *The Sunday Times*, 14th February 1954.

we say timelessly) He was pursuing them, the Hound of Heaven, importuning them with the offer of grace which they were to refuse.' The Old Testament and the New have a unity in their diversity.[1]

However, some discrimination is universally exercised when the Scriptures are read. What should its nature be? In the case of the New Testament, by what right do we say, for example, of the passage in which marriage is commended on the ground that 'it is better to marry than to burn' (1 Cor. vii. 9): St Paul is not so good here? In terms already used, this constitutes a case of 'applied revelation'. In this sphere there is no guarantee against misapplication. Yet a man, witnessing to Christ, does not the less witness even when his application of Christ's doctrine goes astray. It is only when the Bible is regarded as a series of immediately employable commands, and its authority as vested in these taken each in isolation, that real difficulty is encountered. If this is not what authority means and not where it lies, the edge of the difficulty is turned. The authority of the Bible reposes in the fact that, in statements some right and some wrong, and in practical application some of which is disputable and some even more dubious, a unified witness is borne to Him who is at the centre of the Gospel.

Similar and more acute difficulty arises in the case of the Old Testament. By what right, in the singing of the proper Psalm for Whit-Sunday, is the congregation directed to 'omit verses 21 to 23'?: 'But God shall wound the head of his enemies', etc. No doubt the phrases here used fall roughly upon over-refined ears. Yet what is being conveyed in these harsh terms is the undoubted truth that, since God is righteous, unrighteousness is inimical to Him and to His purposes and by the very token of His concern for righteousness His wrath must be visited upon unrighteousness. Two ways of regarding Scripture obscure this truth and make the difficulty insurmountable: first, if the Bible is held to be verbally inerrant; and secondly, if the authority of the Bible is regarded as vested

---

[1] A practical consequence may be mentioned. In many of those Churches where the liturgy followed is not fixed, this unity is obscured or disrupted by the interpolation of all kinds of things, necessary items of worship, no doubt, but at this point irrelevant, between the reading of the Old Testament and the New Testament lessons, e.g. especially by the departure of children to Sunday School before the second lesson is read.

in isolated texts. But if these ways be rejected, there is no reason why, with due explanation and exposition, such rough sentiments should not play a rightful and important part in witnessing to the God and Father of our Lord Jesus Christ. The very character of God makes itself known through the opacity and even distortion of the human witness. Biblical authority thus broadly conceived also gives meaning to other passages commonly neglected as unedifying. What, for example, are we to make of the passages which present the specification of the ark and of the temple, of the detailed legislative regulations in the Book of Exodus, and the long lists of names that occur elsewhere? The answer is that they too bear testimony to the same saving and redeeming God. No doubt we could have done with less of them, or even with their entire omission. But the truth is that witness can be borne to this God only by means of men, by their words or by their deeds, just as the incarnation can only be effected by means of the assumption of 'bone of our bone, and flesh of our flesh'. To object to the contingency and the inadequacy of these means is to quarrel with the possibility of witness altogether. The means do not indeed possess exemplary authority to be obeyed; but they do have all the authority which God concedes to their testimony. The men of the Old Testament are men who have been addressed by God. Forthwith they 'apply' the revelation vouchsafed to them. The temple specifications set on record the kind of amenities provided for the proper worship of God. (How simplified the rebuilding of Iona Abbey and other restored churches would be had similar care been taken to record details of their original construction!) The laws show the chosen people applying to the regulation of their life and conduct what they learned from their encounter with God. In the lists that have come down to us we have the names of men who played their part in testifying to God, some as God's destroyed enemies, and some as founder and early members of the Church of God, of which we are the present-day members. And if the tombs of our ancestors are sacred and the names on our war memorials are revered, those names too have their appropriate place, even if the Sermon on the Mount is read oftener than they.

f) *Witness to Jesus Christ and presence of Jesus Christ.* The Bible witnesses, but does not argue. There is a distinction here which has to be understood or the function of the Bible will not be rightly apprehended; but at the same time, it is one which must not be exaggerated. A. Richardson puts the point forcibly when he says:[1]

> 'We shall fail to understand the Bible if we do not recognize that it is a book of witness, not of argument. It contains no arguments for the existence of God; it simply testifies to what He has done. Indeed, the biblical meaning of the word God would have been destroyed if the Bible had once attempted to argue that He exists. A God whose existence could be proved, or rendered more probable by argument, would not be the God of the Bible. The God of Israel is not an Ultimate Being who appears at the end of a chain of reasoning. He is the God to whom we can testify but whose nature we deny as soon as we begin to argue that He exists.'

This is profoundly true, though one would have to add that argument has a propaedeutic use. But the Bible points; it speaks, but does not debate. And when the Bible speaks, the pattern of its speech is: Look there; it never says: Come on one side a moment, and let me demonstrate to you the existence of God or some other such truth.

While this is true, the Bible is not to be regarded as a mere verbal fingerpost, a kind of perpetual ejaculation, implying that nothing significant can be said about God. The Bible has much to say about God, and to say it the Bible uses of necessity the speech and categories of the thought of its day. When, for example, the Fourth Gospel testifies to Jesus Christ in terms of the Logos, it is indeed far from arguing about Jesus Christ or for the existence of God. But the form in which the witness is cast is itself a commendation to those who understood and used the category of Logos, while at the same time it might well mean a revolution in their thinking. The Bible never supposes that God can be reached by reason; on the other hand, it never supposes that God is totally incommunicable in rational terms, for this would mean that God was wholly above and beyond reason and impervious to reason. The contention that we can say nothing significant about God

[1] *Preface to Bible Study*, 40.

and that the enjoyment of God consists in blank silence, belongs, not to Christianity, but to philosophical absolutism. For the Hindu, *neti, neti* is all that a man can say about God (not this, not this);[1] and typical of its teaching is the story of the disciple who came repeatedly asking his *guru* to tell him about God, to be invariably met with entire silence; and on protesting, he received the rejoinder: I am telling you about God, but you do not understand; the Atman is silence. In sharp contrast to this, the God of the Bible is one who breaks silence and ventures upon speech.

In common parlance, the Word of God is a synonym for the Bible. In many of our churches, we are Sunday by Sunday reminded of this when, to introduce the Scripture Lessons, the solemn declaration is made: Let us read the Word of God, or: Hear the Word of God. To say that the Bible is the Word of God is primarily the affirmation of an ontological relation between the printed words and the speech of God. But it is often manipulated so as to form the basis of a psychological explanation of how this witness comes into existence. The question is legitimate, but its answer can only be inferred from what Scripture says and cannot claim direct scriptural warrant. In other words, we move here into a realm in which our judgment may be at fault. In this realm, it is not surprising that several interpretations compete with each other. The simplest of them holds that the way in which the words of the Bible reach paper is by divine dictation, that the writers of Scripture act as God's amanuenses, and that the Bible is in this sense inspired. Then the Bible and the Word of God are identical terms.

The phrase: Thus saith the Lord, which is so characteristic of prophecy, seems to lend support to this interpretation. Moreover, higher criticism has called attention to the fact that the Old Testament as we now have it was compiled when prophecy was well under way. Pre-prophetic documents certainly find their place, but the framework in which they stand is directly due to the influence of prophecy. In this sense, the prophetic books are normative for the rest of the Old Testament. The characteristic phrase: Thus saith the Lord, becomes all the more significant, and the identification of the Bible with the Word of God even more plausible.

[1] Brihadaranyaka Upanisad, II. 3. 6, IV. 9. 26 (*Sacred Books of the East*, XV).

But the Bible contains other books than those of the prophets. In particular, it contains also the Psalms. Here we find many moods represented. Sometimes it is the record of personal experience—Ps. ciii: 'Bless the Lord, O my soul; and all that is within me, bless his holy name'; and Ps. xlii: 'Why art thou cast down, O my soul? and why art thou disquieted within me?' Sometimes it is pure affirmation of faith—-Ps. xlvi: 'God is our refuge and our strength, a very present help in time of trouble.' And so on. It is excessively difficult to conceive of such words being dictated by the object of worship. A psalm thus written to dictation must on the side of the worshipper appear the height of artificiality. On the side of God, a parallel impropriety appears. It may indeed be difficult or impossible to comprehend what exactly God does with Himself; but, however we answer the problem, it will not do to conceive of Him merely making eyes at Himself in this way.

Yet the key to the matter does seem to lie in the phrase: Thus saith the Lord. We advance more certainly, however, if we abandon the attempt to extract from it a psychological explanation of how the words come to be written, and instead examine what it has to say about the real connexion between the Word of God and the written words. The phrase is certainly no mere *façon de parler*; it means what it literally says, and testifies to the fact that God is a speaking God. Whatever be the psychological mechanism by which this is effected, what follows the formula when it is used is the report of someone to whom God has really spoken.

But it is not only a report. The prophet using this phrase does not merely record a private experience and what God said to him there. He is not only a reporter, but primarily a witness. His function is not merely to make public what God has said, but to point to the God who says it. He does not repeat what he has overheard an absentee God saying; he rather witnesses to a present God who is addressing His people through him. As this happens, the distinction between witness to God and presence of God really collapses. Where and when God is witnessed to, there and then God is present. It is to the presence of this God that the prophet directs the attention of those who listen to him.

If this is the case, then two conclusions follow, one positive and one negative. The all-important thing in the

s

transaction is the presence of God. Through His servants, the prophets, He enters into conversation with men and addresses them, and this whether He come in mercy or in judgment, in forgiveness or in condemnation. But what is this coming, this presence, this conversation of God, but simply the divine action of drawing men into saving relation with Himself? The broken relations are being re-established by the divine action. Men, whether they like it or not, are being brought face to face with crisis which turns either to their eternal salvation or their lasting loss. Here again is revealed the God who contrived the redemption of Israel out of Egypt; here is present the God and Father of our Lord Jesus Christ; here again in non-incarnational mode, is the Christ. He comes as the redeeming God, effecting men's deliverance, not only in history from the enemies of their earthly existence, but spiritually from the enemy of souls.

The second conclusion to be drawn affects profoundly the question of the nature of revelation and of inspiration. If primacy is rightly accorded to the presence of God when the prophet addresses his people in God's name, it is withdrawn from the actual words which are used. First importance no longer attaches to the accuracy of what is said, as though it were needful that the very words of God be reported. There is therefore no need to suppose the complete suppression of the personality and the individuality of the spokesman whom God has chosen. There is thus room for distortion and misrepresentation of God's intention. The embarrassment provided for the literal inspirationist by the contradictory and even immoral injunctions sometimes attributed to God in the Bible is removed. God's witnesses still remain human—very human indeed. But His use of them neither requires nor guarantees their infallibility. The Bible as Word of God is witness to God present and speaking through human, sometimes very human, agents.

It is from the Old Testament that what has been said is drawn. The pattern traced is as follows. The Old Testament witnesses to God, the redemptive and saving God. This witness is not *ipso facto* infallible. Where this witness, incorrect and distorted though it may be, is borne, He to whom it is witness is present. The question now to be asked is whether this pattern applies to the New Testament. The answer is not in doubt: *mutatis mutandis* the pattern applies here too. But the altered circumstances and the new dispensation which the New Testament connotes do involve certain changes: the incarnation has taken place, and this differentia between the Old Testament and the New cannot fail to have its implications. In the New Testament, the 'Thus saith the Lord' of the prophets has dropped out. Of course it has done so: the reason is that the Word of God has become incarnate. Yet the function of the apostles is identical with that of the prophets, though the form in which it is discharged differs. They do not declare: 'Thus saith the Lord'; instead, they point to the Word of God Jesus Christ, and bear continual witness to this Word of God —John the Baptist, and Peter at Caesarea Philippi in the days of his flesh; the disciples 'glad when they saw the Lord' after His resurrection; the apostles looking 'stedfastly toward heaven as he went up'; St Paul on the Damascus road testifying to His continuing exalted activity. This Jesus Christ, they all declare, is God's Word, now made express and explicit; and they know no other duty than to bear continual and complete testimony to Him.

The Word of God in the Old Testament is God speaking, and thereby bringing men into reconciliation with Himself and effecting their deliverance and redemption. The Word of God in the New Testament, first in the flesh, and then by the exercise of the prerogatives of His exalted existence, does just the same thing. Whether speaking to the crowds that 'heard him gladly' in the fields and streets of Palestine, or from the cross where 'lifted up he draws all men unto him', or ascended, exalted and regnant, and 'with you alway even unto the end of the world', He brings men not merely into His own presence, but into the presence of God Himself. Thus the salvific pattern receives new and final exemplification.

When, then, the gospel of Jesus Christ is proclaimed by the apostles, it is not concerning some absent person that tidings are told or reports circulated. To proclaim the gospel is to stretch out the hand and point the finger to Him who is the Word of God; and when this occurs, there Jesus Christ is present. A telling exposition of this point is offered by Oscar Cullmann in a lecture entitled '*Kyrios* as Designation for the Oral Tradition concerning Jesus'.[1] From this one or two

---

[1] See *The Scottish Journal of Theology*, Vol. 3, 180ff.

quotations may be given. 'The words ἀπὸ τοῦ Κυρίου in 1 Cor.
xi. 23 refer back to Christ as the One who stands, not only at
the beginning, but also behind the transmission of the tradition, that is, the One who is at work *in* it.' 'The testimony of
the apostles together constitutes the *paradosis* of Christ, in which
the *Kyrios* Himself is at work.' 'In Col. ii. 6 the *Kyrios* is designated as content of the *paradosis*, but He is *content and author of
the paradosis at the same time*.'

'The designation *Kyrios* not only points to the historical
Jesus as the chronological beginner of the chain of tradition,
as the first member of it, but accepts the exalted Lord as
the real Author of the whole tradition developing itself in
the apostolic Church. Thus the apostolic *paradosis* can be set
directly on a level with the exalted *Kyrios*.'

In other words, the gospel is 'the power of God unto salvation'. But it is so, not in its own right, as if words themselves
could save a man. The power of the gospel lies in the fact that
the Word of God identifies Himself with the gospel when it is
proclaimed, so that where the Word is spoken and witness
borne, He recognizes what is there accomplished, and is present in person and in power. Once again the distinction between witness to the Word of God and the presence of that
Word collapses. He is present when He is proclaimed. The
vessels may be earthen, but they contain the promised treasure.

When men witness to-day, they place themselves beside the
apostolic witnesses. We belong to the same era as the New
Testament witnesses—the same era in which, according to St
Paul, two aeons overlap, the aeon of the former times over
which the wrath of God hangs, and the aeon of the latter
times in which God's grace has been manifested by and in
Jesus Christ. By faith we belong to this new aeon; yet in our
life here we belong at the same time to the older aeon in which
the shattered powers of darkness still carry on a rearguard
action even after the decisive engagement in which they have
in principle been defeated has taken place. Whenever in this
twilit age, where the remnants of darkness still retard the full
victory of the light, men witness to God and Jesus Christ, they
take position with those who in the pages of the New Testament witness for the first time to the event of all events, the
person and the work of Jesus Christ. The witness of today is

the latest stage of the witness begun by the men who wrote the New Testament.

To this extent there is identity between the witness of today and the witness of apostolic times. But there is also a difference. While their witness is that of predecessors to whom none is prior, our witness is that of successors. And again, since there is a first term and a proximate witness to Jesus Christ, to 'all that Jesus began both to do and teach' (Acts i. 1) as St Luke accurately phrases it, and since Jesus Christ is the 'same yesterday, today and for ever', the witness of the successors can only corroborate the substance of the earlier witness. This is why the Bible is normative in Christian life and thought, and why preaching if it is to be Christian must be biblical.

Further, in as much as in witnessing we take our place beside the apostolic witness, our witness is accorded a function of the same astonishing dimensions as that of the apostles. Where witness, derivative from the biblical witness and governed by it as norm, occurs, there again the distinction between witness to Jesus Christ and presence of Jesus Christ collapses, and He to whom witness is borne is really present. It is as true today as it was of the apostolic witness, that 'he that heareth you heareth me' (Luke x. 16), and this precisely because in both cases the free grace of God effects the identification.

Here lies the fundamental misunderstanding of those who think that a line has to be drawn between the 'essential ministry' and the 'derivative ministry'[1] in the sense that the apostolic ministry is continued by means of episcopal transmission and all other ministry is dependent on this.[2] The error here is that what belongs to the free action of the sovereign God is in fact locked up in an office—an exact parallel to the error of those who lock it up in Holy Scripture itself. The one materializes the action of God in an institution, the other in a written book. The truth of the matter is that God retains His freedom of action. He still hesitates to give Himself into the keeping and dispensation of these means. He must indeed apparently communicate Himself to His children through things other

[1] *The Apostolic Ministry*, 8-10 *et passim*.

[2] It does not now appear that much support for this view is to be derived from the ambiguous and unbiblical conception of *shaliach* (cf. with *The Apostolic Ministry*, T. W. Manson: *The Church's Ministry*, 35-53).

than Himself, and the treasure is still in earthen vessels. But by His free and sovereign grace, the treasure is bestowed: the Word preached in this present year of grace and judgment becomes by His action the vehicle of the Incarnate Word.

g) *The locus of the authority of Holy Scripture.* When the question is asked concerning the locus of the authority of Holy Scripture, the first thing to be affirmed is that the Bible has at least the authority of an authentic record of certain facts. Nowhere else can I find a book that tells me so much about Jesus Christ or about the circumstances in which His life was lived. The Gospels stand as testimony to a figure rising to an unusual level of greatness. The books of the Bible that refer to a time subsequent to the completion of His earthly work are in their own way further evidence to the reality as well as to the greatness of this individual. If we go behind His advent, it is discovered that there are books providing sufficient evidence of the historical reality of such facts as the Exodus from Egypt or the restoration of Jersualem after the captivity. Whether these events are rightly regarded as in any sense patterns of a divine activity operating in the world is for the moment beside the point. They are salient moments in the history of the people into which Jesus Christ is born and among whom He lived the years of His natural life. If Jesus Christ, who is the central theme of the Bible, rightly claims authority, then the Bible which is the circumstantial record of Him and of His deeds enjoys a reflected and indirect authority derivative from Him.

But the function which the writers of the books of the Bible really and primarily discharge is rather different. The prophet when he records what God said to him and what He commanded him to do is no doubt recording facts of his experience. But he is not in the first degree interested in the facts of his experience. His aim and intention is witness—to witness to the God who has confronted him in an encounter of which the facts as recorded are only the peripheral circumstances. The Psalmist when he writes his poetry is clearly a poet; and yet his prime intention is not to be a poet, not even to clothe the truth in language that shall communicate beauty through beauty. His primary interest and intention is again to witness—to witness to God and what God has done for him and for his people. The lawyer and the legalist writers in the Old Testament no doubt take reasonable pride in setting down the code by which their people lived and to which their action should conform. Yet once again, their main interest is not in systematizing the code. All the time they are engaged in this work, they are conscious that this code has as its source, its inspiration and its ultimate intention, God Himself; and their recording of it is a witness to One who is behind and beyond it. Or again, the historian certainly puts on record the events of his people's history. But it is not as bare historical events that they are of interest to him. Their prime interest lies in the fact that these events embody a meaning and a divine significance. The events are not merely historical happenings; they are also instinct with the purpose and design of God.

It thus follows that while the Bible, both Old Testament and New Testament, is of indispensable use to the historian and the sociologist, to the *litterateur* and even the scientist, the interests which these students pursue do not rank first in the minds of the writers of the Bible. What the writers of the Bible have to say about these facts is for these students always a little off-centre. The writers do not look at the objects, which both they and, for example, the historian, have in common, from quite the same standpoint. If the historian looks at them straight, the biblical writer regards them obliquely. It is impossible to force what the Bible is saying into the straitjacket of the disciplines mentioned without doing serious damage to the intention and to the actual content of what is written. The Bible is indeed an authority for those interested in history and the like, but this authority is not the sole or essential authority which the Bible possesses.

The authority of the Bible is in fact located in that element within it which from other points of view is eccentric. Where witness is borne, there God, who lives and speaks and in this sense acts redemptively, is present. Here is the sphere where He is accustomed to bestow His presence. The Bible thus becomes the appointed means through which God addresses men, the named place where He confronts them. 'The uniqueness of the Bible consists simply in its being the medium through which God speaks to mankind His word of judgment and forgiveness.'[1] The authority of the Bible similarly consists in

[1] A. Richardson: *Preface to Bible Study*, 37.

the fact that by divine appointment the place where He is witnessed to is the place where His presence is pledged and granted. The Bible has the authority of God who chooses to speak in and through it.[1]

It is of some importance to recognize the nature of the place thus chosen and appointed for His being present. The last thought to be entertained is of some semi-magical device by which God is induced to speak. The power of incantation, the virtue of the reiterated sacred symbol Aum,[2] even the 'much speaking'[3] of the scribes and Pharisees, are not the means that find a place in the Christian religion. In the case of the Bible, the initiative lies wholly with God; while at the same time the means chosen is not a purely arbitrary means. When the record of His saving deeds is set forth, whose course is visible in the history of the chosen people, and whose climax is Jesus Christ, in response to the word of witness the Word Himself is present to save anew. God who is truth communicates Himself not through silence or untruth or nonsense, but through the veracious record of His saving deeds. In this consists the authority of the Bible, and here it is located.

This authority, its nature and its locus, is on the whole well expressed by the phrase which simply says that the Bible is the Word of God. This may be accepted, if only for the reason that any other expression is less satisfactory. That the Bible *contains* the Word of God is also true in a sense, but it conveys a wrong impression. As Flacius says,[4] salvation is not in the Bible like provisions in a sack which one can sling on his shoulder and take home. Nor can the Bible be divided into parts, a Word of God and its container. Since all is witness, there is a unity in the Bible that defies such partition. In fact, God marches up and down through the Bible magisterially, making His Word come to life at any point throughout its length and breadth. So too it is rightly enough said that the Bible *becomes* the Word of God. Yet this does not happen by haphazard but by God's action. Hence underneath this expression must be understood the truth that the Bible *is* the

---

[1] If this is true, is it not quite inappropriate that latecomers to service, church court, or meeting are discouraged from entering during the prayers, but permitted to wander in at will during the reading of Holy Scripture?

[2] Mandukya Upanisad, I. 1; see S. Radhakrishnan: *The Principal Upanisads*, general index, under 'Om'.

[3] Matt. vi. 7.   [4] See Chapter III.

Word of God. Otherwise it is forgotten that the Bible becomes the Word of God by stated and steady appointment. At the same time, the expression conveys the truth that the Word of God really means God speaking, and that the Bible is the Word of God, not in the sense that God's Word is petrified in a dead record, but that the Bible itself is vivified by His living presence to convey what He has to say. Bible and Word of God are not two separate things, though they are distinguishable. The Bible is rightly said to be the Word of God and so to enjoy divine authority.

General Index

Jesus Christ in the Old Testament, 253ff.
  as theme of Scripture, 51ff., 67, 70, 228, 236f., 238f., 276
  His use of the Old Testament, 260ff.
  witness to and presence of, in Scripture, 268ff.
Johnson, H. J. T., 105, 145, 150, 153
Josephus, 168f.
Journal of Theological Studies, The, 19, n.1
Jowett, Benjamin, 16

Kerr Lectureship, 9
Kierkegaard, S., 25, 202, 226
Kittel, *Theologisches Wörterbuch zum neuen Testament*, 180
Knox, R. A., 250, 266f.
  The Belief of Catholics, 11f., 108, 134, 135, 137, n.1, 140f., 142f., 144
Köhler, W., *Dogmengeschichte*, 9, 16, Ch. III *passim*.

Lachmann, Carl, 17
Lagrange, M. J., *The History of the Canon of the New Testament*, 123, n.2, 152f.
Lamentabilis, 145
Langton, Stephen, 159f.
Lattey, C., 104, n.2
Leube, Hans, *Kalvinismus und Luthertum*, 58, 77
Lightfoot, R. H., 15, 24
Lippmann, Walter, 25
Loisy, A., 104, 144, 153
Lowe, John, 179f.
Luther, Martin, 8, 9, 15f., 23f., 29, 32, 51, Ch. III *passim*, 198, 205, 241, 255
  on authority of Scripture, 60ff., 63ff., 71f.
  and Calvin, views of Scripture compared, 29f., 32, 56f., 61, 100
  on Christ as Word of God, 69f., 176
  on critical study of Scripture, 66f., 68
  on humanness of Scripture, 62, 68f.
  on inspiration of Scripture, 65f., 162
  on Karlstadt, 61
  legalistic view of Scripture, 59
  on *predicatio verbi divini*, 63
  on place of reason, 64, 71, 79, 93, 94
  on Scripture distinguished from Word of God, 66ff., 69ff.
  on Scripture as norm, 60
  on Scripture and Spirit, 60f., 64f.
  on Scripture as a 'wax nose', 71
  on *was Christum treibet*, 67, 70, 228
  on Word of God and words of God, 62f.
Lutheran Church, Scripture according to documents of, 72ff.

Mackinnon, J., *Calvin and the Reformation*, 55

Major, G., 95
Mandukya Upanisad, 278
Manning, H. E., 135
Manson, T. W., 22f., 275, n.2
Marsh, John, *The Fulness of Time*, 250f.
Mascall, E. L., *Corpus Christi*, 241, n.3
Marcion, 122, 186, 257
Melanchthon, Philip, 16, 95
  on authority of Scripture, 78ff.
  on individual interpretation of Scripture, 79
  problem of revelation and reason in, 78f., 93
Moldaenke, Günther, *Schriftverständnis und Schriftdeutung im Zeitalter der Reformation*, 89, 90, 91
Munificentissimus Deus, 135

Neal, Daniel, *The History of the Puritans*, 58
Neil, William, *The Rediscovery of the Bible*, 254, n.1
Newman, J. H., 105, 134f., 142, 153
Nielsen, Eduard, *Oral Tradition*, 155, n.4, 260, n.1
Niesel, W., *Die Theologie Calvins*, 38, n.2
Novatian, 158

Occam, 59
Oman, John, 131, 222
Old Testament and New Testament—their relation, 188, 193, 212f., 237ff., 243ff., 256f., 260ff., 273
Oral Tradition, 42f., 125f., 132, 198
Origen, 24, 27, 118f., 122, 140, 159, 230

Pannier, J., 44
Papias, 198
Parker, T. H. L., *The Knowledge of God*, 45, n.1.
Pascendi, 118, 148, n.6, 154
Paul, St, 17, 239f.
Peel, Albert, 31, n.4
Petre, Miss M. D., 144
Phillips, G. F., *The Old Testament in the World Church*, 182, 263ff.
Philo, 168
Phythian-Adams, W. J., *The Call of Israel, The Fulness of Israel*, 254, n.1
Pietists, 97f., 99f.
Polanus, J., 87
Pontifical Biblical Institute, 147
Pope, Hugh, 19, 111, n.1, 142, n.1
Porteous, N. W., 255
Preaching today, 63, 197
Predecessors—Successors, 275f. *See* Barth.
Preiss, Théo, *Das Innere Zeugnis des Heiligen Geistes*, 40, 49f.
Preus, R., *The Inspiration of Scripture*, 9
'Progress' in the Old Testament, 188ff., 228ff.
'Progressive Revelation', 182ff.

Index to Scripture References